Department of Economic and Social Affairs

World Economic and Social Survey 2010

Retooling Global Development

United Nations
New York, 2010

DESA

The Department of Economic and Social Affairs of the United Nations Secretariat is a vital interface between global policies in the economic, social and environmental spheres and national action. The Department works in three main interlinked areas: (i) it compiles, generates and analyses a wide range of economic, social and environmental data and information on which States Members of the United Nations draw to review common problems and to take stock of policy options; (ii) it facilitates the negotiations of Member States in many intergovernmental bodies on joint courses of action to address ongoing or emerging global challenges; and (iii) it advises interested Governments on the ways and means of translating policy frameworks developed in United Nations conferences and summits into programmes at the country level and, through technical assistance, helps build national capacities.

Note

Symbols of United Nations documents are composed of capital letters combined with figures.

E/2010/50/Rev.1
ST/ESA/330
ISBN 978-92-1-109161-8

United Nations publication
Sales No. E.10.II.C1

Printed by the United Nations
Publishing Section
New York

Preface

The global financial crisis has exposed serious weaknesses not only in the world economy but also in global economic governance. Fortunately, a remarkable spirit of multilateralism has prevailed in the responses to this upheaval. Countries have refrained, by and large, from resorting to protectionist measures. Governments have enacted stimulus packages, kept interest rates low and provided additional finance to the International Monetary Fund and the World Bank that is aimed at helping countries in need. These efforts stand in sharp contrast to the approach of the 1930s, when beggar-thy-neighbour policies had pushed the global economy into a prolonged depression and deepened the political crisis that led to the Second World War.

Still, this encouraging multilateralism cannot hide the shortcomings in institutions and rules that were shaped, for the most part, more than 60 years ago. Since then, world conditions have become much more complex and there is much greater interdependence across nations. International economic relations have also changed, with a considerable number of developing countries exerting a much bigger influence on the world economy—a trend that is likely to continue. At the same time, however, we must all be concerned that an even greater number of developing countries are falling behind, and that extreme poverty remains widespread. The global food and financial crises have caused significant setbacks in efforts to achieve the Millennium Development Goals, and have been a painful reminder that a stable global economic environment is a critical precondition for human progress. In the decades ahead, we can expect climate change and demographic changes, including migration and population ageing, to further reshape the patterns of global development.

This year's ***World Economic and Social Survey*** takes stock of development challenges and identifies deficiencies and gaps in global economic governance mechanisms. It also points out promising directions for reform, including strengthening government capacities for formulating and implementing national development strategies; doing more to ensure that official development assistance is aligned with national priorities; and strengthening the international trade and financial systems so that countries with limited capabilities can successfully integrate into the global economy.

Pursuing these and related initiatives will not be easy: we need new types of thinking and a new balance between decision-making processes at the national and global levels. In that spirit, the ***Survey*** offers ideas on how the international community can steer a course towards achieving a more balanced and sustainable globalization and a safer, more prosperous and more just world for all. I therefore commend the body of information and the analyses presented here to a wide global audience.

BAN KI-MOON
Secretary-General

Acknowledgements

The *World Economic and Social Survey* is the annual flagship publication on major development issues prepared by the Department of Economic and Social Affairs of the United Nations Secretariat (UN/DESA).

This year's ***Survey*** was prepared under the general supervision and leadership of Rob Vos, Director of the Development Policy and Analysis Division (DPAD) of UN/DESA. Manuel F. Montes led the team that prepared the report. The core team at DPAD included Christina Bodouroglou, Nazrul Islam, Alex Julca, Mariangela Parra-Lancourt, Vladimir Popov and Shari Spiegel. Administrative and statistical support for the overall report were provided by Lydia Gatan and Nicole Hunt. Substantive inputs were also received from Frank Schroeder of the Financing for Development Office and Marion Barthélemy of the Office for ECOSOC Support and Coordination of UN/DESA.

We gratefully acknowledge background research contributions by Tony Addison, Channing Arndt, Sarah Cook, Giovanni Andrea Cornia, Jane D'Arista, Derrese Degefa, Geske Dijkstra, Daniel Drache, Louis Emmerij, Korkut Erturk, Valpy FitzGerald, James Galbraith, Merilee Grindle, Sara Hsu, Nagesh Kumar, Thandika Mkandawire, Deepak Nayyar, Emmanuel Nnadozie, Alfredo Saad-Filho, Finn Tarp, Lance Taylor, Daniel Titelman, John Toye and Rolph van der Hoeven. The report also benefited from discussions with staff of the Economic Commission for Africa (ECA), the Economic and Social Commission for Asia and the Pacific (ESCAP), the Economic Commission for Latin America and the Caribbean (ECLAC), the United Nations Conference on Trade and Development (UNCTAD), the International Labour Organization (ILO), the World Institute for Development Economics Research of the United Nations University (UNU-WIDER) and the United Nations Research Institute for Social Development (UNRISD). In addition to these contributors, we also owe thanks for the insights provided by other participants at two workshops organized within the framework of the preparation of this report, including Yilmaz Akÿuz, Tariq Banuri, Roy Culpeper, Martin Khor, Richard Kozul-Wright, José Antonio Ocampo, Rizal Ramli, Shahra Razavi and Lan Xue.

Helpful overall guidance was provided by Jomo Kwame Sundaram, Assistant Secretary-General for Economic Development at UN/DESA.

Overview

Globalization at a crossroads

The global economic crisis of 2008-2009 exposed systemic failures in the workings of financial markets and major deficiencies at the core of economic policy making. The rapid spread of the financial fallout in the United States of America throughout nearly the entire world, affecting jobs and livelihoods, underscored the interconnectedness of the global economy. Moreover, the economic and financial crisis came on top of several other crises. Skyrocketing but highly volatile world food and energy prices reflected a decades-long neglect of food agriculture and failure to reign in increasingly speculative energy markets. Climate change is already a clear and present danger whose consequences are being felt in many parts of the world in the form of more frequent and severe droughts and excessive rainfall; its effects are compounding the other crises.

These multiple dramas have unfolded simultaneously and have exposed major weaknesses in our mechanisms of global governance for facing up to these challenges. While the strong desire for quick economic recovery is understandable, getting "back on track" would mean returning to an unsustainable path of global development. Sustained and widespread future prosperity will require major reforms in global economic governance and new thinking about global economic development.

A central concern of the new thinking will be the need for a focus on sustainable development—entailing an approach that would balance material wealth improvements with protection of the natural environment and ensure social equity and justice—rather than a focus narrowly concentrated on economic growth and private wealth generation based on market incentives. Global solutions will be required for global problems and, given the interdependence of these problems, policy responses will need to be highly coherent at various levels if the international community is to achieve the multiple objectives associated with fair and sustainable global development. Because of the complexity of global challenges, pursuit of these solutions will not be easy: it will require a new kind of thinking and the striking of a new balance between decision-making processes at the national level and those at the global level.

Retooling global development along these lines is the main theme of this year's *World Economic and Social Survey*. The study does not pretend to offer a blueprint; it aims instead to present ideas that could become the basis of a new, coherent "toolbox" for guiding development policies and international cooperation.

Times are changing

The present challenges emerge at a time that may well represent a watershed in history. Four major changes in the global economy are likely to be dominant in the foreseeable future.

First, there are important shifts taking place in the global economy. The rapid growth in developing Asia that is shifting the balance of global economic power is likely to continue. At the same time, while quite a few developing countries (mostly in Asia) have experienced a significant "convergence" towards the living standards of the now advanced countries, others, especially in Africa, have fallen farther behind (figure O.1). The number of the poor in the world living on less than $1.25 a day decreased from 1.8 billion in

Figure O.1
Persisting global income divergence,[a] 1950-2007

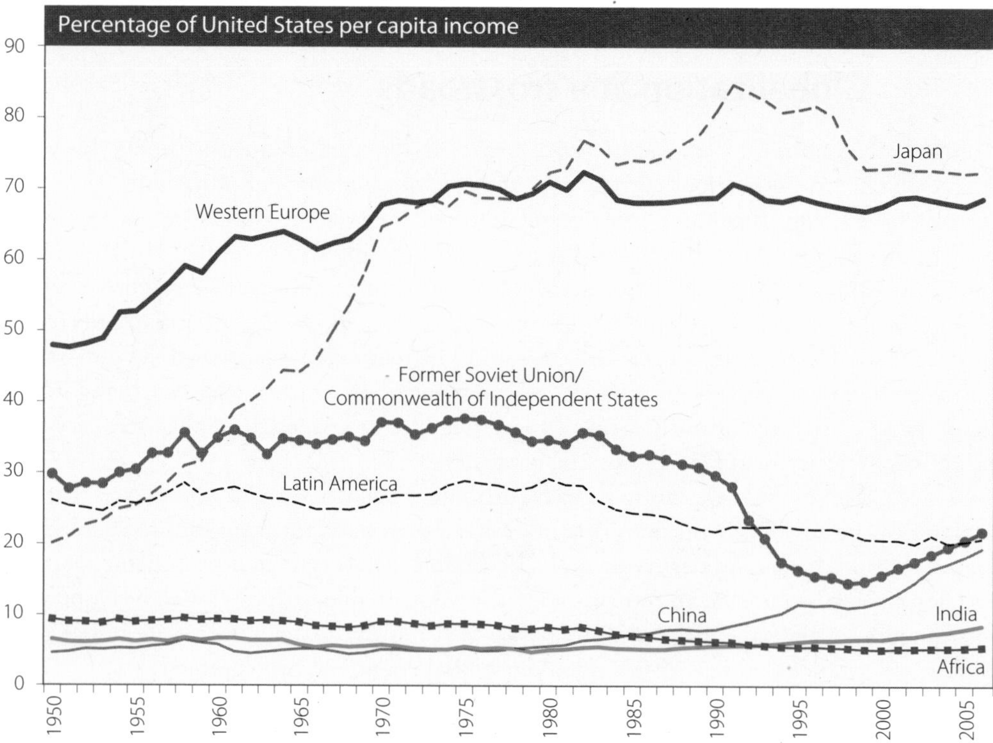

Source: Angus Maddison "Statistics on world population, GDP and per capita GDP, 1-2006 AD" (2008). Available from http://www.ggdc.net/maddison/Historical_Statistics/horizontal-file_09-2008.xls.

a As measured by country or regional income per capita as a proportion of that of the United States of America. Original values were measured in 1990 international Geary-Khamis dollars.

1990 to 1.4 billion in 2005, but nearly all of this reduction was concentrated in China. In sub-Saharan Africa and South Asia, the absolute number of the poor increased (figure O.2). At the same time, with few exceptions, income inequalities within countries have increased since the early 1980s. Redressing this trend in global economic divergence, so as to prevent its becoming a source of new tensions and insecurity, will be a major challenge in the decades ahead.

Second, demographic changes in the coming decades will strongly influence increasing global interdependence. More than 70 million people are added to the world's population every year. This means that, by 2050, the global economy would need to be able to provide a decent living for more than 9 billion people, of which 85 per cent will be living in developing countries (figure O.3). Progress in human development worldwide has helped to drastically reduce mortality rates and allow people to live longer. As a result, the world population is ageing rapidly. By 2050, 1 in 4 persons living in developed countries, and 1 in 7 in what are now developing countries, will be over 65 years of age. This will put pressure on pension and health systems. Further, the presence of declining and ageing populations in developed regions may result in much larger migration flows than occur today.

Developing countries will have to adapt to growing urban populations. By 2050, 70 per cent of the world's population is projected to live in urban areas and mega-cities and undergoing further growth will create problems of their own. This will make the creation of a sufficient number of decent jobs more challenging and, if the challenge is left unaddressed, persistent widespread poverty and inequality among urban-dwellers will be sources of social and political instability. The fact that larger urban populations will also change food and land-use patterns has potentially vast implications. In addition to

Figure O.2
Diverging trends in poverty reduction,[a] 1981, 1990 and 2005

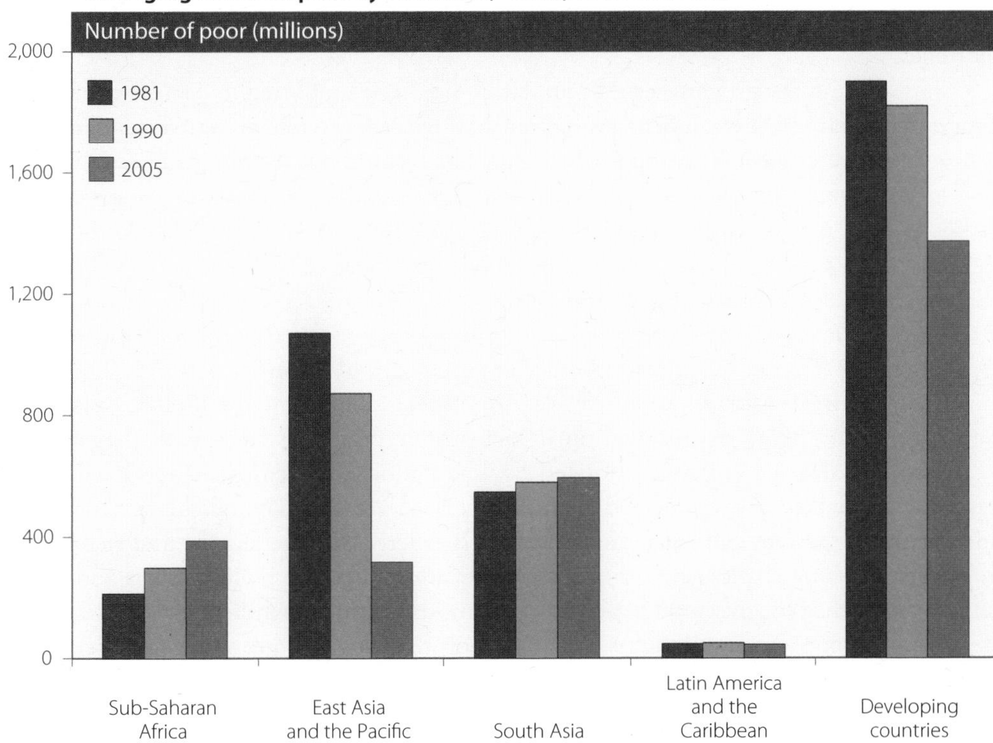

Source: *Report on the World Social Situation: Rethinking Poverty* (United Nations publication, Sales No. E.09.IV.10).

a Poverty being measured as the absolute number of persons living on less than $1.25 per day.

Figure O.3
The growing world population, 1950–2050

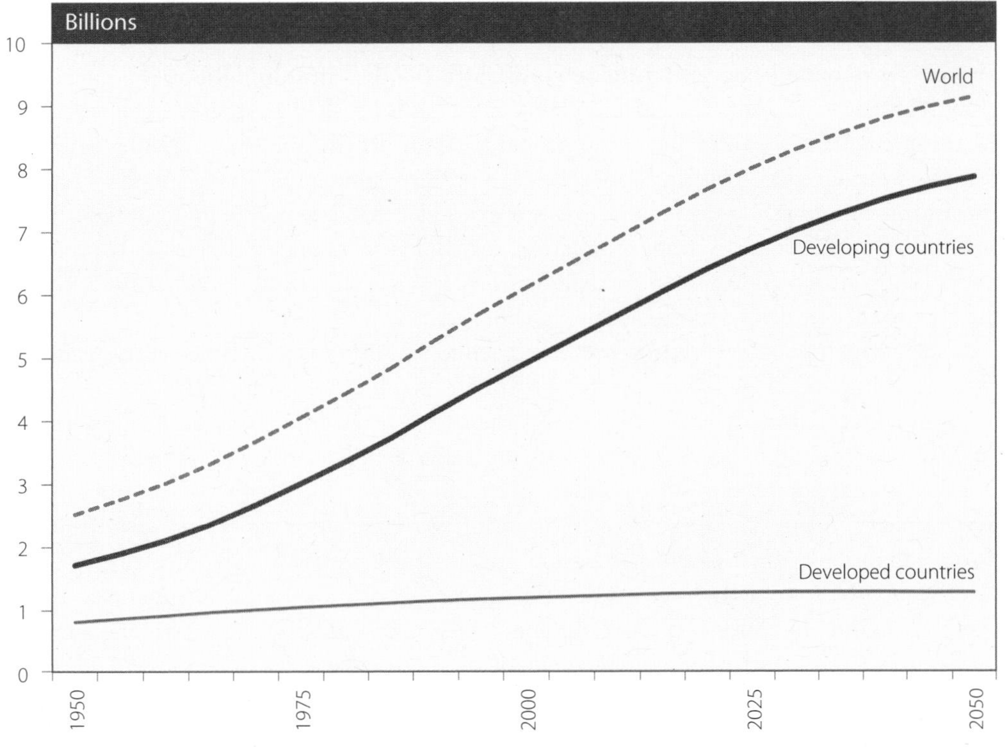

Source: UN/DESA, Population Division "World Population Prospects: The 2008 Revision Population Database". Available from http://esa.un.org/unpp (accessed 12 April 2010).

the decline in agricultural land, there will be a stark increase in the consumption of meat and dairy products, which, under existing production conditions, would lead to land-use shifts and further deforestation, higher energy use, rising food prices and regional food shortages.

Third, the growing world population has been supported in part by the degradation of our natural environment. About one half of the forests that covered the Earth are gone, groundwater sources are rapidly being depleted, enormous reductions in biodiversity have already taken place and, through the burning of fossil fuels, about 30 billion tons of carbon dioxide are currently being emitted each year. Thus, greater prosperity for humanity has come with huge environmental costs having global consequences. The threat of climate change illustrates this and, as demonstrated by the analysis provided in the 2009 *World Economic and Social Survey*, containing this threat will require major transformations of energy systems, industrial production processes and infrastructure.

Fourth, economic processes are increasingly interconnected globally. Agricultural and industrial production is increasingly taking place through largely unregulated global value chains dominated by international companies. The global crisis has made clear how interconnected financial markets are and how quickly problems in one part of the system can cause shock waves elsewhere. Climate change and increasing migratory flows are challenges with global ramifications. Yet, the policies, rules and institutions established to govern these processes are mostly national, while global mechanisms are strongly compartmentalized. Without reform, tensions will grow between decision-making processes at the national level and those at the global level.

The question is how to reform the institutions responsible for global governance so as to make them better equipped to address these challenges coherently while allowing nations and people to have the space needed to determine their own destinies.

Shifting development paradigms

The post-war period has seen fundamental shifts in the thinking about the causes of growth and development. The current global crisis has unleashed another wave of reactions entailing reconsideration of the conventional wisdom. In the 1950s and 1960s, development was perceived as requiring the leadership of Governments in lifting specific binding constraints on growth and development, for example, through public investments aimed at building infrastructure, trade protection and industrial policies designed to promote import substitution and develop entrepreneurial capacity, and through attracting development assistance in lifting foreign-exchange constraints.

Such policies certainly promoted economic growth, sometimes with sustained success, as in parts of Asia, but less successfully in many other instances. Cases of failure to create enterprises that could survive on their own after decades of State support, effectively overcome foreign-exchange constraints and generate sufficient employment, led to reassessments of development policies and cooperation. The "basic needs approach to development", for instance, suggested reorienting Government intervention towards more direct support for employment generation and securing access for all to social services. Another approach argued for reconsideration altogether of a role for Governments in managing economic development. Governments were viewed as distorting markets through their interventions and poor management of public finances. In this context, development policies would need to become more concerned with macroeconomic stability and to rely much more on deregulated markets and private initiative not only in productive activities but also in the provisioning of social services. This approach, which became the dominant paradigm of the 1980s and 1990s, is commonly referred to as the "Washington Consensus", inasmuch as it reflected the policy approach of the multilateral institutions and decision makers based in Washington, D.C.

The United Nations Millennium Declaration, adopted by the General Assembly in its resolution 55/2 of 8 September 2000, embodied a rediscovery of the insight that market-based growth strategies were insufficient by themselves to solve the problem of widespread poverty and that well-functioning institutions and effective social policies were needed to ensure adequate provisioning of health care and education and to prevent social exclusion of many. The global food, energy and financial crises that exposed the systemic flaws inherent in the functioning of deregulated global markets required Governments to step in to address those crises—and in ways that dealt a blow to the conventional wisdom underpinning the Washington Consensus.

Globalization and national policy space

There are no simple recipes for development success. Clearly, none of the dominant paradigms in the realm of development thinking that have emerged over time can take credit for having served as blueprints for successful development. Sustained, rapid economic growth in a number of countries in Asia was held up in the 1980s and 1990s as exemplifying the success of the market-oriented, export-led development strategies advocated by the Washington Consensus. In reality, however, the development policies behind these growth successes, especially in their early stages, resembled much more the recipes associated with the dirigiste paradigm of early development thinking and were not unlike those that had, in earlier times, promoted modern development in Western Europe and Japan. These development policies involved, inter alia, agrarian reforms, investments in human capital, selective trade protection, directed credit and other government support for developing industrial and technological capacity while exposing firms gradually to global competition.

What worked in certain contexts in the past may not work equally well elsewhere. For one thing, the world has become increasingly integrated and the space available to countries for jump-starting their development in relative isolation has become commensurately smaller. The increasing role of foreign direct investment (FDI) and global value chains in driving world production, trade and technology development has limited the scope for the wielding of old-style industrial policies by national Governments; and multilateral trading rules have imposed restrictions on domestic support measures for developing export industries. Further, freely flowing private capital flows have made macroeconomic stabilization much more challenging. Rules for intellectual property rights and quality standards have increased the cost for many developing countries of absorbing new technologies and becoming globally competitive. This does not mean that there is no policy space at all, but rather that the narrowed scope is posing much greater challenges to policymakers today. As discussed below, certain reforms of international rules, which do not conflict with global objectives such as safeguarding global public goods, could help widen margins; but even with those reforms, a high degree of determination and coherent efforts by national policymakers will still be required if development strategies are to succeed.

The future of the poverty agenda

Improving human welfare and eradicating poverty are ultimate objectives of development. The answers to the question how to achieve these objectives through national development policies have moved back and forth between more and less interventionist approaches associated with the shifts in development paradigms.

Trickling down

The modern growth strategies of the 1950s and 1960s assumed that promoting industrial development would accelerate aggregate welfare gains, which would trickle down to the poor through the expansion of formal sector employment and rising real wages. Social policy was seen as a fundamental part of the overall development strategy. In many developing countries, social policy included the widespread distribution of subsidies for goods and services, which not only provided income support, but also contributed to keeping wage costs low in support of industrial development. Urban workers in growing modern industrial sectors and in government services were also the main beneficiaries of expanding social security covering health risks and old-age income insecurity (through pensions), as well as of subsidized and State-provided education and health-care services aiming at universal coverage. Rural producers also received subsidies and other incentives to raise agricultural productivity. However, for the most part, the needs of the structurally poor were neglected by social policies in many developing countries; and, in practice, urban middle-income groups with a stronger voice benefited most in many societies.

Redistribution with growth

Disappointing results from the implementation of this strategy in terms of employment generation and poverty reduction led to the emergence in the 1970s of proposals for promoting more labour-intensive activities, providing greater access by the poor to productive assets (through land reform, access to credit, etc.) and enhancing the coverage of education and health services to include the poor, so that gains from economic growth would be shared among members of the entire population. It was believed that economic growth would become more sustainable with a more equitable income distribution and higher levels of human development. This change in approach was strongly promoted by international organizations, including the International Labour Organization (ILO) and the United Nations, and embedded in "redistribution with growth" strategies, the World Employment Programme and the basic needs approach to development. However, these approaches, while appealing, did not become dominant policy practice in the 1970s or the 1980s.

Back to trickling down

Instead, following the developing-country debt crisis of the early 1980s, the Washington Consensus, together with a renewed focus on aggregate growth objectives, became the new paradigm, according to which market reforms would enhance economic and allocative efficiency and accelerate output growth for employment generation. Social policies also underwent substantial changes. The previous widespread use of subsidies and social transfers was seen as market-distorting and too costly, resulting not only in unsustainable fiscal deficits but also in ineffective delivery of education and health services. Subjecting social services, to a greater extent to market principles (for example, through privatization or the introduction of user fees) would provide greater incentives for efficient service delivery and reduce pressures on Government budgets. Recognition that macroeconomic stabilization and structural adjustment programmes could, in the transition, incur social costs led to the introduction of social safety nets targeted to the poor and vulnerable. Within this framework, the key objective of social policies was no longer to serve a broader development strategy, but to offer up compensatory schemes devised to mitigate painful outcomes of market-oriented economic policies: There was a shift from universalism to selectivity.

A renewed focus on poverty reduction

Through the articulation of the Millennium Development Goals, following the adoption of the United Nations Millennium Declaration, and the decision to put Poverty Reduction Strategy Papers (PRSPs) at the centre of debt-relief initiatives for the poorest nations, poverty reduction and human development were repositioned more explicitly at the forefront of the development effort. Although market reforms and liberalization remained the mainstay of public policies, under these umbrellas, some policy shifts became more visible in the social arena, entailing greater priority for education and health spending, the revisiting of user-fee schemes, the promotion of programmes believed to reduce poverty, for example, in microfinance and land titling, and the introduction of innovative cash transfer programmes, which provided incentives to poor and vulnerable populations to invest in human development by making receipt of the transfers conditional on keeping children in school and/or on use of health facilities by mothers and children. Yet, in many instances, it proved difficult to repair the damage caused by market liberalization, and social policies remained largely marginal to economic policies. Macroeconomic policies, for instance, remained narrowly focused on stabilization of price levels, government budgets and current-account deficits instead of on stabilization of employment. This not only limited scaling up of Millennium Development Goals-oriented public spending but also exacerbated the impacts of external shocks on employment and income growth, causing increased economic insecurity and placing a larger burden of adjustment disproportionately on the poor and vulnerable. Similarly, trade and financial policies remained committed to further integration with global markets, enhancing competitiveness and growth objectives, but in most instances yielding few benefits in terms of employment creation, poverty reduction and enhancement of economic security.

The way forward

As a result, many countries are not on track to achieve the Millennium Development Goals by 2015, the deadline set by the international community. But even should these Goals be achieved, significant human development challenges would remain: millions would still need to be lifted out of extreme poverty, and important educational needs extending beyond access to primary schooling and the high prevalence of acute and chronic diseases would still need to be addressed. These challenges will need to be dealt with in the context of persistent food insecurity, the threat of climate change, population ageing and other demographic shifts. When placed in today's context, the more successful development experiences suggest that the way forward would start with designing national sustainable development strategies tailored to country-specific conditions, the pursuit of coherence across key policy areas, and the recognition that:

- There is a need for a broad, development-oriented approach to macroeconomic policies, based on counter-cyclical fiscal and monetary policy rules supportive of employment creation and protection of household incomes during economic fluctuations, as well as on policy principles that ensure that aggregate price levels and resource flows are consistent with industrial policy incentives promoting economic diversification and sustainable development of the agriculture, forestry, energy, manufacturing and services sectors.
- Agricultural development policies—focusing on access to land, extension services, improved inputs, credits and rural infrastructure for farm smallholders—should be given high priority, especially in countries still facing low agricultural productivity.
- The demands of sustainable development will need to become a main focus of social and industrial policies and the choice of infrastructure and the setting of industrial priorities (not only for manufacturing, but also for agriculture, forestry and energy) will need to be consonant with meeting, simultaneously, the challenges of climate change adaptation and mitigation, sufficient job creation and improving the livelihoods of the poor.
- Social policy itself needs to be coherent, in the sense of avoiding too narrow a focus on social protection and targeting of the poor, and leaning more towards universalism (creating a "social floor" for people of all ages), and ensuring conditions for continuous progress in human development and for household-level social reproduction.

Effectively implementing such strategies will not be feasible without an enabling global environment. National development strategies will need to be supported by stable aid flows, especially for low-income countries with limited access to other sources of financing; by a fair multilateral trading regime allowing the countries space for building domestic production capacity and pursuing sustainable development goals; and by stable and predictable international financial markets. Such coherence between the national and the international arenas of policymaking is not present under today's rules and mechanisms for global governance. Major reforms of the existing international aid, trade and financial architectures are needed.

Towards a new aid architecture

Origins of a fragmented aid architecture

Originally, official development assistance (ODA) had been intended mainly to overcome foreign-exchange constraints on successfully implementing growth strategies. Large shares of bilateral and multilateral aid resources were destined to finance investment in infrastructure. Aid programmes of the 1950s and 1960s had further emphasized technical cooperation and capacity-building. Most, if not all, aid flows were to support Governments in their developmental efforts. This changed in subsequent decades, because of changes in both donor and recipient countries. In some recipient countries, problems of absorption and insufficient governance capacity to manage large aid inflows led to underutilization of foreign assistance. Other countries gained access increasingly to alternative external funding sources, thereby reducing their need to rely on ODA which often came with many strings attached. Donors, for their part, perceived that capacity-building was not taking root in many contexts and increasingly lost confidence both in aid's effectiveness in accelerating aggregate growth and in the ability of recipient Governments to manage aid flows. This loss of confidence in the role of Governments was compounded by the paradigm shift in development policies in the 1980s which resulted in the call for a less activist role for the State. Multilateral development financing became increasingly conditioned on fiscal consolidation, other macroeconomic stabilization measures and market reforms to be enacted by recipient Governments. Bilateral aid often followed suit, especially if aligned behind International Monetary Fund (IMF) and World Bank loan agreements. At the same time, increasing concerns about the social costs of adjustment led to a shift in the focus of aid towards poverty reduction and social programmes, while support for infrastructure (also among the multilateral development banks) was cut back.

In all, aid became much more narrowly focused on poverty programmes and social sectors and moved away from supporting broader, transformative development processes. The shift has also given rise to an enormous proliferation of aid agencies—governmental and non-governmental, multilateral and bilateral—which provide support and resources to developing countries for a multitude of specific-purpose aid projects. Most recently, the expanding roles of private foundations and providers from the South have contributed to this proliferation.

A highly fragmented aid architecture has emerged as a result. This has raised transaction costs and undermined national policy space. Each donor tends to undertake its own identification missions, negotiate the terms of the projects to be sponsored, impose its own accounting methods, define its own conditions, and conduct its own monitoring and evaluation. This not only increases the direct cost of providing aid but also tends to affect the institutional capacity of recipient countries, which complicates the pursuit of coherent, long-term development policies by Governments. Aid fragmentation has also rendered the flow of resources less predictable and more volatile, thereby making the management of budgetary processes highly dependent on aid flows all the more challenging.

Fragmented—and insufficient—aid

A proliferation of donors does not necessarily mean more aid. The average size of aid programmes has become smaller. The major providers of ODA, united in the Development Assistance Committee (DAC) of the Organization for Economic Cooperation and Development (OECD), had contributed about 0.33 per cent of their combined gross national income (GNI) in 1990. This share fell to 0.22 per cent in the late 1990s. By 2010, it was back up to 0.35 per cent, but still fell well short of all existing commitments, including the long-standing United Nations target of 0.7 per cent of GNI.

The delivery gap in respect of fulfilling the commitments to support the Millennium Development Goals development agenda has become all the more poignant with the calls for additional assistance to the poorest countries in addressing their food security problems and climate change. Meanwhile, in many countries, aid flows have been overtaken by other resource flows, including FDI and worker remittances (figure O.4). Delivery gaps in aid commitments are largest for Africa, reflecting the continuing unevenness in the distribution of aid flows which does not strongly favour low-income countries.

These trends raise questions not only regarding the sufficiency of aid, but also about whether the aid that is being delivered is sufficiently aligned with the development financing requirements of the countries most in need of ODA.

Figure O.4
Flows of foreign direct investment (FDI), remittances and official development assistance (ODA) to developing countries, 1980-2007

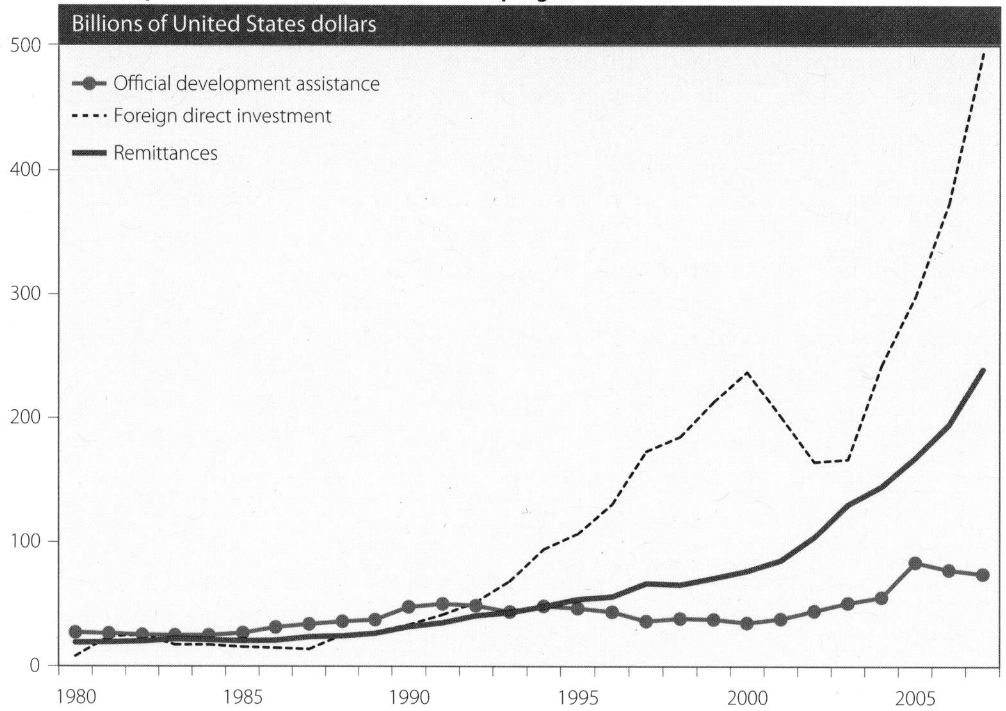

Sources: Organization for Economic Cooperation and Development/Development Assistance Committee and World Bank.

Addressing fragmentation: cures or just Band-Aids?

Donors have been trying to mend the situation. The 2005 Paris Declaration on Aid Effectiveness and the 2008 Accra Agenda for Action[1] have called for greater coherence in aid objectives and for accelerating implementation of agreed principles. The Paris Declaration provides new codes of conduct for donors which aim to reduce fragmentation, and includes targets for harmonization of aid flows aligned behind recipient-country programmes, coordination of donor missions, and reduction of project implementation costs. The quality of aid is to be enhanced by more predictable aid flows programmed at the country level. These efforts at greater coherence are also consistent with the PRSP agenda which ostensibly also aimed to put recipient countries in the driver's seat by aligning donors behind nationally defined development strategies.

Efforts to put these principles into practice have not proved easy. Reconciling national development priorities with the taxpayer-approved objectives of donor countries has been difficult. Less than one quarter of aid flows from DAC donors is provided in the form of budget support and in few instances are aid flows part of multi-annual programmes. In practice, the PRSPs have been perceived as coming with too many strings attached, including macroeconomic policy conditions, and as being donor-driven, effectively undermining country ownership of aid programmes and increased donor alignment behind national development strategies.

1 A/63/539, annex.

The way forward: towards a needs-oriented aid architecture...

Even if attempts so far have not yielded much outright success, putting recipient countries in the driver's seat would seem to constitute a desirable step on the road towards less fragmented and more effective aid delivery. What is needed is a much stronger commitment by donors to accepting the principle of needs-based allocations and alignment of aid flows behind national development strategies, which is consistent with the principles of the Paris Declaration. Rather than the gradual improvements that are currently being attempted, a more radical shift towards full adherence would seem to be needed in order to overcome continued fragmentation and problems of country ownership which undermine aid effectiveness.

Under this approach, sustainable development strategies would provide the framework for policy coherence at the national level and also determine the nature of the financing gaps to be filled by aid flows and the timing required. Bilateral and multilateral as well as non-governmental donors would be aligned and asked to respond to needs through multi-year commitments. Alignment with other sources of development financing could occur as part of the same process (see below). Earmarking of aid funds by donors would become less relevant, although still possible if it served to further specific purposes (as in the case where private sector support would be rallied through vertical global health funds), but such earmarking would always be required to demonstrate its coherence with the priorities and financing needs of the development strategy. Monitoring, evaluation, accountability processes and the updating of funding requirements would be the responsibility of a joint standing committee made up of donors but chaired by the recipient country. Ex ante conditionality would be restricted to recipient countries that had elaborated national development strategies but donors would not attach further policy conditions to their support; instead, the decision to continue support would be based on monitored progress and the outcomes of the implemented strategy.

... with new sources of financing channelled through country-owned trust funds

While the present target of 0.7 per cent of GNI of OECD/DAC countries, set on the basis of estimated foreign-exchange needs of developing countries in the 1960s, has remained unfulfilled in the aggregate, a needs-oriented aid system would probably redefine the amount of aid that needed to be mobilized. Additional targets may need to be set to ensure sufficient resource mobilization for supporting climate change mitigation and adaptation efforts in developing countries, aid for trade and the delivery of global public goods. There will also be a continued need for separate pools of funds for disaster relief and humanitarian aid efforts.

Two further fundamental changes should be considered. The first would aim at better alignment of aid flows with other domestic and external sources of development financing through the use of trust fund mechanisms. The second would entail the increased use of innovative forms of international levies and leveraging of international liquidity for development purposes.

The use of trust fund mechanisms to support individual countries or groups of countries could further facilitate the alignment of donor funding with country priorities, ensure long-term financing, and align traditional ODA resource mobilization with innovative forms of development financing. Bilateral donors and existing global funds would contribute to trust funds which would disburse resources in accordance with the programmatic and budgetary needs of recipient countries. The trust funds could also be allowed to purchase Government securities of developing countries in order to tie aid to future domestic resource mobilization efforts. Experience does exist in this area, as there are a number of cases where multi-year aid commitments have been converted into bond purchases to fund and front-load resources for tropical medicines. Recipient countries, in turn, could also be allowed to periodically deposit budgetary savings earned during economic upswings into the trust funds as insurance against external shocks, and to draw upon them in response to shocks. Another advantage of pooling aid resources in a trust fund is the simplification and harmonization of procedures, and better support of national goals, priorities and strategies. It can prevent duplication and overlapping effects and minimize the burden of integrating aid within recipient institutions. However, the ownership and management mechanisms of trust funds need to be carefully worked out so that country ownership is not undermined. The pledges of funds should not be conditional or earmarked.

New forms of international levies (such as a small levy on international financial transactions) could play an increasing role in providing the resources for a new development finance architecture. The new tax revenues could be channelled via a global fund to country-based trust funds.

Revisiting global trade rules

Present rules insufficiently adhere to the common-but-differentiated principle

The impasse over the Doha Round, launched in 2001 and aiming for more development-oriented multilateral trading rules, reflects the difficulty of striking a proper balance between a desired common set of rules of the game and the principle of accommodating different capacities among countries to competitively engage in trade. The common-but-differentiated approach has been part of the process of designing multilateral rules and strengthening international cooperation ever since the establishment of the General Agreement on Tariffs and Trade (GATT).

Since the establishment of the World Trade Organization, the main emphasis has shifted towards setting common trade rules, as reflected in the trade liberalization that has taken place worldwide over the past two decades. This has progressively restricted the space available to developing countries for utilizing trade policies to foster economic development.

There has been progress in providing developing countries, especially the least developed countries, with greater duty- and quota-free access to developed-country markets for their products through the application of the most-favoured-nation treatment. Yet, important barriers to market access persist for developing countries. Also, agricultural subsidies in advanced countries remain high and continue to limit production and income opportunities for farmers in developing countries.

Creating more space for trade and industrial policies

Countries that have been successfully integrated into world trade over the past half-century all went through stages of trade protection and support to domestic production sectors before opening themselves up to world markets. Present multilateral trade rules leave limited space for newcomers that wish to follow in their footsteps. While further progress needs to be made in enhancing world market access for developing countries and reducing agricultural support measures in developed countries, multilateral rules will need to be recalibrated in order to increase the space available to developing countries for building production and trading capacity.

One key action will be to revisit the current rules limiting the use of subsidies for export promotion. Developing countries should be given more space for applying these subsidies as part of their broader development strategies. To ensure consistency with the common-but-differentiated approach, allowing for the use of such subsidies should be conditioned on their being truly selective (not across-the-board), temporary (not open-ended), performance-related (not unconditional), consistent with the decent-work agenda, and environment-friendly (see below).

A second key action is to significantly expand the Aid for Trade initiative. Resource allocation under Aid for Trade would need to be fully aligned with national development strategies. Aid for Trade emerged as a separate initiative within the context of trade negotiations, designed to compensate for the loss of production, trade and government revenues, as well as to support developing countries in developing an internationally competitive production structure and trade capacity and capabilities.

Trade and climate change

Achieving coherence between trade and climate policies is a recently recognized challenge. In the absence of corrective measures, trade that is more open will likely lead to increased greenhouse gas emissions (for example, those generated through transportation of goods). Conversely, climate change is already affecting the production and trading capacity of some developing countries, inter alia, through the impact of the increased intensity of natural hazards on agriculture and infrastructure.

Furthermore, national policies designed to address climate change may affect world prices and production, trade and livelihoods in other parts of the world. Domestic price subsidies to stimulate biofuel production in Europe and the United States of America, for instance, have impacted on land use, contributed to world food prices' drifting upward and caused increases in poverty in large parts of the developing world.

More generally, at present there is no level playing-field in terms of the capacity of countries to conduct national climate change policies, which will have implications for international competitiveness. For instance, countries lacking resources and affordable access to carbon-efficient technologies possess a competitive disadvantage compared with those that are able to support industries in meeting climate change mitigation targets, inter alia, through duties levied on the basis of the carbon content of products imported from countries not undertaking comparable mitigation efforts. In this way, climate-trade links would be used as a basis for protectionism.

In addition, existing multilateral trading rules constitute hurdles to technology transfers to developing countries. Such obstacles also make the development of industries using green technologies more expensive. Conflicting elements in World

Trade Organization rules and multilateral environmental agreements, including the United Nations Framework Convention on Climate Change,[2] are also a source of many tensions.

Greening global trade and access to technology

A first priority for achieving greater coherence between trade and climate policies will be to resolve the conflicts between multilateral trading rules and multilateral environmental agreements. This will be most urgent in respect of addressing the threat of climate change. Climate objectives should be given primacy when aligning a multilateral climate accord with multilateral trading rules, since the sustainability of material welfare is conditioned by climatic conditions. The alignment should also be consistent with the principle of common-but-differentiated responsibilities underlying multilateral climate accords.

In the area of subsidies, tariffs and environmental standards, action needs to be taken to prevent climate-related border adjustment measures from becoming the basis for protectionism and distorting the level playing-field for fair-trade relations.

The Agreement on Trade-related Aspects of Intellectual Property Rights (TRIPS Agreement)[3] will need to be revisited to allow for the affordable transfer of technologies to developing countries so as to enable them to adapt low-carbon and energy-efficient production methods. To further ensure a level playing-field in the area of policies supporting green production, compensatory schemes will have to be established to cover the incremental costs of introducing cleaner technologies in developing countries.

Tax coordination and global value chains

The predominance of global value chains in international manufacturing and trade has motivated developing-country Governments to provide tax and other incentives to multinational companies in order to attract foreign investment and gain access to these chains. Quite often, there is a tendency to engage in "beggar thy neighbour" tax incentive competition, resulting in a race to the bottom. Tax incentives, however, are not prime movers in respect of decisions on production location made by multinational companies. As a result, Governments tend to lose out on significant tax revenue.

Strengthened international tax cooperation could prevent such tax competition. Tax cooperation should also reduce the scope for the use of transfer-pricing practices by multinational companies which, in order to evade taxes, value intra-firm transaction in such a way as to enable higher profits to be accounted for in locations where taxes are lowest. Effective international tax cooperation may yield significant additional resources for development, possibly exceeding by some margin the present level of annual flows of development assistance.

Regional versus multilateral trade agreements

Discrepancies between the multilateral trading framework, on the one hand, and proliferating economic partnership agreements as well as bilateral and regional free trade agreements, on the other, represent another source of policy incoherence. Consequently,

---

2 United Nations, *Treaty Series*, vol. 1771, No. 30822.

3 See *Legal Instruments Embodying the Results of the Uruguay Round of Multilateral Trade Negotiations, done at Marrakesh on 15 April 1994* (GATT secretariat publication, Sales No. GATT/1994-7).

multilateral discipline regarding free trade agreements and economic partnership agreements needs to be strengthened. At the same time, the negotiation capacity of developing countries adhering to free trade agreements and economic partnership agreements will need to be enhanced. Trade-related technical assistance continues to be inadequate and needs further expansion. Also, in the World Trade Organization, where countries are equal, not all members have the capacity to participate in all negotiations with full-strength teams. Countries whose resources are inadequate for obtaining and utilizing the information required for their engagement in World Trade Organization-related activities need additional assistance.

Refocusing the World Trade Organization

Through the establishment of the World Trade Organization, there emerged the first international enforcement system in economic matters. The dispute settlement mechanism of the World Trade Organization sanctions retaliation through trade measures. It has also encompassed a significant proliferation of multilateral disciplines covering a variety of so-called trade-related issues subject to this legal enforcement weapon. Most of these trade-related issues—especially intellectual property rights, investment measures, and trade in services (particularly financial services)—are of greater direct interest to developed countries. Difficult negotiations over trade-related issues have burdened the World Trade Organization's decision-making machinery and, in effect, have expanded its agenda and extended it into areas that would probably belong more properly within the purview of other agencies.

Coherence in global governance may require rethinking the scope of World Trade Organization disciplines. For instance, the financial crisis has highlighted the pressing need for better international financial regulation and better instruments for countries' management of capital flows. These regulatory needs create tensions with the General Agreement on Trade in Services,[4] which aims at easing cross-border financial services flows (Modes 1 and 2). Such inconsistencies can be avoided by defining multilateral rules on trade in financial services as part of a reformed international financial regulatory framework looked after by a specialized body (see below). Similarly, the complexity of regulatory needs regarding cross-border movements of people could justify the consideration of a separate multilateral framework for consular practices and immigration laws so as to create a transparent and non-discriminatory system of migration for people who wish to move, temporarily or permanently, across borders.

Making dispute mechanisms more equitable

Enforcement mechanisms for trade commitments have to be made more equitable. Serious deficiencies remain at every stage of the World Trade Organization dispute settlement process. Given the substantial cost, poorer nations are deterred from bringing cases into that process. Retaliation is the only possible sanction. Since all economic sanctions are costly to the initiator, a poor country's ability to impose a sanction on a rich one is much more limited than that of a rich country seeking to impose a sanction on a poor one. Ensuring the viability of the World Trade Organization process and its enforcement mechanism in the long term requires the counteracting of existing biases. In domestic litigation, legal aid is used to provide the poor with better access to justice which is costly: the injured party is

4 Ibid.

awarded its costs by the court while centrally organized sanctions spare the injured party from having to bear all the costs of punishing the violator. Analogously, the inclusion of compensatory mechanisms in the World Trade Organization dispute settlement process could introduce greater justice into the enforcement of multilateral trading rules.

Reforming the international financial system

Fundamental weaknesses in the international financial system played a key role in the current global economic crisis. Financial deregulation and lifting of capital controls in most countries had supported greater global financial integration during the 1990s and 2000s. It also facilitated the move of financial innovation into the area of new, complex derivatives and the increased distancing of financial instruments from more tangible and productive assets. This fed a rapid expansion of short-term capital movements. Financial markets also became increasingly interwoven with insurance, commodity and real estate markets through complex instruments that could be easily transacted internationally. In large part, this process of "financialization" expanded beyond the control of regulators. In addition to fostering an illusion of asset diversification, the system promoted excessive risk-taking and asset inflation bubbles which stimulated what proved to be an unsustainable pattern of global economic growth. Unregulated financial expansion also fed pro-cyclical capital flow volatility and speculation in commodity markets. The latter played some role in the fuel and food crises.

The central function of a financial system is to intermediate efficiently between savers and investors and to provide reliable and adequate long-term financing for investment. Financial growth of the past decades clearly lost track of that function. The rate of (productive) investment stagnated in most parts of the world, despite the explosive growth in finance (figure O.5). Greater capital mobility has given developing countries greater access to financial resources, but it has also made macroeconomic policy management more challenging because of the volatile and boom-bust nature of financial flows in deregulated markets.

In today's world of increased economic and political interdependence, achieving a broad-based, rapid and sustained growth in employment and incomes involves even more complex policy challenges than those of the past. The multilateral arrangements designed at Bretton Woods did not include a global regime for capital movements, as capital mobility was expected to be limited. However, even after the breakdown of those arrangements, and despite the surge in private capital flows, no such regime emerged. Clearly, a renewed Bretton Woods system will be needed to help both developed and developing countries mitigate the damaging effects of volatile capital flows and commodity prices.

Strengthening international financial cooperation

A number of options are available for creating a more stable financial system and a better environment for sustainable growth. Some are being addressed as part of the responses to the 2008-2009 global crisis, but probably all will need to be adopted, and simultaneously, to bring about the desired outcome.

First, improved international financial regulation is needed to stem excessive risk-taking and capital flow volatility, including through appropriate capital controls and macro-prudential regulatory reforms imposing counter-cyclical biases in rules for reserve requirements and loan-loss provisioning.

Figure O.5
Rapid financial growth but stagnant fixed investment, 1970-2008

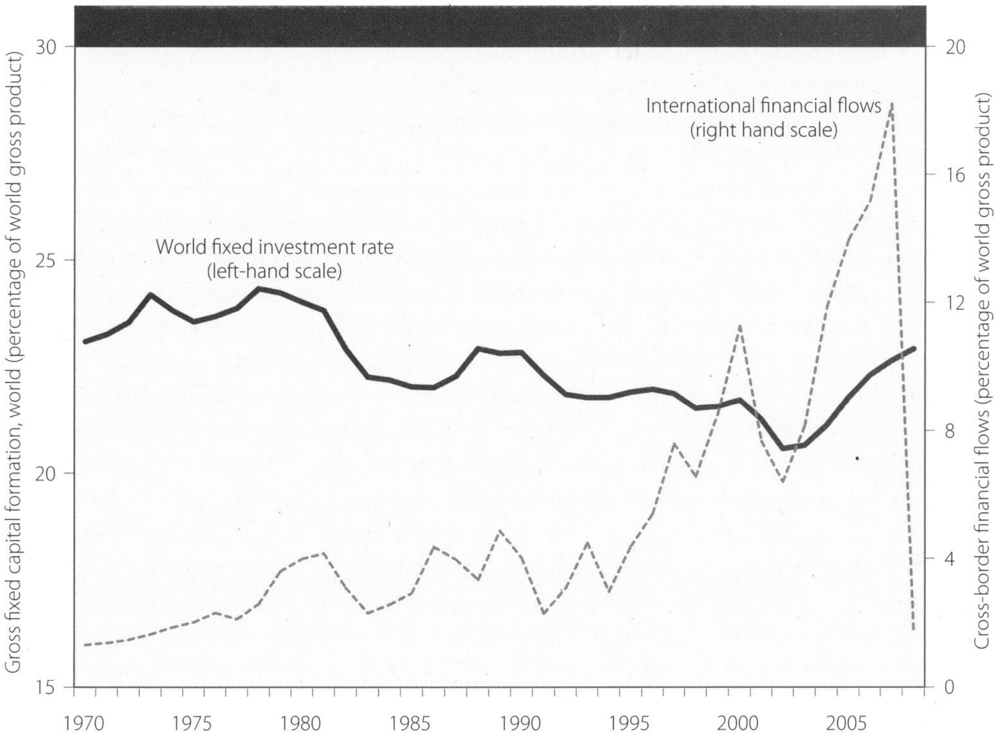

Source: UN/DESA, based on United Nations Statistics Division, National Accounts Main Aggregates; and, International Monetary Fund, *International Financial Statistics.*

Second, strengthened international tax coordination and lifting of bank secrecy are needed for comprehensive financial regulatory and supervisory reforms so as to ensure that oversight extends to offshore banking centres which currently are unregulated and operate as tax havens.

Third, as new systems of regulation are being elaborated, there is a need for a fundamental revision of existing mechanisms of compensatory financing designed to cope with external shocks. Such revisions should ensure more adequate availability of and easier access to international liquidity, especially for developing countries, by modifying the terms of access to such resources along the lines of recent reforms of IMF credit facilities but with a further easing of access, especially for low-income countries, through alignment with national development strategies and new aid modalities, as proposed above.

Fourth, multilateral surveillance will need to be revised so as to include within its purview all possible international spillovers of national economic policies. Surveillance for crisis prevention and safeguarding of global financial stability remains a key responsibility of IMF, which has centred its efforts on external stability and exchange-rate assessment. It did not prove effective in preventing the recent global crisis, in part because the existing mechanism did not differentiate among countries in terms of their influence on systemic stability—that is to say, surveillance was not more rigorous for countries issuing major reserve currencies. Such differentiation should be an essential part of surveillance; but, more importantly, perhaps it should be embedded in a strengthened and institutionalized mechanism for coordinating macroeconomic policies internationally. As the crisis has made clear, such a mechanism is needed in order to moderate swings in the global business cycle and address the problem of global financial imbalances. The promise of the Group of Twenty (G-20) to establish a framework for generating strong, sustainable and balanced world economic growth should be fleshed out and operationalized urgently. However, as sustainable rebalancing of the world economy will take many years, the implementation of such a framework cannot be left to informal consultations at the level of the G-20: it will require proper institutionalization within the multilateral system and establishment of enforcement mechanisms to make policy coordination effective and accountable.

Fifth, a new global reserve system could be created, one that no longer relies on the United States dollar as the single major reserve currency. The dollar has proved not to be a stable store of value, which is a requisite for a stable reserve currency. Nonetheless, motivated in part by needs for self-insurance against volatility in commodity markets and capital flows, many developing countries accumulated vast amounts of such reserves during the 2000s. Hence, a new system needs to be developed. That system should allow for better pooling of reserves at the regional and international levels; it must not be based on a single currency or even multiple national currencies but, instead, should permit the emission of international liquidity (such as SDRs) to create a more stable global financial system. Such emissions of international liquidity could also underpin the financing of investment in long-term sustainable development, as suggested above.

Reforming governance of the international financial architecture

None of these reforms will work effectively, however, if the democratic deficit undermining the credibility of the Bretton Woods institutions is not repaired. The governance structure of IMF and the World Bank must be reformed so as to more adequately reflect changes in the weights of actors in the world economy, and to be more responsive to current and future challenges, thereby strengthening the legitimacy and effectiveness of these institutions. It is important not only to rebalance voting power in these institutions but to fundamentally restructure their functions and to equip them with the resources necessary to enable them to effectively safeguard global financial stability, coordinate macroeconomic policies and provide adequate long-term development financing.

A new multilateral agency would need to be created to enforce the rules to be established for better and more comprehensive international financial regulation and supervision. Existing institutions, such as the Basel Committee on Banking Supervision and the Financial Stability Board, are too limited in terms of the scope of their functions and instruments and they lack sufficient representation. The new multilateral financial authority would also need to ensure coherence between the global financial regulatory framework and multilateral trade rules.

Is fair and sustainable globalization feasible?

The present set of institutions and rules for managing the world economy were established more than 60 years ago together with the founding of the United Nations and the creation of IMF, the World Bank and the General Agreement on Tariffs and Trade (GATT). Since then, the world has changed beyond recognition, while, in contrast, institutions for global governance have changed little or have adapted slowly. National economies have become ever more closely integrated through trade, investment, finance, international migration, and the technological revolutions in transport and communications.

It is clear that development outcomes in the twenty-first century will be shaped, to a large extent, by the international context. It is also clear that the inequities, both in formal terms and in practice, in the ground rules operating throughout the world economy is unduly restricting the policy space essential for promoting development. This year's *World Economic and Social Survey* argues that there is a need to eliminate inconsistencies in multilateral rules-setting related to different spheres and to international versus national objectives. This can be achieved through progress in achieving the following key actions:

- Empowering national authorities to deploy a much broader range of development policies than those implemented in the last two decades through reform of aid mechanisms, international trade disciplines and financial regulations
- Significantly expanding the access of developing countries to technology so as to render it comparable with the access provided to the international trade in goods
- Establishing just, predictable and comparable regulatory regimes to facilitate the international movement of both labour and capital
- Institutionalizing counter-cyclical macroeconomic coordination through reforms in surveillance mechanisms and the global payments and reserve system
- Achieving effective coordination in financial regulation and tax cooperation, which will require abandoning the self-defeating State competition over foreign investment flows that has gone on for years
- Averting the threat of climate change through globally coordinated action, which will require adjustments, through the aid, trade and financial architectures, in rules-setting and priority-setting so as to make them coherent with global sustainable development objectives

Retooling the rules of the game for a fair and sustainable global development is necessary, but not sufficient. It is also about the players. Providing developing countries having weaker initial conditions with more time, resources and policy space for becoming full participants is not to be regarded as an act of charity or goodwill on the part of the powerful but as an imperative for realizing the shared goal of expanding international commerce. The principle of common-but-differentiated rights and obligations defined as a function of level of development will need to be applied in practice and embedded within a system of clear rules.

Reshaping rules is easier said than done. Players will need to agree on the common global sustainable development goals to be pursued and will need to be convinced that cooperation will provide net benefits for all—benefits serving present and future generations. However, within any scheme of international cooperation, net benefits may be perceived as not being equal for all; and any expected unevenness in outcomes may impede the reaching of effective global solutions. Because of differences in living standards, and therefore in capacity to pay, some countries will be expected to shoulder larger shares of the total costs of providing global public goods, which may reduce their incentive to cooperate in providing them. Hence, with respect to establishing multilateral agreements, the proposed pattern of burden-sharing is as important as the extent of the benefits to be conferred by the public goods.

The international community must face a key fact, namely, that the pattern of uneven development brought about by globalization so far has been sustainable neither economically nor environmentally, nor has it been feasible politically. As this time around, developing countries are much more significant and much better integrated into the world economy, the global crisis has profounder implications and more serious consequences for development.

While the present crisis only highlights the ever-present risks associated with the deeper integration of national economies into the world economy, the issue concerns not so much a retreat from globalization, although in quantitative terms the current crisis is forcing such a trend, as a feasible reshaping of the globalization process. The proposed means of retooling the existing aid, trade and financial architectures aim at overcoming present shortcomings. It is equally important to overcome institutional shortcomings in current decision-making in the key organizations of global economic governance, such as IMF and the World Bank, and to eliminate inequities in respect of the access to participation in other organizations, such as the World Trade Organization.

There is a need to strengthen the global coordination of economic decision-making so as to minimize the number of cases where rules dealing with trade, aid, debt, finance, migration, environmental sustainability and other development issues come into conflict. At present, there is no international agency dealing systematically with questions of coherence and consistency in multilateral rules-setting. Although in 1995, it was proposed that a reformed United Nations Economic and Social Council exercise this directive role, the proposal received only modest support at the time.

The global crisis has provided painful evidence of the weaknesses of the present system. The issues of climate change and demographic changes demand even greater coherence among the spheres of global governance and between decision-making processes at the global and national levels. Whatever its shape, the foundation to be established for international coordination based on shared principles and transparent mechanisms is more urgently needed than ever.

沙祖康

Sha Zukang
Under-Secretary-General
for Economic and Social Affairs
June 2010

Contents

Boxes

Figures

Tables

Explanatory notes

The following symbols have been used in the tables throughout the report:

..	**Two dots** indicate that data are not available or are not separately reported.
–	**A dash** indicates that the amount is nil or negligible.
-	**A hyphen (-)** indicates that the item is not applicable.
-	**A minus sign (-)** indicates deficit or decrease, except as indicated.
.	**A full stop (.)** is used to indicate decimals.
/	**A slash (/)** between years indicates a crop year or financial year, for example, 2009/10.
-	**Use of a hyphen (-)** between years, for example, 2009-2010, signifies the full period involved, including the beginning and end years.

Reference to "dollars" ($) indicates United States dollars, unless otherwise stated.

Reference to "billions" indicates one thousand million.

Reference to "tons" indicates metric tons, unless otherwise stated.

Annual rates of growth or change, unless otherwise stated, refer to annual compound rates.

Details and percentages in tables do not necessarily add to totals, because of rounding.

The following abbreviations have been used:

ASEAN	Association of Southeast Asian Nations
DAC	Development Assistance Committee of the Organization for Economic Cooperation and Development
EU	European Union
FDI	foreign direct investment
G-8	Group of Eight
G-20	Group of Twenty
GATT	General Agreement on Tariffs and Trade
GDP	gross domestic product
GNI	gross national income
GVC	global value chain
HIPCs	heavily indebted poor countries
IBRD	International Bank for Reconstruction and Development
ILO	International Labour Organization
IMF	International Monetary Fund
ODA	official development assistance
OECD	Organization for Economic Cooperation and Development
PPP	purchasing power parity
PRSPs	Poverty Reduction Strategy Papers
SDRs	special drawing rights
UNCTAD	United Nations Conference on Trade and Development
UNDAF	United Nations Development Assistance Framework
UN/DESA	Department of Economic and Social Affairs of the United Nations Secretariat
UNFCCC	United Nations Framework Convention on Climate Change
UNU-WIDER	World Institute for Development Economics Research of the United Nations University
WGP	world gross product
WIPO	World Intellectual Property Organization

The designations employed and the presentation of the material in this publication do not imply the expression of any opinion whatsoever on the part of the United Nations Secretariat concerning the legal status of any country, territory, city or area or of its authorities, or concerning the delimitation of its frontiers or boundaries.

The term "country" as used in the text of this report also refers, as appropriate, to territories or areas.

For analytical purposes, unless otherwise specified, the following country groupings and subgroupings have been used:

Developed economies (developed market economies):

Australia, Canada, European Union, Iceland, Japan, New Zealand, Norway, Switzerland, United States of America.

European Union (EU):

Austria, Belgium, Bulgaria, Cyprus, Czech Republic, Denmark, Estonia, Finland, France, Germany, Greece, Hungary, Ireland, Italy, Latvia, Lithuania, Luxembourg, Malta, Netherlands, Poland, Portugal, Romania, Slovakia, Slovenia, Spain, Sweden, United Kingdom of Great Britain and Northern Ireland.

EU-15:

Austria, Belgium, Denmark, Finland, France, Greece, Germany, Ireland, Italy, Luxembourg, Netherlands, Portugal, Spain, Sweden, United Kingdom of Great Britain and Northern Ireland.

New EU member States:

Bulgaria, Cyprus, Czech Republic, Estonia, Hungary, Latvia, Lithuania, Malta, Poland, Romania, Slovakia, Slovenia.

Economies in transition:

South-eastern Europe:

Albania, Bosnia and Herzegovina, Croatia, Montenegro, Serbia, the former Yugoslav Republic of Macedonia.

Commonwealth of Independent States (CIS):

Armenia, Azerbaijan, Belarus, Georgia[a], Kazakhstan, Kyrgyzstan, Republic of Moldova, Russian Federation, Tajikistan, Turkmenistan, Ukraine, Uzbekistan.

Developing economies:

Africa, Asia and the Pacific (excluding Australia, Japan, New Zealand and the member States of CIS in Asia), Latin America and the Caribbean.

Subgroupings of Africa:

Northern Africa:

Algeria, Egypt, Libyan Arab Jamahiriya, Morocco, Tunisia.

Sub-Saharan Africa:

All other African countries, except Nigeria and South Africa, where indicated.

Subgroupings of Asia and the Pacific:

Western Asia:

Bahrain, Iraq, Israel, Jordan, Kuwait, Lebanon, Occupied Palestinian Territory, Oman, Qatar, Saudi Arabia, Syrian Arab Republic, Turkey, United Arab Emirates, Yemen.

South Asia:

Bangladesh, Bhutan, India, Iran (Islamic Republic of), Maldives, Nepal, Pakistan, Sri Lanka.

East Asia:

All other developing economies in Asia and the Pacific.

Subgroupings of Latin America and the Caribbean:

South America:

Argentina, Bolivia (Plurinational State of), Brazil, Chile, Colombia, Ecuador, Paraguay, Peru, Uruguay, Venezuela (Bolivarian Republic of).

Mexico and Central America:

Costa Rica, El Salvador, Guatemala, Honduras, Mexico, Nicaragua, Panama.

Caribbean:

Barbados, Cuba, Dominican Republic, Guyana, Haiti, Jamaica, Trinidad and Tobago.

a As of 19 August 2009, Georgia officially left the Commonwealth of Independent States. However, its performance is discussed in the context of this group of countries for reasons of geographical proximity and similarities in economic structure.

Least developed countries:

Afghanistan, Angola, Bangladesh, Benin, Bhutan, Burkina Faso, Burundi, Cambodia, Central African Republic, Chad, Comoros, Democratic Republic of the Congo, Djibouti, Equatorial Guinea, Eritrea, Ethiopia, Gambia, Guinea, Guinea-Bissau, Haiti, Kiribati, Lao People's Democratic Republic, Lesotho, Liberia, Madagascar, Malawi, Maldives, Mali, Mauritania, Mozambique, Myanmar, Nepal, Niger, Rwanda, Samoa, Sao Tome and Principe, Senegal, Sierra Leone, Solomon Islands, Somalia, Sudan, Timor-Leste, Togo, Tuvalu, Uganda, United Republic of Tanzania, Vanuatu, Yemen, Zambia.

Small island developing States and areas:

American Samoa, Anguilla, Antigua and Barbuda, Aruba, Bahamas, Barbados, Belize, British Virgin Islands, Cape Verde, Commonwealth of the Northern Mariana Islands, Comoros, Cook Islands, Cuba, Dominica, Dominican Republic, Fiji, French Polynesia, Grenada, Guam, Guinea-Bissau, Guyana, Haiti, Jamaica, Kiribati, Maldives, Marshall Islands, Mauritius, Micronesia (Federated States of), Montserrat, Nauru, Netherlands Antilles, New Caledonia, Niue, Palau, Papua New Guinea, Puerto Rico, Saint Kitts and Nevis, Saint Lucia, Saint Vincent and the Grenadines, Samoa, Sao Tome and Principe, Seychelles, Singapore, Solomon Islands, Suriname, Timor-Leste, Tonga, Trinidad and Tobago, Tuvalu, United States Virgin Islands, Vanuatu.

Group of Eight (G-8):

Canada, France, Germany, Italy, Japan, Russian Federation, United Kingdom of Great Britain and Northern Ireland, United States of America.

Group of Twenty (G-20):

Argentina, Australia, Brazil, Canada, China, France, Germany, India, Indonesia, Italy, Japan, Mexico, Republic of Korea, Russian Federation, Saudi Arabia, South Africa, Turkey, United Kingdom of Great Britain and Northern Ireland, United States of America, European Union.

Chapter I
Introduction

As the world emerges from its worst recession since the Second World War, it is important to remind ourselves that interdependence across nations is an essential feature of economic development. Over the past few years, many have come to feel that interdependence is the carrier of economic distress. Skyrocketing food and energy prices have affected the livelihoods of many. The strong rise in food prices during 2007 and 2008 exposed not only the structural basis of food insecurity—the result of decades of underinvestment in agriculture, especially in developing countries—but also the interconnectedness of such insecurity with other global problems. The effects of climate change are already being felt in many parts of the world in the form of more frequent and intense droughts and excessive rainfall which have exacerbated food insecurity and intensified price volatility.

Climate change, financial integration and global value chains are making for increasing interdependence throughout the world

Efforts to mitigate climate change, like the promotion of biofuels, have led to shifting land-use patterns and have crowded out food production for human consumption. World commodity markets, having become intertwined with financial markets through derivatives trading, have also become increasingly speculative. Owing to largely unfettered deepening of global financial integration, systemic financial distress in one country has spread quickly to many countries. Trade channels have always served as vehicles for the spillover of a recession in one country into another; but at the height of the present crisis, global trade collapsed precipitously because of the dominance of global value chains in today's production and trade.

It was not meant to be this way. With the fall of the Berlin Wall, there were hopes that a new rising tide of globalization would bring about enough peace and prosperity to lift all boats. There have certainly been gains: inflation has been contained, international trade has expanded, capital has flowed across borders on an unprecedented scale, and there has been substantial progress in reducing global poverty. Still, the growth and poverty reduction record has been uneven and the achievement of such gains is bound up with widening global macroeconomic imbalances and the degradation of the world's natural environment.

New thinking about global economic development is necessary

The food, energy, financial and climate crises that unfolded simultaneously at the end of the first decade of the twenty-first century have exposed major weaknesses in existing mechanisms designed to manage the process of global development. While the strong desire for quick recovery from the present world economic and financial crisis is understandable, getting "back on track" does not seem to be an option, as it would mean returning to an unsustainable path of global development. Sustained and widespread future prosperity will require major reforms in global economic governance and new thinking about global economic development.

Policy responses will need to be highly coherent at various levels

A central concern of the new thinking will be the need for a focus concentrated on sustainable development—entailing an approach that would balance material wealth improvements with protection of the natural environment and ensure social equity and justice—rather than one narrowly centred on economic growth and private wealth generation based on market incentives. Global solutions will be required for global problems and, given the interdependence of these problems, policy responses will need to be highly coherent at various levels if the international community is to achieve the multiple objectives associated with fair and sustainable global development.

Globalization at a crossroad

The balance of global economic power is shifting

The fact that the world is changing rapidly poses additional challenges in respect of finding pathways towards a feasible fair and sustainable development. First, there are important shifts taking place in the global economy. The rapid growth in developing Asia which is shifting the balance of global economic power is likely to continue, thereby moving further towards a world economy with multiple engines of growth. Apart from the recent crisis, this has been due not so much to the decline of the economies of the United States of America and the European Union (EU) as to the growth in strength of the economies of other countries. Brazil, the Russian Federation, India and China (the so-called BRIC countries) have become the new economic giants and are already making their presence felt in global forums, such as the platform of the Group of Twenty (G-20), and through their own interaction.

Per capita income of developing countries measured in terms of purchasing power parity (PPP) has more than quadrupled over the past half-century (figure I.1). Also in PPP terms, the weight of Brazil, China and India in the world economy increased from 10 per cent in 1950 to 27 per cent in 2008 (figure I.2). The Russian Federation is adding another 2.5 per cent. Measured this way, the weight of each of today's major economic powers, the United States and Western Europe, has dropped from over one quarter to less than one fifth.

Redressing global inequality will be a major challenge in the decades ahead

While several developing countries (mostly in Asia) have experienced a significant "convergence" towards the living standards of the now advanced countries, others, especially in Africa, have fallen farther behind (figures I.1 and I.3). The number of the world's poor living on less than $1.25 per day decreased from 1.8 billion in 1990 to 1.4 billion in 2005, but nearly all of this reduction was concentrated in China. In sub-Saharan Africa

Figure I.1
Diverging per capita income growth[a] among developing countries, 1950-2010

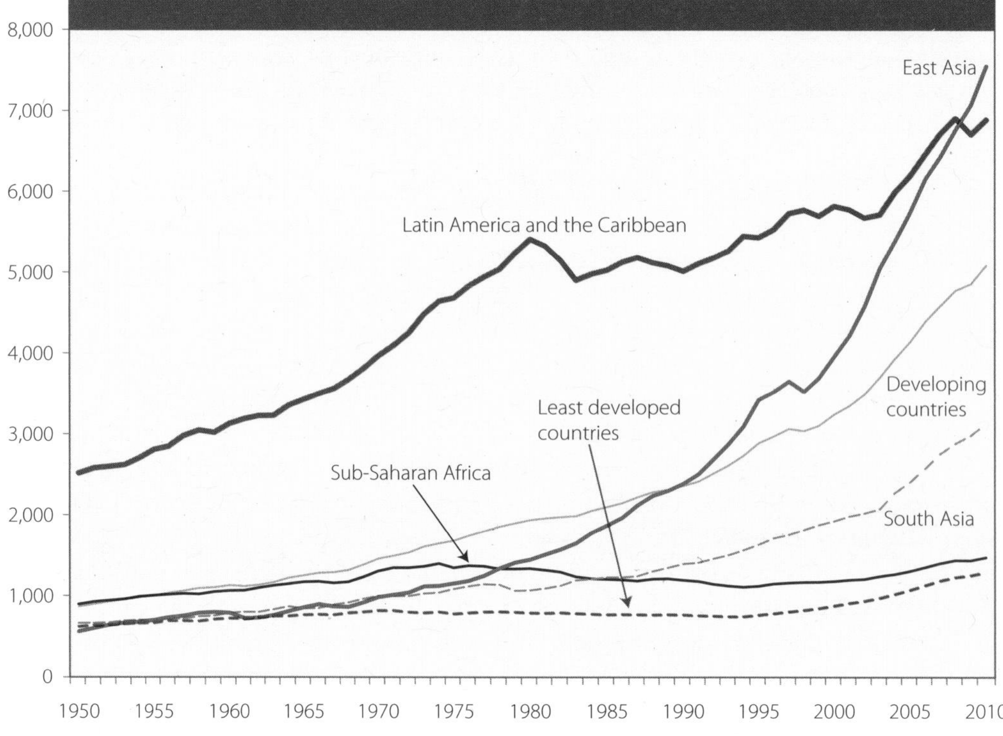

Sources: UN/DESA calculations, based on Angus Maddison, Historical Statistics of the World Economy: 1-2008 AD (2010) (available from http://www.ggdc.net/maddison); and UN/DESA, World Economic Situation and Prospects database (available at http://www.un.org/esa/policy/link/global_economic_outlook.htm).

a Gross domestic product (GDP) per capita in 1990 Geary-Khamis international dollars.

Figure I.2
Shifting global economic power measured as shares of world gross product,[a] 1950-2008

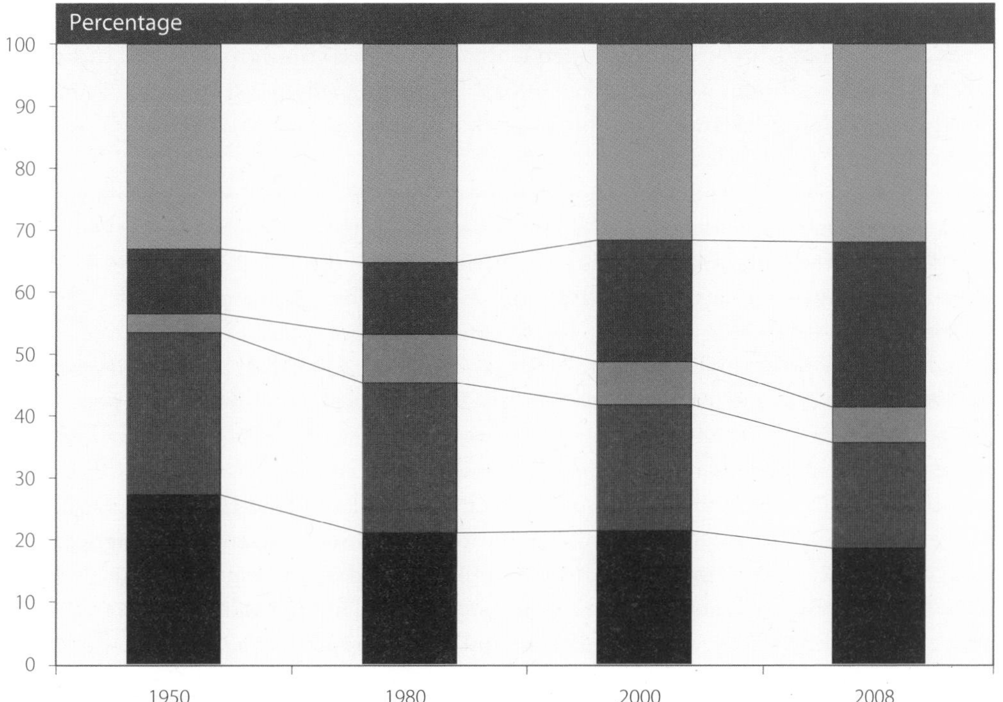

Source: UN/DESA calculations, based on Angus Maddison, Historical Statistics of the World Economy: 1-2008 AD (2010). Available from http://www.ggdc.net/maddison.

a In 1990 Geary-Khamis international dollars.

Figure I.3
Global income divergence,[a] 1950-2008

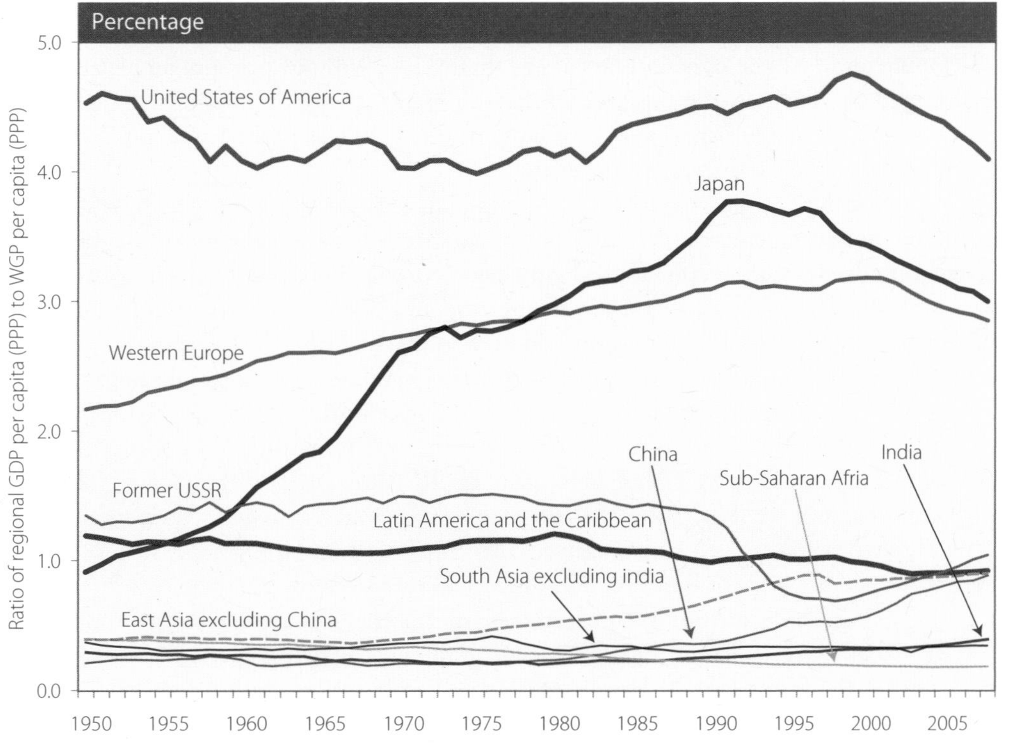

Source: UN/DESA calculations, based on Angus Maddison, Historical Statistics of the World Economy: 1-2008 AD (2010). Available from http://www.ggdc.net/maddison.

a Measured as the ratio of regional gross domestic product per capita (purchasing power parity (PPP)) to world gross product (WGP) per capita (PPP).

and South Asia, the absolute number of the poor increased (see chap. II). At the same time, with few exceptions, income inequalities within countries have increased since the early 1980s. Aggregate measures for global inequality, which combine within- and between-country income disparities, show clearly increasing trends over the past decades—trends revealed to be starkly unambiguous when China is excluded (Bourguignon and Morrison, 2002; Milanovic, 2005; World Bank, 2006a). Redressing this trend in global economic divergence, so as to prevent its becoming a source of new tensions and insecurity, will be a major challenge in the decades ahead.

Demographic changes will strongly influence the nature of global interdependence

Second, demographic changes in the coming decades will strongly influence increasing global interdependence. World population is projected to grow by another 2 billion-3 billion over the next four decades. This means that, by 2050, the global economy would need to be able to provide a decent living for more than 9 billion people, of which 85 per cent will be living in developing countries. These changes need not create a Malthusian dearth of food, but they will put further pressure on the world's ecosystems. Developing countries will have to adapt to growing urban populations. By 2050, 70 per cent of the world's population is projected to live in urban areas, and mega-cities that are undergoing further growth will create problems of their own. A growing global middle class added to fast developing-country growth and larger urban populations will also change food and land-use patterns, with the implications being potentially vast. In addition to the decline in the amount of agricultural land, there will be a stark increase in the consumption of meat and dairy products, leading, if the phenomenon is not addressed in a timely manner, to land-use shifts and further deforestation, higher energy use, rising food prices and regional food shortages.

Population pressures will also increase such current problems as high unemployment and underemployment. Rapid urban growth will amplify the challenge of redressing persistent widespread poverty and inequality among urban-dwellers. Progress in human development worldwide has helped to drastically reduce mortality rates and allow people to live longer. As a result, the world population is ageing rapidly. The fact that, by 2050, 1 in 4 persons living in developed countries, and 1 in 7 living in what are now developing ones, will be over 65 years of age (figure I.4), will put pressure on pension and health systems. Further, the presence of declining and ageing populations in developed regions and continued disparity in economic opportunities across nations may result in much larger migration flows than occur today.

Greater prosperity for humanity has come with huge environmental costs having global repercussions

Third, the growing world population has been supported in part by the degradation of our natural environment. About one half of the forests that covered the Earth are gone, groundwater sources are rapidly being depleted, enormous reductions in biodiversity have already taken place and, through the burning of fossil fuels, about 30 billion tons of carbon dioxide are currently being emitted each year. The impact of climate change is already being felt through the occurrence of more frequent and intense floods and drought, which, inter alia, is affecting the food situation of many of the world's poorest, especially in parts of Africa and Asia. Thus, greater prosperity for humanity has come with huge environmental costs having global consequences. The threat of climate change illustrates this and, as demonstrated by the analysis provided in *World Economic and Social Survey 2009* (United Nations, 2009a), containing this threat will require major transformations of energy systems, industrial production processes and infrastructure.

Without reform, tensions will grow between decision-making processes at national and global levels

Fourth, as already mentioned, economic processes are increasingly interconnected globally. Agricultural and industrial production is being carried out more and more within the framework of largely unregulated global value chains dominated by international companies. The global crisis has made clear just how interconnected financial

Figure I.4
An ageing world population, developed and developing countries, 2000-2050

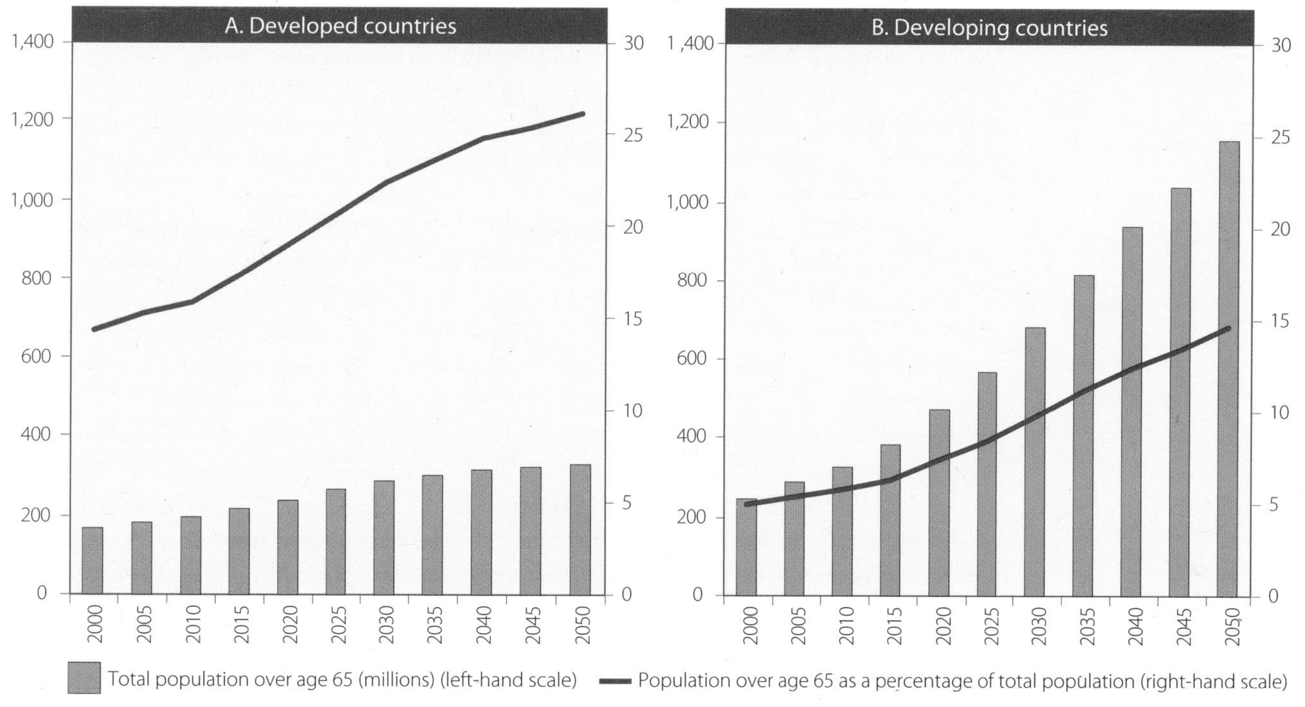

Source: Population Division, UN/DESA, World Population Prospects: The 2008 Revision Population Database. Available from http://www.esa.un.org/unpp. See also *World Population Prospects: The 2008 Revision*, vol. I; *Comprehensive Tables* (United Nations publication, Sales No. 10.XIII.2).

markets are and how quickly problems in one part of the system can cause shock waves elsewhere. Climate change and increasing migratory flows are challenges with global ramifications. Yet, the policies, rules and institutions established to govern these processes are mostly national, while the global mechanisms that do exist are compartmentalized and in need of better coordination. Without reform, tensions will grow between decision-making processes at the national level and those at the global level.

The question is how to reform the institutions responsible for global governance so as to make them better equipped to address these challenges coherently while allowing nations and their people to have the space needed for determining their own destinies.

Development in an interdependent world

The emergence of the post-war international financial and trade architecture

Globalization has been with us since dawn of history, but the desire to exert control over its ramifications is of more recent vintage. As the immediate post-was period was marked by the creation of the International Monetary Fund (IMF) and the International Bank for Reconstruction and Development (IBRD) (both in 1944) and the United Nations Organization (in 1945), it is often regarded as the time when international economic cooperation reached its peak. The special circumstances of the time, with many of the countries involved in the creation process having being exhausted by the War while still living in the shadow cast by the Great Depression of the 1930s, became the source of a great willingness to forge a new international financial architecture, although its design was left largely to an inner circle comprising two countries, namely, the United States and the United Kingdom of Great Britain and Northern Ireland (Toye, 2010).

The post-war system of global governance sought to avoid the "beggar thy neighbour"-type policies of the 1930s

In the 1930s, the "beggar thy neighbour"-type policies of most Governments—entailing the use of currency devaluations to increase the competitiveness of a country's export products and reduce balance-of-payments deficits—worsened national deflationary spirals, which resulted in plummeting national incomes, shrinking demand, mass unemployment, and an overall decline in world trade. To overcome the weaknesses embedded in the pre-war international monetary system, a system of fixed exchange rates was introduced with the United States dollar as the reserve currency and with the dollar pegged to the price of gold. Short-run balance-of-payment difficulties would be overcome by IMF loans. The new system would facilitate stable currency exchange rates, and a country with payment deficits would not have to induce a cut in national income to bring it to a level low enough for import demand to finally fall within that country's means. The agreement made no provisions for the creation of international reserves.

A dollar shortage limited post-war reconstruction and development financing

As the United States, the country with the reserve currency, was running large trade surpluses in the immediate post-war period, a dollar shortage arose in the international payment system which then restricted the financing available for post-war reconstruction and development. The International Bank for Reconstruction and Development, then the most important institution within the World Bank Group, initially had too limited a lending capacity to offset this shortage (Mason and Asher, 1973). To remedy the situation, the United States encouraged capital outflows and set up the European Recovery Program (better known as the Marshall Plan) to provide, largely through grants rather than loans, large-scale financial and economic aid for the rebuilding of Europe. IBRD lending and Marshall Plan-like support, as conceived, subsequently became central in meeting the needs of developing countries for development assistance and long-term financing.

Inconsistencies between multilateral rules and national policy space have been a continuing source of controversy

The trade-related component of the envisaged post-war international architecture—an International Trade Organization—was not established until a much later date. Instead, international trade arrangements were governed by the interim General Agreement on Tariffs and Trade (GATT) of 1947, which lasted until 1995, when it was replaced by the World Trade Organization. The GATT was mainly concerned with modalities for negotiating reductions in industrial tariffs on a non-discriminatory basis, albeit with safeguards erected against trading arrangements that would be detrimental to industrial employment (Toye, 2010). Tariff reduction was a matter of considerable interest to the advanced economies, but had less appeal for the developing countries, many of which had gained independence only during the 1950s and 1960s and wished to pursue economic development strategies through the use of industrial and trade policies. Such perceived inconsistencies between the virtues of having a common set of multilateral rules and the need for the policy space required to pursue national development objectives have been a continuing source of controversy in the course of shaping the international economic architecture.

Shifting development paradigms

Early development thinking focused on modern economic growth and strong government leadership

Views about what types of international arrangements would best serve global and national development goals have changed with the shifts in the thinking about the factors conducive to growth and development in countries at low levels of development. In the

1950s and 1960s, development had been perceived in terms of a process of economic growth. Lack of capital and lack of industrial and entrepreneurial capacity were seen as major obstacles to growth. To overcome these obstacles, what was required was strong government leadership, which would steer the development process in the right direction by conducting the policies and mobilizing the resources needed to lift binding constraints on economic growth. This was to be achieved through, for example, public investments aimed at building infrastructure, trade protection and industrial policies designed to promote import substitution and develop entrepreneurial capacity, and through attracting development assistance in lifting foreign-exchange constraints.

In the aftermath of the Great Depression, public management of the economy had emerged as a primary activity of Governments, including in the developed countries. Building on Keynesian theoretical insights, Governments made employment, stability and growth important subjects of public policy and took responsibility for assuring their citizens a degree of economic well-being, with such steps leading to the creation of the welfare State. In Europe and Japan, industrial policies were key elements in post-war reconstruction.

The first generation of development economists, many of whom were associated with the United Nations system, such as Paul Rosenstein-Rodan, Michal Kalecki, W.A. Lewis, Gunnar Myrdal, Hans Singer, Raúl Prebisch and Jan Tinbergen, likewise thought in terms of broad, integrated macrostrategies (Meier and Seers, eds., 2001) and saw development as a transformational process. Poor countries would need to move away from a dependence on primary exports and the rural economy and develop manufacturing industries in order to foster more dynamic growth processes; major investments in infrastructure and new activities would be needed to create the right initial conditions. To describe the non-marginal changes that would need to occur, these economists used metaphors like the "snowball" (Lewis), the "big push" (Rosenstein-Rodan), "dynamic linkages" (Hirschman) and the "take-off" (Rostow). Different views existed on how best to induce the necessary change, but the dominant one was that the developmental State should be the prime mover.

Exceptions to multilateral trade rules addressed mainly short-term adjustment issues of developing countries

In the 1950s and 1960s, some modifications to the GATT and IMF policies aimed at accommodating developing-country interests. In 1955, for example, developing countries were granted special treatment in the GATT, allowing them to protect particular industries and introduce quantitative restrictions so as to address balance-of-payments difficulties. In 1963, the Compensatory Finance Facility was introduced by IMF for countries suffering sudden shortfalls in export revenues. Rather than facilitate industrial capacity-building over the long-run, these exceptions to multilateral trade rules addressed mainly short-term adjustment issues. The European Economic Community also granted trade preferences to its former colonial territories and set up a fund to offset commodity price fluctuations (Stabex), thereby moving further away from the original GATT principles towards a multiplicity of uncoordinated preference regimes (Toye, 2010).

As discussed in chapter II, a number of developing countries managed to successfully navigate their way amid such hurdles in international rules-setting and pragmatically implemented sets of policies promoting modern growth strategies. High rates of economic growth were achieved in large parts of the developing world, sometimes with sustained success, as in parts of Asia. The industrial development that was behind high tariff protection and other government support also led to substantial average welfare increases in Latin America during the 1950s and 1960s, followed, however, by relative stagnation starting in the 1980s and 1990s (figure I.1).

Yet, the many instances of failure to create industries in developing countries that could survive on their own after decades of State support, to effectively overcome foreign-exchange constraints, to generate sufficient employment and to reduce poverty and inequality, led to reassessments of development policies and cooperation. The "basic needs approach to development", for instance, suggested reorienting Government intervention towards more direct support for employment generation and securing access for all to social services (International Labour Organization, 1976). Similar approaches emphasized interventions on behalf of the poor to reduce income inequality and increase gains from aggregate economic growth (Chenery and others, 1974).

Perceived inequities in global economic governance led to a struggle in the 1970s for a New International Economic Order

Inequities in the rules and mechanisms for global economic governance were seen by some as constituting another key factor accounting for the lack of success of the development effort, which perception led to the struggle in the 1970s for a New International Economic Order (NIEO). Under this banner, there were calls for, inter alia, more national policy space for developing countries, regulation of foreign direct investment (FDI), international commodity agreements to protect the purchasing power of developing-country exports, lowering of the costs of technology transfers, more development assistance and greater voting power for developing countries in the multilateral institutions (Jolly and others, 2004). However, none of these proposals would become dominant in actual policy approaches.

In the meantime, significant shifts took place in the global context. The confidence in the dollar's peg to gold ebbed during the late 1960s, with persistent, and widening, United States balance-of-payments deficits and with European countries running increasing surpluses while remaining reluctant to revalue their exchange rates. This situation also exposed the inherent weakness of a global reserve system effectively linked to the national currency of just one country (see chap. V). The system of fixed exchange rates and capital controls was abandoned, but the dollar standard in effect remained. Exchange rates were allowed to float—or not—by country choice and major countries agreed to hold dollar reserves in the United States.

The lifting of many restrictions on cross-border financial transactions led to a surge in private capital flows, including to developing countries. As real interest rates were low in the period of high inflation of the 1970s, international borrowing from private sources, lending banks in particular, became an attractive external financing option for Governments in many developing countries, especially middle-income countries, compared with aid flows and multilateral bank lending which were often subject to restrictive policy conditions. As private capital flows proved strongly pro-cyclical and as borrowing conditions abruptly changed at the end of the 1970s, many developing countries ended up saddled with unserviceable debts.

The Washington consensus emerged as the dominant paradigm in the 1980s

The debt crisis had come to be perceived as another failure in the development effort, reflecting unsound fiscal management and failure to create dynamic export sectors which could have kept debt service-to-export ratios within sustainable bounds. Influenced by these events, another, diametrically opposite approach—commonly referred to as the "Washington Consensus", inasmuch as it reflected the policies of the multilateral institutions and decision makers based in Washington, D. C. (Williamson, ed., 1990)—gained prominence in the 1980s and 1990s. It argued for reconsideration altogether of a role for Governments in managing economic development for Governments were viewed as having distorted markets through their interventions and poor management of public finances. In this context, development policies would need to become more concerned with macroeconomic stability and to rely much more on deregulated markets and private initiative not only in productive activities but also in the provisioning of social services.

The market reforms would be conducive to "getting the prices right" and provide the necessary incentives for businesses and households to improve efficiency and invest in a better future. Different levels of success in achieving development were no longer explained by differences in initial conditions, but rather by whether the right policies (market-friendly, fiscally sound) or the wrong ones (interventionist) had been conducted.

Market reforms were not the key to growth successes in Asia

Sustained rapid economic growth in a number of countries in developing Asia was held up in the 1980s and 1990s as exemplifying the success of the market-oriented, export-led development strategies advocated by the Washington Consensus. In reality, however, the development policies behind these growth successes, especially in their early stages, resembled much more the recipes associated with the dirigiste paradigm of early development thinking and were not unlike the policies that had, in earlier times, promoted modern development in Western Europe and Japan. These development policies involved, inter alia, agrarian reforms, investments in human capital, selective trade protection, directed credit and other government support for developing industrial and technological capacity while exposing firms gradually to global competition.

Many other developing countries were strongly hit by the debt crisis and had to turn to IMF and the World Bank for structural adjustment loans which came attached with strict conditionality regarding fiscal adjustment and the initiation of market-oriented policy reforms. Trade liberalization and capital-account liberalization were key components of the reforms. Together with a further lifting of remaining restrictions on cross-border capital flows, this approach set off a new wave of growth in private capital flows to developing countries and further strengthened the trend towards production within global value chains.

Deregulated financial globalization and pro-cyclical private capital flows enhanced the risk of financial crises

The advance of deregulated financial globalization and the pro-cyclical nature of private capital flows also enhanced the risk of financial crises—crises witnessed by many emerging market economies during the 1990s and 2000s. As these crises inflicted hardly any hurt on the economies of developed countries, many analysts determined their cause to have been the policy mistakes made by the Governments of the (Asian and Latin American) countries affected. The crises served to expose the limited capacity of IMF to signal the risks whose build-up could lead to financial crises, as well as its limited lending capacity and consequent inability to come to the rescue when a crisis of significant magnitude did strike. Developed-country Governments, especially that of the United States, had to contribute resources in an ad hoc fashion to make up for this deficiency. Few saw the emerging market crises as evidence of growing systemic risks with potentially global repercussions and of the need for a fundamental reform of IMF to enable it to fulfil its function as guardian of the financial stability of the global economy (see, for example, De Gregorio and others, 1999). Although IMF did move to strengthen its early warning information system, little else was done to build in better safeguards against financial crises.

In fact, after the Asian crisis of the late 1990s, further measures were taken to liberalize financial sectors worldwide, giving greater scope to financial innovation and permitting high leverage ratios. Successful Asian exporters with large trade surpluses had already been accumulating dollar reserves on an increasing scale before the financial crises in their region, and continued on an even larger scale thereafter, motivated in part by the desire to provide greater self-insurance against future external shocks and crises. The reserve accumulation undervalued the currencies of the countries concerned, contributing to widening trade deficits in the United States, while at the same time helping to finance those deficits. Asian trade surpluses were thus recycled through the financial system in the United States which recycled portions back again to emerging market economies in the form of cross-border financial investments. This dynamic helped keep inflation and interest rates down worldwide and contributed to strong global growth during much of the 2000s; at the same time, however, it also inflated asset bubbles, induced excessive risk taking in financial sectors and was conducive to widening global imbalances, thereby planting the seeds of the global financial crisis of 2008.

The World Trade Organization moved further in the direction of reducing barriers to international trade in goods, services and investment and of enforcing property rights

The World Trade Organization (within which the GATT was subsumed in 1995) became the most substantial addition to the mechanisms of global economic governance during the period of the 1990s. The World Trade Organization moved towards setting tighter common rules designed to reduce barriers to international trade. Under the World Trade Organization, trade negotiations were broadened to encompass issues of importance to development prospects, such as trade in agricultural products heavily subsidized by developed countries; and some types of industrial policy for development, especially for the poorest countries, were permitted. While the World Trade Organization has become a near universal body, negotiations under the so-called Doha Round have stalled not only owing to disagreements over the issue of creating more space for developing countries to enable them to use subsidies and other measures in support of the build-up of their export industries, but also because of the question how to level the playing field for developing countries in respect of intellectual property rights so as to ease their access to technology, among other controversial areas. Meanwhile, a proliferation of economic partnership agreements and bilateral and regional free trade agreements has been complicating the multilateral trading system and generating inconsistencies, thus making achievement of a fairer trading system all the more challenging.

The United Nations Millennium Declaration has been responsible for a renewed focus on poverty reduction and human development

Adopted by the United Nations General Assembly at the turn of the new century, the United Nations Millennium Declaration[1] conveyed the rediscovery of the insight that market-based growth strategies were insufficient by themselves to solve the problem of widespread poverty and that well-functioning institutions and effective social policies were needed to ensure adequate provisioning of health care and education and to prevent the social exclusion of many. The decision to put Poverty Reduction Strategy Papers (PRSPs) at the centre of debt relief initiatives for the poorest countries was a reflection of the same insight. Nonetheless, trade and financial liberalization and fiscal prudence remained central to policy reforms in developing countries and the policy conditionality attached to multilateral lending. Policy shifts were more visible in the social arena, as reflected, inter alia, in greater priority for education and health spending, the introduction of innovative cash transfer programmes and support for microfinance schemes. Despite the existence of a broader development strategy as embodied in PRSPs, these social policy changes were often not well coordinated with economic policies. Macroeconomic policies, for instance, remained, for the most part, narrowly focused on price stabilization and fiscal consolidation, thereby constraining the required scaling up of Millennium Development Goals-oriented spending and/or failing to protect employment during economic downturns.

Where do we go from here?

There are no simple recipes for success in development

The experiences of the past decades have shown that there are no simple recipes for development success. Clearly, none of the dominant paradigms within the realm of development thinking that have emerged over time can take credit for having served as a blueprint for successful development. What worked in certain past contexts may not work equally well elsewhere. For one thing, the world has become increasingly integrated and the space

1 See General Assembly resolution 55/2.

available to countries for jump-starting their development in relative isolation has become commensurately smaller. As explored in chapter IV, the expanding role of FDI and global value chains in driving world production, trade and technology development has resulted in a limiting of the scope for the wielding of old-style industrial policy instruments by national Governments; and multilateral trading rules have imposed restrictions on domestic support measures for developing export industries. Further, freely flowing private capital flows have made macroeconomic stabilization much more challenging. Rules for intellectual property rights and quality standards have increased the cost for many developing countries of absorbing new technologies, becoming globally competitive and introducing greener production processes to combat and adapt to climate change. This does not mean that there is no policy space at all but, rather, that the narrowed scope in this regard is posing much greater challenges to policymakers today.

The role of the State is being reassessed

With the exposure by the global food, energy and financial crises of the systemic flaws inherent in the functioning of deregulated global markets, there has been a turn of the tide in the thinking about public policies. By intervening in the ways required by the crises, Governments have dealt a blow to the conventional wisdom underpinning the Washington Consensus. Their actions have led to a reassessment both of the role of the State in driving national development processes and of how national policies should be coordinated at the regional and global levels in order to engender outcomes consistent with objectives of global financial stability, shared prosperity and sustainability of the world's natural environment.

The mechanisms for achieving global economic governance have adapted insufficiently to global changes

The present set of institutions and rules for managing the world economy were established more than 60 years ago. Since then, the world has changed beyond recognition while the mechanisms for achieving global economic governance have either changed little or adapted but slowly.

Because of the complexity and interconnectedness of today's global challenges, a new balance must be found between international rules-setting and the provisioning of global public goods, on the one hand, and the creation of the space needed by nations to determine their own destiny, on the other. Striking such a new balance will not be easy: it will require a new kind of thinking and the striking of a new balance as well between decision-making processes at the national level and those at the global level. Retooling global development along these lines is the main theme of this year's *World Economic and Social Survey*. The study does not pretend to offer a blueprint but aims instead at presenting ideas that could become the basis for a new, coherent "toolbox" designed to guide development policies and international cooperation.

The chapters that follow address issues of coherence and incoherence among the different spheres of operation of multilateral rules and mechanisms for global economic governance and between global and national development objectives.

National development policies will need to seek a high degree of coherence which cuts across policy areas

Chapter II provides an overview of the evolution of development thinking, focusing in particular on the shifting paradigms elaborated to illustrate how best to achieve poverty reduction and higher levels of human development. Lessons from successful development experiences suggest that national policies will need to seek a high degree of coherence which cuts across policy areas and that the objective of achieving human and sustainable development will need to be mainstreamed into macroeconomic, sectoral, labour-market and social policies. Effectively implementing such national sustainable strategies will not be feasible without an enabling global environment. Low-income countries with limited access to other sources of financing, especially, will need the support of stable and predictable flows of development assistance.

The aid architecture needs to become needs-oriented

Chapter III demonstrates how the international aid architecture has become increasingly fragmented over time and, as is most likely, less effective. The analysis presented suggests that resolving these shortcomings may require going beyond the commitments set out in the 2005 Paris Declaration on Aid Effectiveness in order to put recipient countries much more securely in the driver's seat and align development assistance much more explicitly behind national development strategies. This would enable the aid architecture to become needs-oriented and could also facilitate alignment of official development assistance (ODA) with other sources of development financing in a more predictable manner, including through the use of trust fund mechanisms.

The multilateral trading system needs to seek greater coherence with other areas of global governance

Chapter IV describes the progress that has been made since the 1990s in setting *common* responsibilities within the framework of the multilateral trading system, while emphasizing that insufficient attention has been paid to the *differentiated* responsibilities of those economies having more limited capabilities for gainfully integrating into the global trading system. Broadening participation in global trade will require a fair multilateral trading regime, one that provides poorer countries with space for building domestic production capacity and pursuing sustainable development goals. It will also require significantly improving the access of developing countries to technology, to the point where it is comparable with the access that they have provided to their markets.

Just as significantly, that trading regime will have to deal with other frameworks for global governance and economic cooperation in key instances of incoherence, including between itself and the plethora of regional and bilateral free trading agreements, between multilateral trading rules and multilateral environmental agreements (especially those on climate change) and between rules on trade in services and international regulatory reforms and international tax cooperation. One may question whether, in the latter two areas, the World Trade Organization should be a prime mover or whether, instead, the main competency should lie eventually with specialized environment frameworks and an international financial authority.

The international financial architecture needs to undergo reform in five related areas

Chapter V analyses the fundamental shortcomings in the international financial architecture that were contributory to the present global financial crisis and suggests five key areas where fundamental reform is needed in order to create a system that will be more stable and conducive to sustainable global growth. The key areas encompass new mechanisms of international financial regulation; international tax coordination; international liquidity provisioning and compensatory financing; mechanisms for multilateral surveillance and effective macroeconomic policy coordination; and the global reserve system. Several of the proposed reforms are under consideration, including at the level of the Group of Twenty (G-20) and the policymaking bodies of the Bretton Woods institutions themselves. The analysis suggests, however, that the reforms in all these areas will, by and large, need to be conducted simultaneously in order to be effective.

A fairer and sustainable globalization may not be feasible without better coordination and greater equity in global economic governance

Chapter VI discusses whether a fairer and sustainable process of global development is feasible. Reshaping rules and seeking greater policy coherence are easier said than done. Players will need to agree on common global sustainable development goals that are to be pursued and will also need to be convinced that cooperation would serve present and future generations and provide net benefits for all. However, in any scheme of international cooperation, net benefits may not be (or may be perceived as not being) equal for all, and any unevenness in expected outcomes may impede the achievement of effective global solutions. Because of differences in living standards, and therefore in capacity to pay, some countries will be expected to shoulder larger shares of the total costs of providing global public goods, which may reduce their incentive to cooperate. Hence, in respect of establishing multilateral agreements, the proposed pattern of burden-sharing is as important as the extent to which the benefits conferred by the public goods are or are perceived to be evenly distributed. Equally important is the need to overcome democratic deficits in current decision-making within the key organizations of global economic governance, such as IMF and the World Bank, and to eliminate inequities in access to participation in other bodies, such as the World Trade Organization.

The chapter goes on to assess whether the proposals for retooling the existing aid, trade and financial architectures could result in a more coherent system, one that would overcome the shortcomings inherent in the present compartmentalized mechanisms for achieving global economic governance. There is a need to strengthen the global coordination of economic decisions in order to eliminate possibilities of conflict among the rules governing trade, aid, debt, finance, migration, environmental sustainability and other development issues.

However, as the eminent United Nations-affiliated economist Sidney Dell pointed out a quarter-century ago (see Dell, 1985, p. 19):

> There is no international agency dealing systematically with global questions of consistency and inconsistency. In matters of economic policy, the triumvirate of the IMF, the World Bank and the GATT/WTO as they function at present is not up to the task. There have been proposals to set up an Economic Security Council to no avail so far. Thus the mechanism of global control has remained the same; that is unsatisfactory.

In 1995, it was proposed that a reformed United Nations Economic and Social Council assume this directive role, but the proposal received only modest support at the time.

The current global crisis has provided painful evidence of the weaknesses of the present system. Further, the phenomena of climate change and demographic shifts demand an even greater coherence among the spheres of global governance and between global and national-level processes of decision-making. In consequence, the need to establish a framework (its shape still to be determined) for international coordination based on shared principles and buttressed by transparent mechanisms has become more urgent than ever.

Chapter II
Retooling poverty reduction strategies: towards a new consensus?

Summary

- The recent financial crisis and the accompanying recession have given further impetus to rethinking development and poverty reduction strategies, reorienting them in a direction away from market fundamentalism and towards a revitalized government role in guiding the economy.
- The Millennium Development Goals provide the most recent overarching framework for poverty reduction and human development. While providing a clear set of targets, the Millennium Development Goals agenda does not spell out any specific strategy. Poverty Reduction Strategy Papers, introduced alongside the Goals agenda, do spell one out, but they have been criticized for a lack of coherence with economic development policies.
- Achieving policy coherence for poverty reduction and sustainable development requires integrating a broad approach to macroeconomic policies with sector policies, environmental policies and social policies.
- Such coherence should be sought through national sustainable development strategies. Those strategies should be developed locally. However, for this to be done effectively, changes will also be needed in global governance in order to provide sufficient space for national self-determination, while preserving coherence with shared global development objectives.

See-saw movements in thinking about poverty

Initial development theories did not focus on poverty reduction directly…

While it was always an underlying aspiration, poverty reduction was not an explicit *direct* goal of initial development programmes. Rooted in modern growth theory which dominated early development theory, development policies of the 1950s and 1960s focused on promoting modern industrial development to accelerate overall economic growth. Industrial growth was supported through trade protection, cheap credits and subsidies and large-scale public investments in infrastructure. Output growth was expected to "trickle down" to the entire population and reduce poverty through rising wages and employment generation, even if initially poverty reduction might not be commensurate with the rate of output growth, as rising income inequality was expected to be an inevitable, although temporary side effect of industrialization. Capital productivity growth would lead to rising profit shares and allow for higher savings to finance domestic investment. Over time, at higher levels of development, gains from growth would be shared more broadly with faster real wage growth and dynamic employment expansion.[1]

1 Kuznets (1955) suggested an inverted U-shaped relationship between level of development (generally measured by per capita income level) and the degree of inequality (in what was subsequently known as the Kuznets hypothesis).

...and strategies based on those theories failed to reduce poverty sufficiently

In practice, however, job creation under the industrialization strategies proved to be rather unsatisfactory in many developing countries, as biases in policy incentives favoured the adoption of capital-intensive technologies (imported from developed countries). In many instances, new industries also tended to rely more heavily on imports than on inputs provided by other domestic sectors, thereby limiting the coming into play of employment dynamics through inter-industry linkages. Furthermore, the focus on industrialization led to an urban bias and a relative neglect of agriculture, despite the fact that most of the population would depend on agriculture for employment and income. It should be noted that such downsides were not present in all early development experiences. The newly industrializing countries of East Asia also relied on import substitution and imported technologies at the initial stage of their development. However, unlike those in Latin America and Africa, their industrial policies tended to be more selective and oriented towards the building of export competitiveness and the creation of domestic linkages, while raising agricultural productivity, which was a central policy objective in the early stages. As a result, these countries achieved a much more integrated growth and development outcome.[2]

New development ideas established poverty reduction as a direct goal

Because employment growth and poverty reduction stayed below expectations in most developing countries, mainstream development thinking moved away from the trickle down approach and put greater emphasis on targeted interventions for employment generation, redistribution of incomes and investment in human capital. In large parts of Asia and Latin America, the previous neglect of the agriculture sector was redressed through the so-called green revolution, aimed at increasing land productivity through use of high-yielding varieties of crops and other modern inputs (such as mechanized irrigation, chemical fertilizers and insecticides). In some instances, the green revolution also helped increase rural employment, as the new technology required more labour, especially on small-scale farm units. This was much less the case in situations where mechanization set in. New paradigms emerged such as the "redistribution-with-growth" and "basic needs" approaches to development (see box II.1). In these approaches poverty reduction not only became an explicit goal of development, but also came to be seen as a means to accelerate growth.

Box II.1

The basic needs approach to development[a]

The basic needs development strategy grew out of the work of the International Labour Organization (ILO) World Employment Programme of the 1970s. It brought employment—and people and human needs—back to the centre of development strategy. This was directly in line with the centrality of the issue of employment to the United Nations in the early days and the International Monetary Fund (IMF) as well; however, ILO work in the 1970s elaborated and enriched the earlier concept of employment and the policies for dealing with it by relating both concept and policies directly to the situation and needs of developing countries.

Origins

By the middle of the 1970s, when ILO was in the midst of preparing for the World Employment Conference—with assistance from other organizations of the United Nations system and the World Bank—the idea of a basic needs development strategy was born. The idea of basic needs had originated in the psychology literature of the 1940s and more specifically in an article by Albert Maslow in the *Psychological Review* of March 1942 in which he distinguished a hierarchy of five needs starting

2 See, for example, Amsden (1991; 2003) and Wade (1990) for detailed analyses of the industrialization processes of the East Asian newly industrializing countries.

Box II.1 (cont'd)

with the physiological and ending with self-actualization (Maslow, 1943). Later, in India, during the 1950s, the concept of "minimum needs" was developed by Pitambar Pant of the Indian Planning Commission. Still, the basic needs approach did not become a mainstream approach in development, even if the attractiveness of the concept was clear.

In the 1970s, however, actual applications of the concept were "suddenly" carried out simultaneously in three different contexts: in the Bariloche project in Latin America, in the 1975 Dag Hammarskjöld Foundation publication entitled *What Now?* (Dag Hammarskjöld Foundation, 1975) and in the ILO World Employment Programme. It became clear that employment creation was not an end in itself but rather served to fulfil the basic needs of individual human beings—corresponding more or less to the first of Maslow's five rungs. Many people were already on the second, third, fourth and even fifth rungs, but a significant proportion were not even in sight of the ladder. And so the idea arose of designing a development strategy that had as its main objective the meeting of basic needs, including those of the poorest 20 per cent of the population.

Practicality

The report of the 1976 World Employment Conference (International Labour Organization, 1976; 1977) defined basic needs in terms of food, clothing, housing, education and public transportation. Employment was both a means and an end, and participation in decision-making was also included. The first task was to quantify basic needs for a target year (in this case, 25 years into the future (1975-2000))—to determine, in other words, what the level of GDP should be in *t*+25 years to ensure that even the poorest 20 per cent of the population would have enough to eat, have decent housing and enjoy high-quality education? Without going into all the details of the numbers and calculations, one may state that this quantification was found to be feasible. Having quantified GDP for the target year, one could calculate the annual rate of economic growth required between the base and the target years. This approach reversed conventional practice, which was to project a desirable annual rate of per capita economic growth into the future. The latter was a forward rolling approach, while the basic needs approach achieved more precision by setting specific production targets and deriving the desirable rate of economic growth implied. In this sense, the basic needs development strategy was also more practical than conventional strategies.

Not surprisingly, in most cases, the rate of economic growth required to fully meet basic needs targets had been unrealistically high by historical standards—well above 8 per cent per annum over 25 years. East Asia, and later China and India, subsequently achieved such rates, but in the mid-1970s, the miracles of East Asia and China lay ahead. Hence, the only option for achieving the basic needs targets was to work with two parameters: the rate of economic growth *and* income distribution. Indeed, if income distribution improves (becomes less unequal), then the overall rate of economic growth does not need to be so high. It was shown that with "redistribution from growth", that is, marginal redistribution of future increase of income rather than redistribution of existing wealth, basic needs targets could be reached with an annual rate of economic growth of 6 per cent.

When this package was presented to the World Employment Conference, it was greeted with enthusiasm, except by the tripartite United States delegation and some employer delegates from other industrialized countries. Opposition may have reflected ideological suspicions rather than well-founded fears; in any event, with the election of Jimmy Carter as President a few months later, Washington's official views changed so much that the United States Agency for International Development (USAID) started preaching aggressively the gospel of "basic human needs". The President of the World Bank, Robert McNamara, adopted the basic needs approach wholesale, asked Mahbub ul Haq and his team to work further on it, and tried hard to steer his operational departments in that direction (Kapur, Lewis and Webb, 1997).

By the middle of the 1970s, it looked as though a more appropriate development strategy had been designed which effectively combined economic growth, productive employment creation and basic needs. At the core of the strategy was a shift to a pattern of economic growth that was more employment-intensive, more equitable and more effective in the battle against poverty.

On the other hand, viewed from a distance of 35 years, the strategy had been weak on gender and the environment, although the historical context is important, because it had only just

Box II.1 (cont'd)

started to receive attention at the time of the United Nations Conference on the Human Environment, held in Stockholm in June 1972, and the World Conference on the International Women's Year, held in Mexico City in June and July 1975. On the other hand, the strategy was strong in that it had a quantified macroeconomic framework and quantified sector frameworks and was placed within an international context.

The use of overarching concepts

Employment, basic needs and many other issues were pushed to the sidelines with the onset of the debt crisis. The succeeding "lost decade" of the 1980s was characterized by the enforcement of "mean and lean" policies which resulted in a tragic loss of growth opportunities for millions of people. The return of laissez-faire in the early 1980s unleashed a strong political and academic offensive against the "predatory State". Development strategies, including the basic needs strategy, that implied the involvement of an activist State no longer had a raison d'être because it was determined that the magic of the market would bring back national growth and prosperity. The overarching development concept shifted its focus to development without the State at the country level and globalization without a countervailing power at the international level. This approach was labelled the Washington Consensus.

The concept of basic needs lived on, but without the strategy and the macroeconomic framework. What were retained were specific goals, for example, achieving universal primary education by year X or eradicating a certain illness by year Y. This approach has been generalized by the United Nations in the Millennium Development Goals. The Goals are, of course, important but without a quantified macro- and sector framework, this approach has little to do with the meeting of basic needs as originally conceived.

The concept of basic needs reappeared on the world scene in the 1990s incorporated in the *Human Development Reports* and the approach reflected therein (United Nations Development Programme, 1990). The presentation was more sophisticated than that of the basic needs strategy of the 1970s but, alas, the concept once again lacked a quantified macro- and sector framework. Nevertheless, this represented progress compared with the situation in the 1980s.

Now, in 2010, and several national and regional financial crises and a "Great Recession" later, where do we stand? We are obviously moving towards a better balance between the role of the market and the role of the State, at least at the national level. This is not the case, however, at the global level because globally there is no effective equivalent of the State.

The current priorities are the creation of a new financial architecture at the national and global levels, climate change, and the realization of the Millennium Development Goals. The remarkable fact is that, while overarching development concepts are obviously necessary for the realization of these priorities, one observes a return to microeconomics with its focus on specific problems at the local level. Obviously, all politics are local and in the end all problems have to be solved locally, but consistency between priorities and the policies needed to realize these priorities is of the essence. And that is why we need both macroeconomic and global frameworks. In order to meet the basic needs of the world population, such frameworks must still take into account the "old" objectives of better global and national income distributions. This course of action could be stimulated at the macrolevel by making development policies greener and at the microlevel by focusing on the creation of a new financial structure.

a Box II.1 was specially prepared for this report by Louis Emmerij, former President of the Organization for Economic Cooperation and Development (OECD) Development Centre, Paris; special adviser to the President of the Inter-American Development Bank, Washington, D.C.; Rector of the Institute of Social Studies, The Hague; and Director of the ILO World Employment Programme during the 1970s. At present, he is Co-Director of the United Nations Intellectual History Project (UNIHP).

However, these new ideas were implemented only partially and faced fiscal constraints

To be sure, neither the basic needs nor the redistribution-with-growth approaches ever became dominant in actual policy practices. Many countries continued to push for modern industrial growth but started at the same time to put more emphasis on agriculture, for example, by introducing green revolution and other agrarian reforms, to increase Government subsidies for basic needs and to invest more in social development. In some cases, where a basic needs-type strategy had been implemented in practice, as in Sri Lanka in the 1970s, it was seen (by some) to hamper growth by de-emphasizing investment and industrial development (Grindle, 2010). In other cases, generous subsidies and expanding government spending led to widening fiscal deficits and, together with adverse external factors, to mounting external debt burdens which proved unsustainable in the early 1980s.

With the "Washington Consensus", poverty reduction once again became an indirect goal

Perceived failures in State interventions led to the emergence of a new growth orthodoxy in the 1980s. This orthodoxy, which eventually came to be referred to as the Washington Consensus, laid strong, if not exclusive, emphasis, on market mechanisms as the main vehicles for achieving prosperity. The activist government policies of earlier development strategies were seen as having been faulty and, in many instances, steered by rent-seeking behaviour of government officials rather than as having served development objectives. Industrial protection and subsidies for many basic needs were perceived as distorting the proper functioning of markets, hampering not only output and employment growth, but also efficiency in the delivery of social services and poverty reduction. Industrial policies were to make way for trade liberalization, subsidies for basic goods and public utilities were to be eliminated, directed credit schemes were to make way for deregulated financial intermediation, and social services were to be properly priced through the introduction of user fees or private delivery systems. Equity and poverty reduction once again became aspirations, that is to say, *indirect* goals of development policies. Inasmuch as stabilization policies and market reforms came with visible social costs, compensatory social policies (including emergency employment programmes, social investment funds and other targeted poverty reduction programmes) were introduced in the 1990s, often with heavy support from the international community. This reflected the recognition by the Washington Consensus that markets would not immediately resolve the severest equity and poverty problems. However, by and large, the focus remained on aggregate growth, to be achieved primarily by relying on markets.

With the introduction of the Millennium Development Goals agenda, poverty reduction became a direct goal yet again

Disappointingly, the market reforms did not produce the expected sustained and strong output growth (Ocampo, Jomo and Vos, 2007), let alone significant poverty reduction. Moreover, in most instances, the elimination of subsidies, introduction of user fees and privatization of services did not prove to be particularly successful in either reducing costs or enhancing the coverage of social service delivery. By the end of the 1990s, these disappointing outcomes had led to a rethinking of development goals and strategy. The focus shifted once again back to defining poverty reduction as an explicit goal, rather than as an implicit or indirect one. Through the adoption of the United Nations Millennium Declaration by the General Assembly on 8 September 2000,[3] the United Nations introduced a concrete set of development targets embodied in the Millennium Development Goals. Poverty reduction was featured as the first and pre-eminent goal. At the end of the 1990s, the World Bank and the International Monetary Fund had incorporated a linkage between market-oriented structural adjustment policies and the poverty agenda within the revised framework for the heavily indebted poor countries (HIPCs), making the formulation of Poverty Reduction Strategy Papers (PRSPs) a precondition for the receipt of debt relief under the heavily indebted poor countries Initiative.

Fractured consensus and little policy coherence

The Millennium Development Goals identify clear targets, but do not come with any specific strategy

The Millennium Development Goals reintroduced poverty reduction and other human development objectives and placed them at centre stage, which was a significant development. However, the Goals, per se, do not encompass any particular strategy for achieving those objectives. For instance, while productive employment creation is generally considered a

3 See General Assembly resolution 55/2.

main vehicle for poverty reduction, targets for the creation of decent employment were not initially part of the Millennium Development Goals agenda; employment indicators were introduced only after 2005.[4] The Goals provide no more than a set of targets, which, though they may provide a focus for a coherent strategy, do not as such offer any guidance on what combination of policies would be most effective in fostering the simultaneous achievement of the Goals. In the absence of any well laid out strategy, the focus of the implementation of the Goals agenda has often been on raising budgetary allocations for education, health and other basic social programmes.

A lack of policy coherence has hampered poverty reduction efforts

The PRSPs came closer to embodying the concept of an integrated national development strategy with an explicit focus on poverty reduction and achievement of the other Millennium Development Goals. They were meant to be comprehensive and ensure greater coherence between economic and social policies and to serve in positioning donor support behind a nationally defined development strategy. However, PRSPs have been criticized for failing in practice to make macroeconomic, trade and financial policies integral and explicit parts of a strategy aiming to generate sufficient productive employment, reduce poverty and enhance access to social services (see, for example, Gottschalk, 2005; North-South Institute, 2004; Stewart and Wang, 2003; and Vos and Cabezas, 2006). Instead, core elements of the Washington Consensus, including orthodox macroeconomic stabilization policies and liberalized trade and domestic finance, have remained preconditions for qualifying for debt relief and bilateral and multilateral donor support. In cases where those conditions meant imposing strict fiscal requirements or where trade liberalization failed to support employment creation and reduce income inequality, PRSPs turned out to be more a set of compensatory social policies constrained by external pressures related to fiscal consolidation than examples of coherence over the broader range of development policies. In practice, such macroeconomic constraints have been found to set ceilings capping Millennium Development Goals-motivated public spending, even when direct funding for such purposes would have been available from external donors. This has reportedly led to instances where donor aid was redirected towards an increase in international reserves or not disbursed at all, despite the existence of domestic needs and the ability of the Government to absorb it.[5] This example illustrates incoherence between national development objectives and international policy agendas.

The poverty challenge remains daunting

About one quarter of the developing world's population is still poor

It is likely that lack of policy coherence has slowed progress in poverty reduction. Using the new international poverty line of $1.25 per person per day in 2005 purchasing power parities (PPPs), as defined by the World Bank, 1.4 billion people, representing about 26 per cent of the developing world's population, lived in poverty in 2005 (see figure II.1; and box II.2 for a discussion of the thorny issue of defining poverty). There are, however, large regional variations in the poverty trends (see figures II.2 and II.3). The incidence of poverty is still highest in sub-Saharan Africa, where more than half of the population

4 See the 2005 World Summit Outcome (General Assembly resolution 60/1).

5 The experiences of Uganda and Ethiopia under PRSPs offer examples in this regard. The problem of budget allocation of official development assistance (ODA) proceeds in Uganda is discussed in Van Arkadie (2006); the sterilization of ODA proceeds is assessed in Lister and others (2006). In the case of Ethiopia, some controversy emerged over the issue of why the International Monetary Fund would not permit the Government to count unpredictable ODA as part of Government revenue (Stiglitz, 2003).

Figure II.1
World population and the number of the poor, 1981-2005

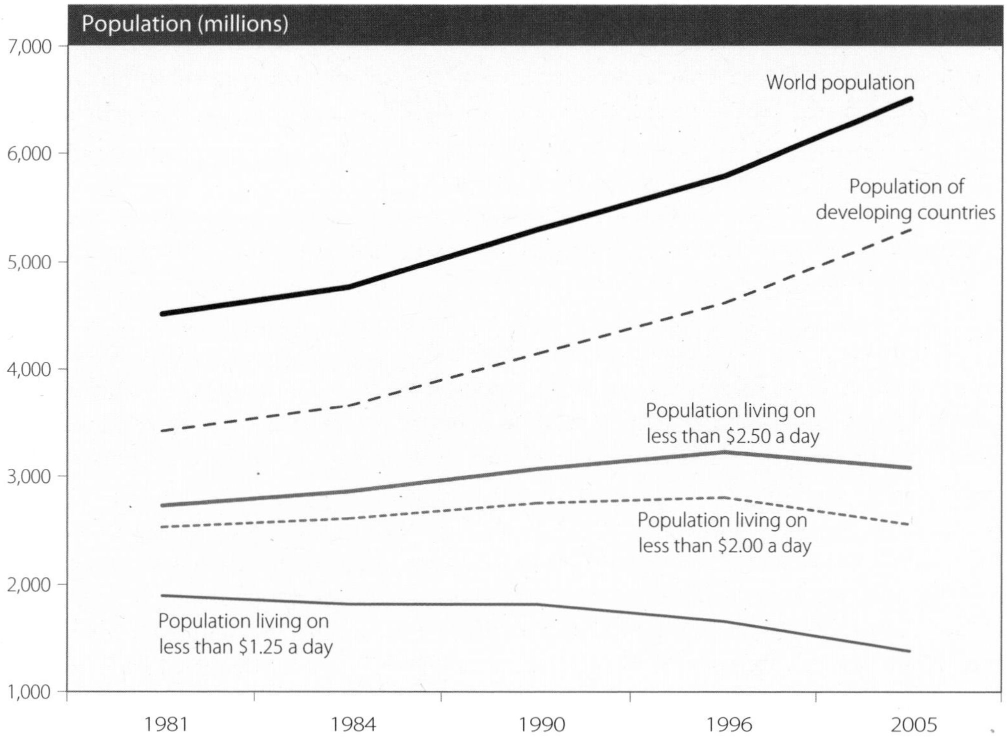

Source: United Nations (2009b, figure II.1), based on Chen and Ravallion (2008).

Box II.2

The poverty of poverty definitions

Defining poverty remains a thorny issue. In particular, the use of the 1-dollar-a-day poverty line has been subject to much criticism, as discussed at some length in the 2010 *Report on the World Social Situation* (United Nations, 2009b). Nonetheless, it has been adopted as a benchmark for measuring progress towards Millennium Development Goal 1. The establishment of the $1-a-day poverty line arose from the effort to derive a common measure of absolute poverty that could be used across all countries of the world for both aggregation and international comparison purposes. To do this, researchers at the World Bank (see Ravallion, Datt and van de Walle 1991) had looked at national poverty lines and found that the minimum income thresholds for the poorest 6 countries (in a sample of 33 countries) almost coincided, at $1 per day per person (at 1985 PPP prices). In 2008, the World Bank revised the threshold upward to $1.25 per day based on the new set of PPP values derived from 2005 prices and computed on the basis of a larger sample and improved data. The new $1.25-per-day measure basically represents, as was the case with the previous threshold of $1.08, an income level that is needed (in poor countries) to ensure a minimum amount of caloric intake, along with a few basic necessities.

Both the $1 and the $1.25 poverty lines have drawn much criticism. A close analysis shows that this criticism is directed at a variety of disparate issues. It is often argued that, conceptually, poverty is multidimensional and hence cannot be reduced to the single dimension of a lack of income. The main difficulty with this criticism lies in how to operationalize the multidimensional notion of poverty. Responding to this issue, some offer to reduce multidimensionality to a few "basic" dimensions. The United Nations Development Programme (UNDP) human poverty index is an attempt to go beyond income in constructing a composite poverty index. The Millennium Development Goals also recognize the multidimensional nature of human well-being through the deployment of a broad range of objectives and targets.

Box II.2 (cont'd)

The use of a common international income threshold has also been subjected to criticism. The contention here is that the nature of poverty is country-specific. Along these lines, it has been argued that by using a common international poverty threshold that would be applicable to the poorest countries, one would necessarily underestimate global poverty. It has also been observed that the relationship between income and life achievement (measured, for example, by life expectancy at birth) is non-linear. Based on this non-linear relationship, an "ethical poverty line" has also been proposed which would correspond to an "ethically" necessary living standard (measured, again, by an acceptable life expectancy). Although country-specific poverty lines are likely most relevant for national policymaking, their use would entail a different meaning of poverty in each context and thereby severely limit cross-country comparisons and aggregations across countries.

A more traditional critique (see, for example, Sen (1973)) questions the focus on poverty incidence as the key indicator for assessing progress towards poverty reduction, inasmuch as poverty is a matter not just of how many people are below the poverty line, but also of how poor they actually are and whether the income gap with respect to the poverty line is narrowing or not. In the same vein, policymakers should also consider gauging the "depth" of poverty and taking a dynamic view of poverty instead of a static one, based on snapshots.

The third critique focuses on the measurement and interpretation of purchasing power parity (PPP) conversion factors which aim at putting the cost of living in one country at par with that in another. Those conversion factors refer to the average cost of living, rather than that faced by the poor. People with lower incomes tend to spend a larger share on food and, when living in remote rural areas, incur higher living expenses than others, because of transportation costs, for instance. Hence, the poor may encounter price levels different from those encountered by the average population. Data limitations typically impede such differentiation. Also, PPP measures are not available for all countries, though the extent of coverage is changing. In this regard, as mentioned above, the initial $1-a-day poverty line was based on the *common* (national) poverty lines of 6 of the poorest countries out of a sample of 33 developing countries studied by Ravallion, Datt and van de Walle (1991) who used 1985 Penn PPP values. However, Chen and Ravallion (2001), after having recomputed this line using 1993 Penn PPP values and taking the *median* of the lowest 10 national poverty lines of the same country sample, suggested a poverty line of $1.08 per day. They later switched to a new set of PPPs (for 2005) computed by the World Bank and suggested a poverty line of $1.25 per day based on the *mean* of the poverty lines of the 15 poorest countries of the sample (Chen and Ravallion (2008)).

Despite its shortcomings, the international poverty line remains the benchmark used by the international community to assess trends in global poverty. One can always determine (as did Chen and Ravallion (2008)) whether use of a higher or lower poverty line (but one commonly applied to all countries) would reveal different trends. Also, the same information used to produce internationally comparable estimates of the incidence of poverty (or the number of the poor) can also be used to assess the "depth" of poverty (in other words, how poor the poor actually are). Data on other dimensions can also be used to produce a multidimensional picture of poverty and deprivation. In fact, the Millennium Development Goals encompass a considerable number of the dimensions that are often discussed within the context of the definition of poverty. In the end, of course, what matters most for national policymaking is how each society defines the decent level of living that should be achievable by all.

(50.4 per cent) was found to be poor in 2005. Poverty remains deep in South Asia, where 40.3 per cent of the population remained below the poverty line in 2005. By contrast, in East Asia and the Pacific, the rate of poverty was 17.9 per cent; and in Latin America and the Caribbean, it was even lower (8.2 per cent).

Yet, significant poverty reduction has been achieved

The existence of persistent widespread poverty should not obscure the fact that there has been a significant achievement in poverty reduction during the past few decades. For example, the total number of poor (according to the definition above) had been 1.8 billion in 1990 and 1.9 billion in 1981 (compared with 1.4 billion in 2005). However, these numbers mask the actual progress achieved: the fact that the total size of the population

Figure II.2
Regional trends in poverty, 1981-2005

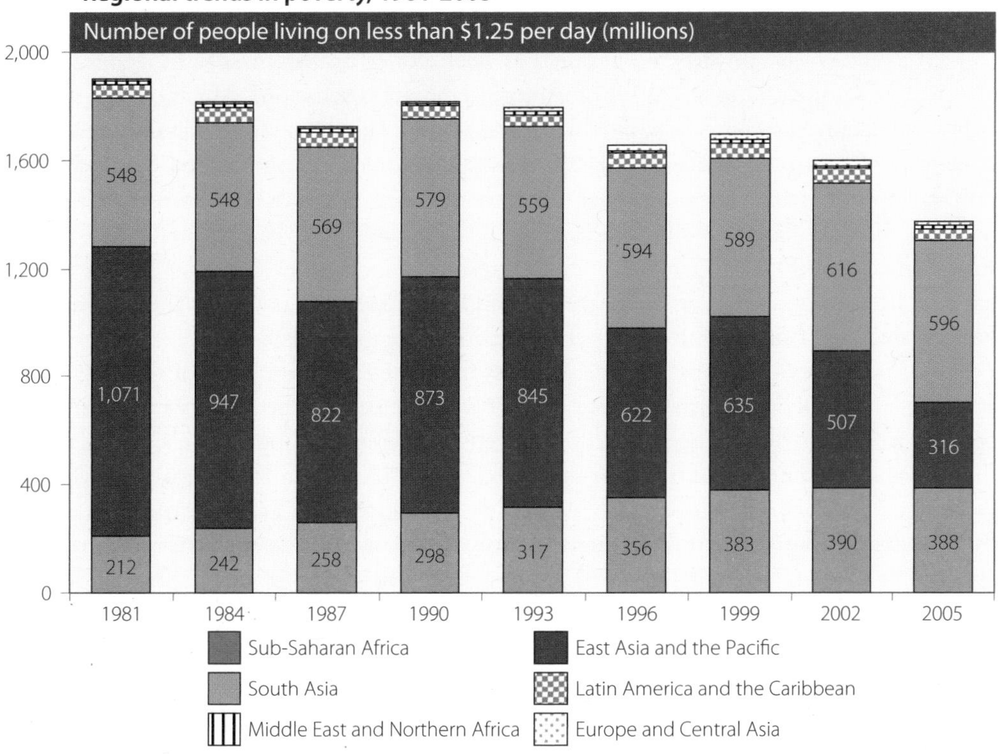

Source: United Nations (2009b, figure II.2), based on Chen and Ravallion (2008).

Figure II.3
Global poverty trends, with and without some major developing regions and countries, 1981-2005

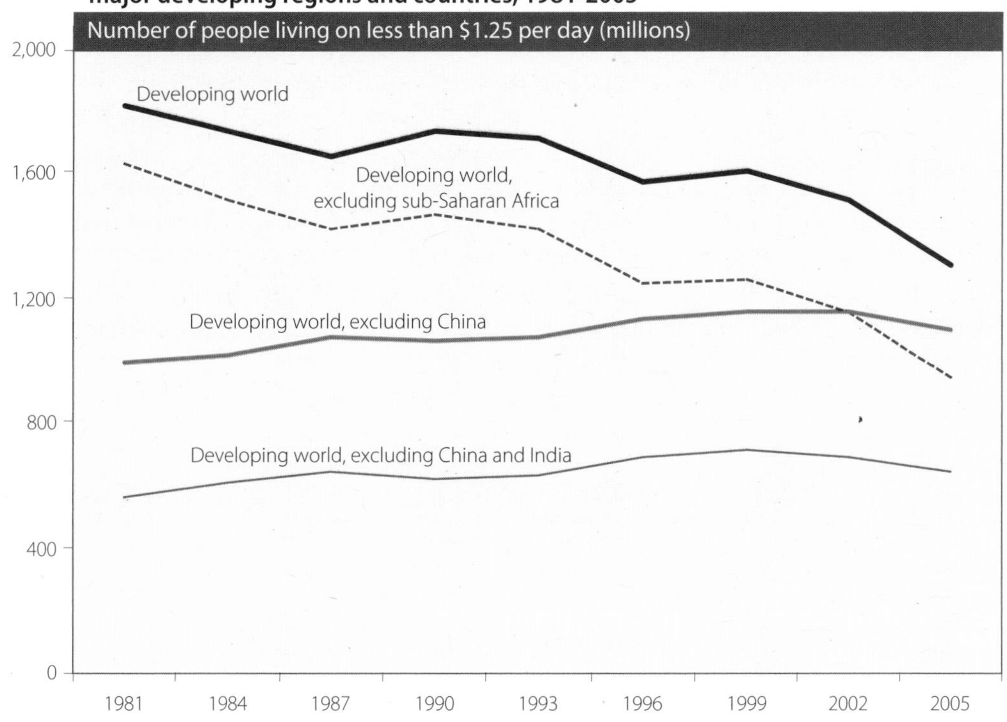

Source: United Nations (2009b, figure II.3), based on Chen and Ravallion (2008).

also increased significantly during the same time span means that the share of the poor in the total population has decreased sharply. For the developing world as a whole, the incidence of poverty dropped from 52.0 per cent in 1981 to 24.7 per cent in 2005.

Poverty reduction has been most significant in East Asia

However, poverty reduction has been concentrated in specific geographical regions (see United Nations (2009b) for more elaborate discussion). Much of the poverty reduction occurred in East Asia, particularly in China. In China alone, the number of the poor (according to the above definition) decreased from 835.1 million in 1981 to 207.7 million in 2005, which meant a sharp decrease of China's poverty rate from 84.0 to 15.9 per cent. In Viet Nam as well, the decrease in the poverty rate over the same period was staggering: from 90.4 to 17.1 per cent. Progress in several other countries of the region has also been impressive. For the East Asia and Pacific region as a whole, the incidence of poverty declined from 66.8 to 24.4 per cent during the period 1981-2005.

Less progress has been made in South Asia and sub-Saharan Africa…

Poverty reduction has been far less impressive in other parts of the world. For example, although South Asia has seen a significant decrease in the poverty rate (from 59.4 per cent in 1981 to 40.3 per cent in 2005), given the increase in population size this means that the absolute number of the poor increased from 548 million to 596 million over that period (figure II.2). In sub-Saharan Africa, the absolute number of the poor increased from 212 million to 388 million in the same period, while the poverty rate remained almost unchanged, having fallen to 51.2 per cent in 2005 from 53.7 per cent in 1981.

…where most of the world's poor live

As a result of these differences in the pace of poverty reduction, the regional distribution of the poor has changed significantly. Whereas in 1981, poverty had been concentrated in East Asia and the Pacific, with 56.5 per cent of the world's poor living in that region, by 2005 the concentration of poverty had shifted to South Asia and sub-Saharan Africa, which now account for 43.3 per cent and 28.4 per cent, respectively, of the world's poor. By contrast, East Asia and the Pacific now account for only 23.0 per cent of the world's poor.

Without determined efforts, sub-Saharan Africa and South Asia may not achieve the poverty reduction target by 2015

The marked regional variation in the pace of poverty reduction puts at some risk the achievement of Millennium Development Goal 1 (halving the poverty rate by 2015, as compared with 1990). While East Asia has already met Goal 1, several regions, particularly South Asia and sub-Saharan Africa, are still struggling. In fact, leaving aside China, the developing world is not poised to reach Goal 1. In order for South Asia and sub-Saharan Africa to reach Goal 1, these two regions would be required to reduce their poverty rates by 22.1 and 14.5 percentage points, respectively, relative to the rates of 2005. Given that over the period 1990-2005, South Asia and sub-Saharan Africa reduced their poverty rate by only 0.8 and 1.6 percentage points per year, respectively, the challenge remains formidable (United Nations, 2009b). Thus, even if the world as a whole achieves the target set for Goal 1, important regions, especially sub-Saharan Africa and South Asia, may not achieve that target unless very vigorous steps are taken soon.

A vast number of people live just above the $1.25-a-day poverty line

The weak poverty reduction performance of the past decades is also evidenced by the fact that many people remain very close to the poverty line, even though they have managed to cross it. Indeed, the total number of the poor in 2005 increases to 2.6 billion when an income threshold of $2.00 per day is used, which indicates that there were 1.2 billion people with an income per capita of between $1.25 and $2.00 per day and that, using the $2-a-day poverty line, almost half (47.6 per cent) of the population in developing countries would be considered poor.

The presence of a vast number of people living just above the $1.25 poverty line implies that a large number of them risk being pushed down below the official poverty line (used for the purpose of monitoring Goal 1) by negative income shocks, as was the case in many East Asian countries as a result of the Asian financial crisis. In Indonesia, for example, the poverty rate increased from 15 per cent in mid-1997 to 33 per cent by end-1998, thus pushing about 36 million more people below the poverty line and wiping out a large part of the gains in poverty reduction achieved in previous decades.[6] Thus, a large number of people remain vulnerable to poverty even though their present incomes may be higher than the international poverty line.[7]

Lessons learned from poverty reduction strategies

What are the main factors that determine the success of growth and poverty reduction strategies? Theories of development have often tried to point out specific factors and identify the main obstacles, which have changed over time. Development policies and foreign assistance programmes were then designed to overcome capital, infrastructure and/or foreign-exchange constraints, through addressing inequalities in asset or income distributions, investing in human capital, strengthening social protection systems and improving governance and market institutions.

Yet, country contexts differ and history has taught that there exist many pathways to overcoming obstacles to development. The more successful countries, however, have not been those that followed strategies focusing on overcoming a single major constraint, but rather the ones able to effectively find a degree of coherence among different levels of development policy effective enough to usher in the conditions necessary for poverty reduction. The main determinants in the more successful cases are discussed below. While they do not necessarily constitute a blueprint for guaranteed success in other contexts, they do provide lessons on how to tailor development strategies to national requirements.

Distribution matters

Aggregate growth helps to reduce poverty, but it does so more effectively when there is less inequality

Experience shows that, while rapid aggregate growth makes possible a rapid reduction in poverty, the extent to which such a potential is actually realized depends upon on the situation with regard to income distribution. In their in-depth study of several developing economies, Besley and Cord, eds. (2007, p. 1) note that "[g]rowth is less efficient in lowering poverty levels in countries with high initial inequality or in which the distributional pattern of growth favours the non-poor".[8]

A more egalitarian initial asset distribution is, in the long run, an advantage for growth and poverty reduction

Thus, both equality of initial endowment distribution and equality of distribution of current income are important for poverty reduction. However, initial equality may be more important for if growth proceeds from an initial egalitarian distribution, then it has a greater poverty reduction effect. This has been borne out by countries that have proved successful in reducing poverty despite rising income inequality during periods of growth acceleration, with China being the most prominent example, along with Viet Nam. Close scrutiny shows that the acceleration of growth in these countries had its roots in a relatively egalitarian initial distribution of assets. Of course, the poverty reduction

6 See, for example, Harrison and McMillan (2007); Suryahadi, Sumarto and Pritchett (2003); and Culpeper (2005).

7 Many have argued that "insecurity" should be incorporated in the definition of poverty. See, for example, Morduch (1994; 1999) and World Bank (2001). On the basis of such an expanded definition of poverty, many people lying just above the poverty line will also be regarded as poor.

8 Bourguignon (2004), Ravallion (1997; 2001) and other researchers have come to similar conclusions.

effect of rapid growth is greatest when both initial and current inequalities are relatively low, as was the case, during their early development stages, of other East Asian countries and areas such as the Republic of Korea and Taiwan Province of China. Their experience also shows that it may not be necessary for inequality to first rise with development before falling, thereby contradicting the Kuznets' hypothesis of an inverted U-shaped relationship between income level and degree of inequality (see note 1).

Land reforms proved very important to growth accelerations in East Asia

A major factor behind the initial egalitarian asset distribution in East Asian countries and areas was land distribution. The Republic of Korea undertook sweeping land reform during 1945-1950, as did Taiwan Province of China in the 1950s. China undertook radical land redistribution in the years prior to and after the 1949 revolution. Viet Nam carried out land reform in its northern part during 1953-1956 at the time of the Viet Cong's rise to power (in 1954). As a result of these reforms, the vast majority of the population of these three countries and area became endowed with physical capital in the form of land.[9]

Possession of land and other earning assets allows more people to benefit directly from the output that can be produced, using, in the case of land, even existing technology. Often, with additional government support, wider ownership has also facilitated the broader application of "modern inputs", such as chemical fertilizers, high-yielding seeds, irrigation systems, storage, marketing and so on.

The obstacles to the implementation of an egalitarian distribution of assets through redistribution of physical assets are well known. The above-mentioned East Asian examples show that successful redistribution of land has been possible only in wake of victories in war, decolonization or revolution. Under ordinary conditions, such redistribution proves difficult owing to the political barriers encountered. However, recent experiences have shown that, even under such ordinary conditions, redistribution of assets, if it is properly designed with adequate compensation and incentives, can still be carried out.[10]

Investment in human capital matters

Education is critical for poverty reduction in the long run

It may not be entirely fortuitous that East Asian countries proved more successful than countries elsewhere at achieving growth and poverty reduction, since in addition to the attainment of egalitarian physical asset distribution (through land reform), they also put great emphasis on education (see, for example, Cummings (1995); and Booth (1999)). The recent experience of some Latin American countries, which have striven to promote education through the implementation of innovative targeted programmes, points to the importance of education in reducing inequality and poverty. Cornia (2010), for example, notes that the rise in enrolment rates at all education levels since the early 1990s contributed to a significant fall in inequality in Latin America during the 2000s. He further indicates that two thirds of the observed reduction in per capita income inequality and poverty in Brazil between 2000 and 2006 was due to narrowing wage gaps among workers, which in turn had resulted from lower levels of inequality in education.

Large premiums for education are observed in labour markets

The results from cross-country studies show at best a weak impact of investment in human capital on long-term growth (see, for example, Benhabib and Spiegel (1994); Bils and Klenow (2000); United Nations (2006b); and Pritchett (2001)). The same

9 See, for example, Sobhan (1993) for a comprehensive discussion of land reforms and their impact on the growth of East Asian and other countries.

10 See, for example, United Nations (2008, box V.2) for a discussion of the experience of land redistribution through market incentives in South Africa.

studies emphasize, however, that those findings should be viewed with a certain degree of caution, as they may underestimate the true impact, because of problems with regard to data accuracy, model specifications and estimation techniques. The findings also contrast with much more robust evidence of the positive impact of education on output which is provided by the significant wage premiums for education as earned in the labour market. Global integration has amplified such wage premiums. Based on his review of the research, Glewwe (2002) reports positive labour income effects of skills acquired through schooling. Thus, there are clear pay-offs for individuals who invest in education. With the rising role of science and technology in actual production processes, the importance of education and skills is likely only to increase. Education also enhances a person's capability to pursue entrepreneurship.

Human capital formation is an expedient means of reducing inequality

Acquisition of human capital may also provide a way around the difficult problem of achieving a more egalitarian distribution of earning assets. Unlike physical capital, human capital cannot be redistributed by taking from one and giving to another. The only way to ensure the attainment of an equitable distribution of human capital is to allow more people to attain that capital through education and training. In this sense, attaining an egalitarian distribution of human capital is similar to attaining an egalitarian distribution of physical assets through pro-poor distribution of *incremental* income. Both are time-consuming processes. However, allowing more people to acquire more human capital (by providing them with access to education and training) may be less of a source of conflict than directing more incremental income to the poor in order to build up their physical assets. In this sense, acquisition of human capital may provide an easier route to the attainment of a more egalitarian distribution of assets.

Moreover, education also helps the poor in *indirect* ways through enhancing their access to public goods and resources and to the socio-political and decision-making processes. Education, particularly of females, has also proved to be helpful in altering fertility behaviour and facilitating a demographic transition even at a low income level. Smaller family size, in turn, makes it easier to save and accumulate both physical and human capital. Thus, a virtuous cycle can flow from investment in human capital. Thomas (1999), in a study of women in South Africa, finds a strong and statistically significant negative correlation between years of schooling and number of children born, even after controlling for potential confounding variables, as does Oliver (1999) in his study of women in Ghana.

The pattern of growth matters

Economic diversification and structural change encompassing a shift from low- to high-productivity activities are key factors in ensuring sustained robust growth

Early thinkers on development emphasized that growth and development are generally associated with structural transformation of the economy, manifested in the gradual fall of the share of the primary sector of the economy and rise of the shares of the secondary (manufacturing) and tertiary (service) sectors. Empirical studies have found that such regularities do exist but that more dynamic economic growth (and poverty reduction) are associated with transformations arising from rapid agricultural productivity growth and industrial growth built on strong backward and forward linkages across sectors (see Chenery (1986); and United Nations (2006b)).

Recent experiences suggest a similar pattern of transformation. For example, East Asia, the region most successful in poverty reduction, was also the region witnessing the most dynamic pattern of structural change. In China, for example, between 1970 and 2003, the share of manufacturing and mining in overall output increased from 28 to 60 per cent, while the share of agriculture dropped from 49 to 12 per cent, following a push in agricultural productivity and the development of diversified industries. By comparison, South Asia showed less dynamism, with its share of manufacturing and mining peaking in the 1990s to 22 per cent (compared with 14 per cent in 1970). Sub-Saharan Africa achieved little structural transformation, with agriculture continuing to be the mainstay of the economy. Many countries of Eastern Europe and the former Soviet Union even experienced deindustrialization during 1990s, with the share of manufacturing falling; they also experienced increases in poverty during that period. Thus, there is a clear association between success in structural transformation and success in poverty reduction.

One basic reason why growth is generally associated with structural transformation is that demand for agricultural products is of a relatively limited nature, as formalized by Engel's law stating that the share of income devoted to food declines with the rise of income. Thus, a growing economy has to have larger shares of non-agriculture sectors. Additionally, the scope for technological innovation and accompanying productivity increase is much greater in non-agriculture sectors (in particular industry) than in agriculture. Hence, growth leads to expansion of non-agriculture sectors (via demand) and expansion of non-agriculture sectors leads to faster growth (via their generally higher productivity). The question is why certain countries prove more successful than others in bringing about dynamic structural transformation (accompanied, that is, by an overall rise in productivity) and what the latter can do to emulate the former.

Dynamic structural transformation requires coherence between macroeconomic, industrial and social policies

Agricultural development (see below) and industrial policies have been key drivers of dynamic structural transformations. All developing countries that have witnessed sustained successful economic growth since 1960 used active industrial polices to support the economic diversification and technological upgrading of their economies. These policies involved a significant degree of coherence among supportive macroeconomic policies, (selective) infant industry protection, export subsidies, directed credit schemes, local content rules and large investments in human capital, as well as strategic alliances with multinational companies. Support measures were often clearly tied to specific export performance criteria. Further, these policies provided the basis for dynamic structural transformation which also proved successful in taking advantage of globalization.

Economic growth in these cases was founded on sustained increases in labour productivity and labour movement from low- to high-productivity sectors. Importantly, labour also moved to modern service sectors showing significant productivity improvements, which allowed for continuous real wage increases and substantial poverty reduction over time. In the regions with low growth performance, the employment shift to the service sector has been even stronger. In contrast with those of Asia, the service sectors in sub-Saharan Africa, Latin America and many of the transition economies have shown declining productivity as many workers sought employment in informal service activities for a lack of job creation in other parts of the economy (Ocampo and Vos, 2008). This was not conducive to significant poverty reduction, involving instead the shifting of part of the poverty problem from rural to urban areas. Dynamic structural change thus involves strengthening economic linkages within the economy and ensuring productivity improvements in all major sectors.

Dynamic structural transformation also helps to make growth pro-poor

Such a perspective may also provide a more meaningful means of assessing whether economic growth is pro-poor or not. Assessments of the PRSP approach led to considerable discussion regarding the exact definition of pro-poor growth.[11] The general view that seems to have prevailed is that growth is pro-poor when it leads to the improvement of

11 See Filho (2010) for a recent review.

not only the absolute but also the relative position of the poor in the income distribution. It may be evident from the previous discussion that whether growth is pro-poor or not depends to a significant extent on the pattern of growth in terms of sectoral composition and technological characteristics. An approach that begins with improving agricultural productivity and labour-intensive industrialization helps to create more employment opportunities for the poor and to raise their income. However, it is only dynamic structural transformation and investment in human capital that can enable labour to climb up the technological ladder and thereby move to higher-productivity industries, earn higher wages and lift their families out of poverty.

Agriculture and rural development matters

Most of the poverty reduction successes began with a transformation of agriculture

As indicated above, strongly increasing agricultural productivity has been the common starting point of successful strategies directed towards dynamic structural transformation. Indeed, China's growth acceleration began in the late 1970s with agricultural reform that sharply raised productivity and freed significant amounts of labour and savings for industrial development. While China's agricultural reform is generally known more for the shift from collectivistic farming to household farming, in actuality the reform was a more broad-based package, including the lifting of price controls on agricultural products, institutional support to the marketing of farm output, and Government support for the use of modern inputs such as fertilizers and high-yielding varieties of seeds, among others (see United Nations, 2006b, chap. V). Similarly, in their early stages of development, the Republic of Korea, Taiwan Province of China and, more recently, Viet Nam combined land reform with a range of other support measures to boost agricultural productivity. These experiences also point to the importance of policy coherence. Clearly, none of these policies would have been as successful in isolation as it was as the result of having been formulated and implemented together with the others.

By contrast, the agricultural sectors in many countries in sub-Saharan Africa and South Asia, received little effective policy support; as a result, agricultural productivity growth has been weak at best and the sector continues to provide employment to the major share of the workforce.

Neglect of agriculture also hampers efforts to reduce urban poverty

Most of the poor in developing countries live in rural areas and depend on agriculture for survival. Hence without the achievement of a breakthrough in agriculture, it is almost impossible to make significant progress in poverty reduction. Neglect of the agricultural and rural economy makes it difficult to reduce even urban poverty, because it results in the flocking of the rural poor and unemployed to the cities. By contrast, a rise in agricultural productivity can both generate economic surplus and release the labour needed for industrial development.

Integration in the global economy: the means matter

Economic diversification enhances gains from globalization

Increased integration into the world economy seems to have widened the divergence in growth performance among countries. Trade can help stimulate growth, but in this regard, it is a matter not so much of *how much* countries export, but rather of *what* they export. Faster overall economic growth driven by trade is associated with more dynamic export structures, which are characterized by an export mix that not only allows countries to participate in world markets with products having greater growth potential (most often high-tech products with a high income elasticity of demand) but also helps strengthen productive links with the rest of the domestic economy and generate increased value added for a wider range of services and products. The East Asian countries managed to diversify their economies in this manner, as was already evident from the pattern of structural change. The slower-growing developing countries relied on export activities that had less value added and were rooted in a less integrated domestic economy. Many of these countries remain heavily dependent on exports of primary commodities and have lost market shares in world trade. They also have suffered from larger adverse trade shocks as primary commodity prices have been more volatile than those of other export products (United Nations, 2008).

Sudden, across-the-board globalization has been disruptive of growth in low-income countries

In view of the above, sudden across-the-board globalization may not produce the desired results, inasmuch as an economy needs time both to diversify and to transform its current structure: what was possible under previous tariff conditions must be made compatible with globalization. Yet, diversifying into high-technology exports may not be an immediately feasible option for many developing countries. Low-income countries typically lack adequate basic manufacturing capacity, infrastructure and human capital, as well as the international trading capacity needed to develop such dynamic export activities. These countries do, however, have some capacity to compete in world markets for primary goods and would need to consider industrial strategies for diversifying exports so as to include processing natural resource-based products and other light manufactures. Even so, building up new comparative advantages through promotion of backward linkages will be crucial. Yet, even if backward linkages are initially absent, concerted efforts can help in developing such linkages over time, as the East Asian newly industrializing economies demonstrate (see Wade, 1990). In fact, emphasis on backward linkages is often necessary even for the very survival of the current lines of production. For example, the experience since the elimination of the international quota regime on textiles and clothing suggests that poverty reduction through labour-intensive exports is not sustainable without the development of backward linkages. In some African countries, clothing exports have been wiped out by competition from backwardly integrated countries like Pakistan engaged in domestic cotton and textile production and those countries that have built up labour skills in specific areas, like Sri Lanka with its advantage in producing women's undergarments (see the discussion in Adhikari and Yamamoto (2007) and United Nations (2006b)).

Footloose industries are less capable of withstanding negative shocks

Thus, when job creation takes place in production enclaves with shallow linkages to the surrounding economy, workers and the economy at large are vulnerable to unexpected shocks, and suffer unemployment and recession when firms decide to reduce or shift their activities in response to changes in perceived global market conditions and production cost differentials across developing economies. When social protection mechanisms are inadequate, such negative downturns can increase poverty sharply.

Capital-account liberalization has been a source of greater growth volatility...

Similarly, the liberalization of the capital account can be disruptive of growth and poverty reduction. Capital-account convertibility has made countries vulnerable with respect to large surges in capital inflows. These surges often inflate domestic asset price bubbles, which may then burst thereby causing sudden capital outflows. Capital-account opening has also limited the macroeconomic policy space for counteracting such booms and busts. The exchange-rate movements that accompany both large-scale inflow and large-scale outflow of capital can be harmful for sustained poverty reduction. For example, sharp currency depreciation brought about by the sudden outflow of capital in relatively undiversified economies can be contractionary, raising the costs of imported basic foods and medicine and pushing them beyond the reach of the poor. On the other hand, the beneficial impact of such depreciation on exports may not be immediate and, in fact, may ultimately fail to materialize owing to the implementation of policies meant to prevent the currency depreciation. Similarly, large-scale capital inflows may cause the currency to appreciate, thereby harming the country's exports and leading to employment losses and a rise in poverty. Although the rise in the real exchange rate may favour the non-tradable sectors, those sectors generally suffer from home market constraints and hence cannot serve as the engine for a rapidly expanding economy. Also, since they are generally characterized by low wages and low productivity, the real wage appreciation effect of currency appreciation in the non-tradable sectors proves not to be particularly high.

... and where it occurred, has been harmful to poverty reduction

Most importantly, boom-bust cycles tend to affect progress towards poverty reduction in particular since employment is generally more strongly affected than output by downturns. Also, recovery of employment from recessionary low levels takes much longer than does recovery of output (resulting in jobless growth). Using Turkey as his example, van der Hoeven (2010) presents evidence showing that economies that experienced a large incidence of capital-account crises, exhibit a rising rate of unemployment in the medium term despite a rising trend in respect of per capita gross domestic product (GDP) (figure II.4). Similar trends have been found in parts of Latin America (see figures II.5 and II.6 for the cases of Brazil and Chile).

Some East Asian economies have successfully used capital controls to reduce financial volatility

In view of the above, it is not surprising that most successful East Asian countries have generally exercised control over capital flows. Many of them even maintained and some continue to maintain significant Government ownership of the banking sector in order to have control over capital flows not only across borders but also within borders. The contrasting experience of Malaysia and Indonesia during the Asian financial crisis shows the importance of retaining control over capital flows, as Malaysia did, in order to protect the domestic economy from the deep recession resulting from sudden large-scale outflows of capital (see figures II.7 and II.8).

Figure II.4
Turkey: medium-term effects of financial crises on unemployment, 1990-2007

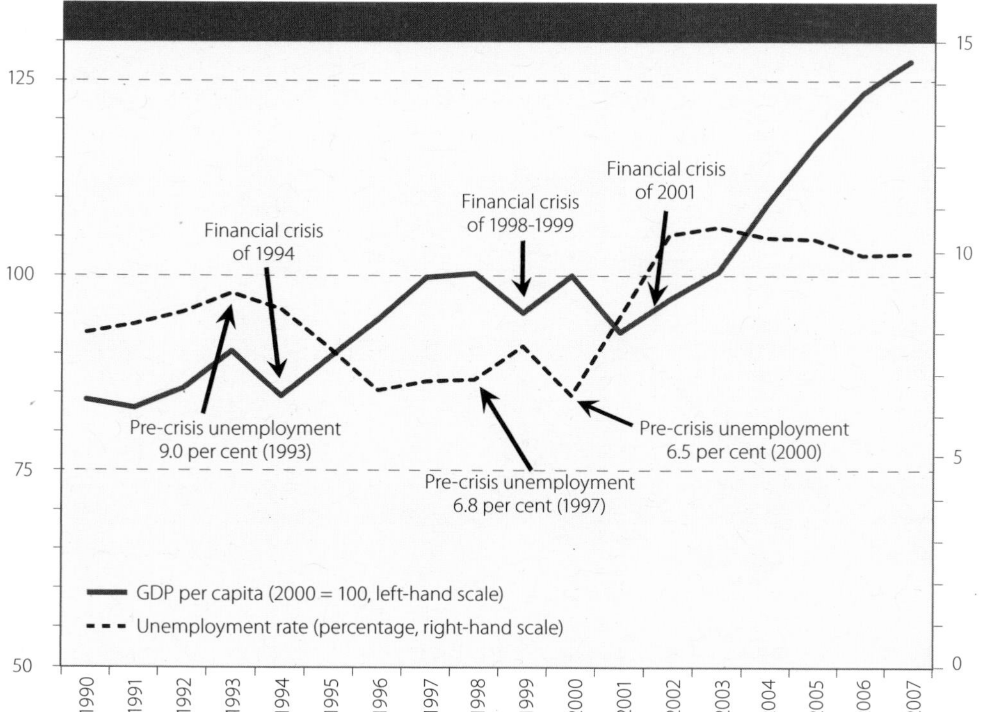

Source: van der Hoeven (2010).

Figure II.5
Brazil: medium-term effects of financial crises on unemployment, 1990-2007

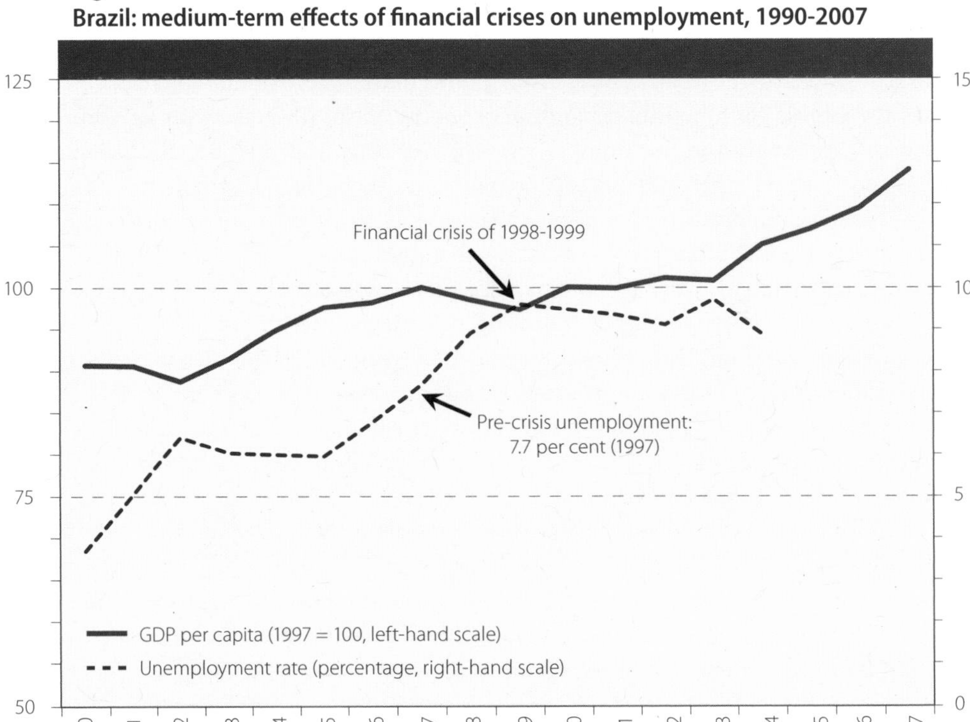

Source: van der Hoeven (2010).

Figure II.6
Chile: medium-term effects of financial crises on unemployment, 1990-2007

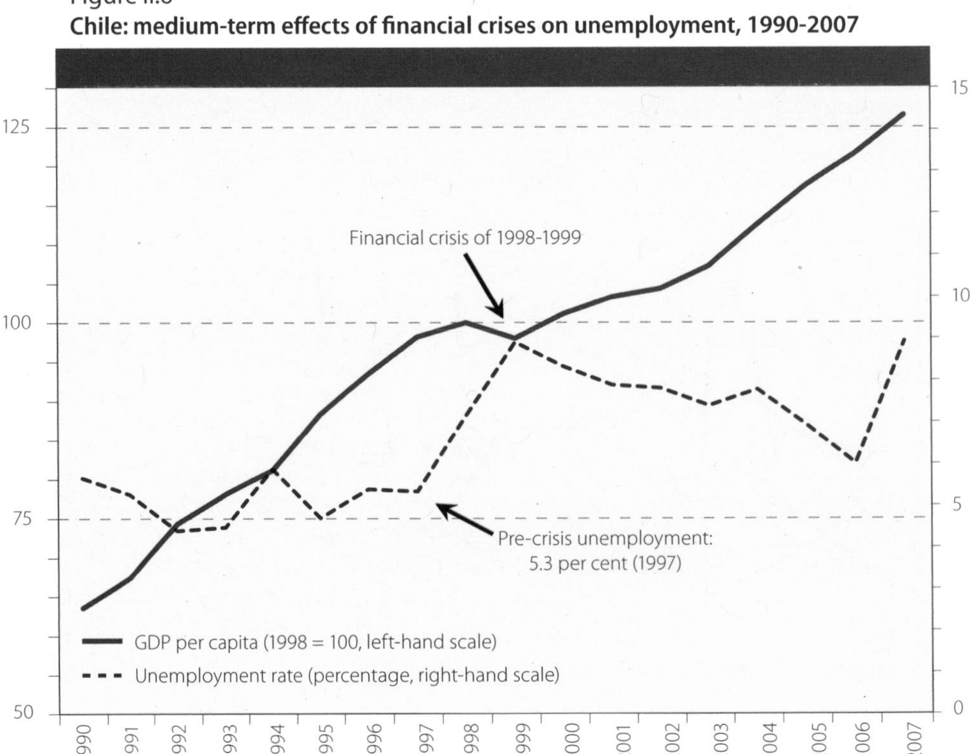

Source: van der Hoeven (2010).

Figure II.7
Indonesia: medium-term effects of financial crises on unemployment, 1990-2007

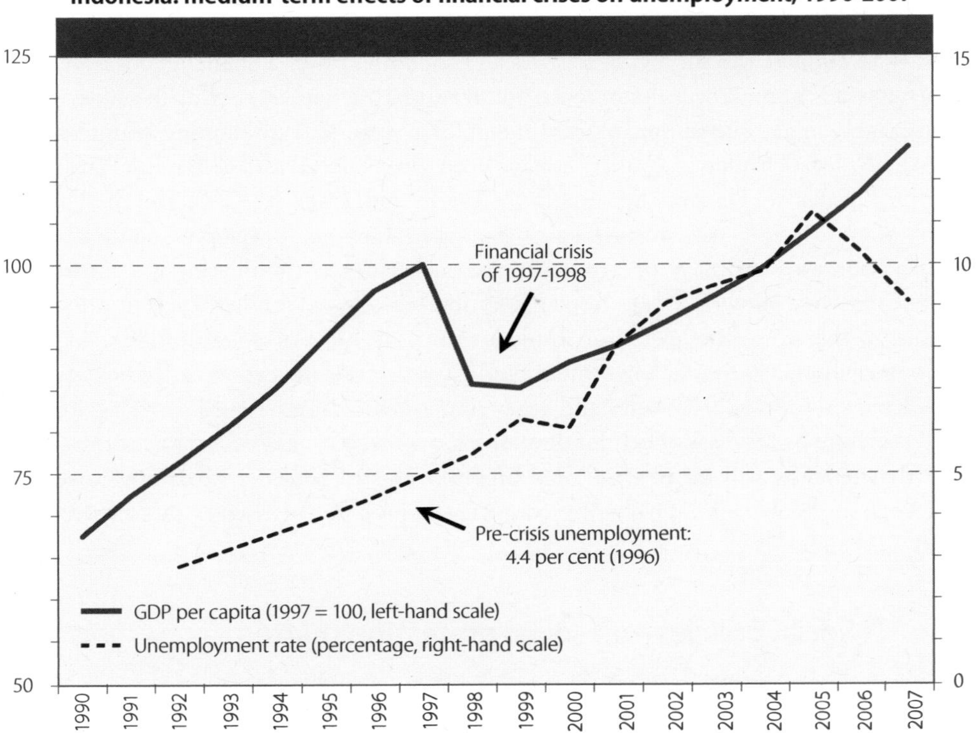

Source: van der Hoeven (2010).

Figure II.8
Malaysia: medium-term effects of financial crises on unemployment, 1990-2007

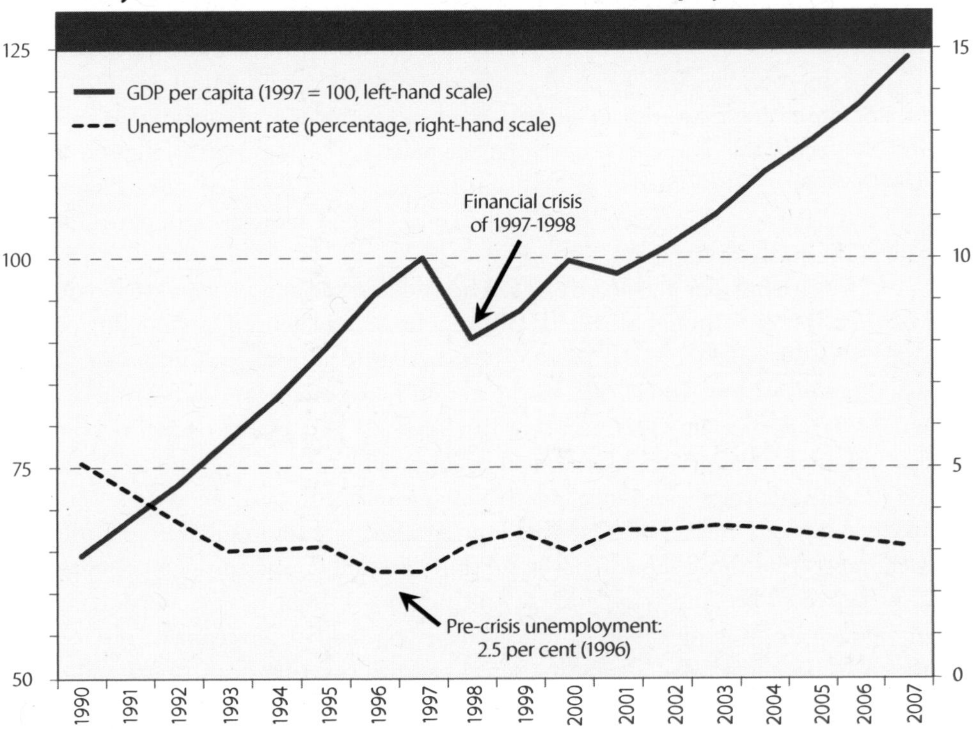

Source: van der Hoeven (2010).

As noted earlier, the East Asian economies, India and some countries of Latin America that have proved more successful in adapting to globalization owe part of their success to prior diversification of the economy achieved under more protectionist regimes.[12] To emulate the success of East Asian economies poses a challenge for developing countries when, at present, rules of multilateral regulating bodies, such as the World Trade Organization, make protection more difficult. It is true that developing countries, particularly the least developed countries, have been given special and differential treatment, as defined under the General Agreement on Tariffs and Trade (GATT) and the Uruguay Round of multilateral trade negotiations. In practice, however, developing countries, aside from the poorest ones, have had to apply the same rules as the developed countries, although they were allowed longer implementation periods and higher levels of protection. In general, therefore, the space for implementing the kind of active production sector development policies that involve infant industry protection, export subsidies, directed credit schemes, local content rules and other components has narrowed. In going forward, it will therefore be necessary both for developing countries to make better use of the policy space that remains and for international organizations to consider expanding the policy space so as to allow more developing countries to prepare themselves to succeed in the global marketplace.

Social policies and social protection matter

East Asian economies have been more successful in aligning their economic and social policies

In a review of social policy making in developing countries, Grindle (2010) notes that Costa Rica, Sri Lanka, China and the State of Kerala in India made significant commitments to social investments at the early stage of development, albeit, according to some, at the cost of growth. Brazil and South Africa, on the other hand, focused primarily (during the 1950s and 1960s) on growth, while not paying sufficient attention to the use of social expenditures to achieve a better spreading of welfare among the population, and later came to face large problems of inequality and poverty. Grindle (2010, p.13) suggests that East Asian countries (the Republic of Korea, Singapore and Malaysia) and Taiwan Province of China could be seen as "perhaps the best examples of countries that have been able to bring economic and social development policies into significant alignment". She notes further that China's current growth spurt is supported "by the ready availability of a literate and healthy labour force" (ibid., p. 12) and yielded a longer-term pay-off to early investment in social development.

Social policymaking in developing countries has gone through several stages

From a broader perspective, it can be said that social policy making in developing countries has gone through distinctly different stages, influenced by changing perspectives on the development process and on how best to deal with conditions of poverty, vulnerability and income insecurity. In the period between the Second World War and the late 1970s, social policy was seen as a fundamental part of the overall development strategy, although it varied in character across countries.

An important element of social policy consisted of the widespread provision of subsidies on goods and services, although, in practice, urban population groups tended to benefit most from those subsidies. The subsidies not only provided income support but also contributed to keeping wage costs low in support of industrial sector development. Urban workers in growing modern industrial sectors and in government services were also the main beneficiaries of expanding social security covering health risks and old-age

---

12 Also, East Asian economies penetrated the United States market at a time when competition was less intense.

income security (pensions), as well as of subsidized and State-provided education and health-care services aiming at universal coverage. Rural producers also received subsidies without, however, offsetting the urban bias in social transfers.

There were various attempts at land reforms with a view to minimizing the idleness of resources and the underutilization of land so as to raise agricultural productivity and support industrial growth. For the most part, however, the needs of the structurally poor, especially in rural areas, were a neglected part of social policies. Relying heavily on public borrowing, the industrial growth strategy and the subsidies ultimately proved unsustainable.

Under the Washington Consensus, universal social programmes were often viewed as unsustainable and inefficient

With the debt crisis of the early 1980s and fiscal consolidation as part of the new macroeconomic policy orthodoxy, social policy underwent substantial changes. The widespread subsidies and social transfers were seen as being too costly, and as causing unsustainable fiscal deficits and undermining efficiency in production, rather than as constituting a powerful engine of development as in the past. Low growth and the pressure to reduce fiscal deficits combined to severely restrict new investments in health and education. Social spending, however, did not decline as a proportion of the budget in most countries, as the political pressure to sustain civil service jobs and wages, which account for the bulk of social expenditures, was considerable. In addition, user fees introduced to cover the costs of complementary inputs—for example, books and medicines—were viewed as serving not only to reduce the fiscal burden, but also to improve the efficiency and quality of social service delivery. Although the remnants of the old policy provided limited job guarantees for that proportion of (generally urban) workers employed in government services or large modern enterprises, the policy adjustments left most of the rural and urban poor with hardly any form of social protection.

In the 1990s, targeted social programmes were introduced

Evidence of growing inequality and persistent poverty and vulnerability, especially in Africa, Latin America and South Asia, led to the recognition that macroeconomic stabilization and structural adjustment programmes came at a high social cost. New, targeted social programmes were therefore introduced to protect the poor from the unfavourable macroeconomic environment. The new programmes included social emergency and social investment funds that received financial support from the multilateral banks. While targeted at the poor, in practice the programmes proved to be limited in coverage and too rigidly designed to be able to adjust coverage and benefits in response to macroeconomic shocks (Lustig, ed., 1995). In fact, social policy and the overall development and growth strategies of many developing countries became totally disconnected. At the same time, emphasis continued to be placed on fiscal consolidation and social sector reforms, including wider application of user fees; and privatization of education and health services, as well as of public pension systems, continued. Evidence of the impact of the pension reforms on coverage is mixed (see Mesa-Lago, 2007; and Vos, Ocampo and Cortez, eds., 2008), but it is generally agreed that they did little to provide additional protection to the poorest.

New forms of social programmes emerged in the late 1990s

Towards the end of the 1990s, a fourth phase of social policy emerged. Many countries saw some recovery of growth and had created greater fiscal space for real increases in public spending on broad social programmes. Trade liberalization increased the demand for more skilled workers and pressures to raise productivity in order for countries to stay competitive in global markets. Continued high economic volatility and several financial and currency crises during the 1990s, and the failure of social investment funds to provide effective protection, gave rise to new forms of social programmes which provided the poor and vulnerable populations with incentives to invest in human capital. Cash transfer programmes were targeted at the poor and not only designed to provide income support but also conditioned upon the keeping of children in school and/or visits paid by mothers and children to health centres. The programmes also addressed a failure of previous education and health policies, namely, their focusing too much on supply-side issues (as in the 1960s and 1970s) or on efficiency and the assumption of adequate "willingness to pay" (and, implicitly, ability to pay) by entire populations. Many evaluations show the (conditional) cash transfer programmes have indeed helped increase school enrolment and the use of health services by the poor, and in this way have helped mitigate income insecurity both by investing in education and health and by providing income support (for surveys, see, for example, Coady, Grosh and Hoddinott, 2004; Morley and Coady, 2003; Standing, 2007; de Brauw and Hoddinott, 2008; Fiszbein and Schady, 2009; and Filho, 2010). Such programmes have now been implemented in a large number of developing countries, and in several cases also include social pension schemes. One evident advantage of these programmes is that they are relatively easy to implement, have an immediate impact and are affordable, typically costing a few percentage points of GDP (United Nations, 2008). This makes them highly attractive politically.

Many of the new social programmes do not fundamentally address the underlying, structural causes of poverty

There are also significant drawbacks, however. Most importantly, this approach to social policy does not effectively address the underlying causes of persistent high poverty and economic insecurity. For instance, increased spending on education may help increase schooling levels among poor children, but will not raise future income if broader economic policies fail to generate sufficient employment and there are no complementary policies that address idiosyncratic determinants of economic vulnerability, including ethnic, racial and gender discrimination, which keep wage returns to some of the poor low. Nor will social investments raise incomes if the poor cannot accumulate physical and financial capital, or if recurrent economic downturns force periodic de-cumulating of their limited assets. Social policy alone cannot change the economic environment or the underlying elements in the structure of the economy that are contributing to poverty and volatile employment and income conditions for vast numbers of households.

Institutions and governance matter

Good governance is needed for success in poverty reduction

Past experience suggests that success in growth and poverty reduction requires capable developmental States. In this sense, there has been a return to early development theories which implicitly assumed the existence of strong developmental States capable of carrying out the suggested coordinated investment programmes. However, times have changed and the tasks that are contemplated for developmental States today are much more complicated than those conceived in the 1950s.

Utilization of policy space requires capable States

It has been widely recognized that developing countries need some policy space in order to formulate and implement policies geared towards consolidation and diversification of their economies. However, policy space cannot be of much use unless there is a Government capable of using it. Wade (1990) has documented the important role that States played in "governing the market" in the first-tier East Asian newly industrializing economies as they went about achieving catch-up growth and poverty reduction. In recent years, the role of Governments has also been vindicated by the experience of Latin America, where Government activism has proved very crucial not only in reducing external dependence and promoting aggregate growth, but also in reducing poverty directly through various innovative social policies (see, for example, Cornia (2010)).

At the same time, it is necessary to be alert to the possibility of "government failures", particularly in view of the fact that formulation and implementation of policies have been rendered more difficult by globalization. While there seems to be agreement about the importance of the role of capable developmental States, it is not clear how such States can emerge in countries that lack them. Grindle (2010) shows that developing countries vary widely with regard to the capability of their States, which range from "very capable" to "failing". A major challenge before the development community is to find the means through which a "failing" State can change into a "capable" one.

Transformation of weak States into capable ones is a major challenge

Ingredients for a new consensus?

Formulation of the Millennium Development Goals represented a great step forward in establishing consensus social development goals. However, the Millennium Development Goals per se do not constitute a development strategy. On the other hand, the recent financial crisis and recession have further undercut the validity and appeal of the Washington Consensus; and thus there is currently a vacuum, so to speak, in the thinking about appropriate growth and poverty reduction strategies. Against this backdrop, can the broadly agreed lessons discussed above provide the ingredients for a consensus regarding the features that are desirable in country-specific national development and poverty reduction strategies? Before considering this question, however, it is necessary to examine the new challenges that have emerged in the interim.

Poverty reduction strategies need to take account of additional emerging challenges

New emerging challenges

Several other challenges, all of which have an inherent international dimension, are affecting poverty reduction efforts. Among these are population ageing, migration and climate change which will compound the poverty challenge, while also providing new opportunities.

Population ageing and international migration

As noted in chapter I, population ageing is occurring in both developed and developing countries, although it is much further advanced in industrialized countries. It is the result of progress in human development, which has meant a lowering of child mortality and improvements in health conditions, resulting in a rise in life expectancy. Societies will have to adjust to increasing proportions of older persons in their population. In this regard, in developed countries, concerns about rising costs of health care (partially related to ageing) and viability of pension systems are already at the centre of policy debates. In many developing countries, population ageing is occurring in an accelerated fashion and life expectancy has risen considerably. Poverty reduction policies will increasingly have to consider this demographic change and include measures to ensure that health care is kept affordable and that guaranteed pension benefits can provide a decent living for older persons.

Population ageing is a global phenomenon that provides opportunities and poses challenges

The fact that developed and developing countries occupy different positions along the population-ageing arc raises the possibility that an increased flow of the younger workers to rich countries could help reduce poverty in developing countries through remittance flows. However, at best migration flows can be only a part of the response to this challenge (see United Nations, 2007). Migration is already creating enormous economic,

Migration provides some opportunities, but limited ones, for addressing poverty as well as problems associated with ageing political, cultural and religious tensions in developed-country societies. The extent to which developed societies will be willing to absorb additional large inflows of labour migrants may be limited. On the sending side, remittances bring benefits, but emigration can also lead to an increasing brain drain and shortages of skilled workers, which may limit domestic economic and social development. Workers returning to their home countries, in contrast, may help increase the skill level of the workforce, but they may also become a force that demands better-quality social services.

Climate change and poverty reduction

Food production in poor countries will be disproportionately affected by climate change

Because of where they live and the nature of their livelihoods, it is the poorer segments of the global population that face the greatest risk of being adversely affected by the effects of climate change. Many of the poor live in rural agricultural areas where climate change induces increased drought in some places and flooding in others. Climate change will also have a strong impact on food production and hunger. Nelson and others (2009) estimate that, by 2050, global rice production will have fallen by 12-13 per cent and wheat by 23-27 per cent relative to a scenario without climate change. Taking into account the impact of climate change on availability of all key crops and meat, calorie availability in 2050 will not only be lower than in the scenario of no climate change but will actually decline, relative to 2000 levels, throughout the developing world and cause a 20 per cent increase in child malnutrition. Further, this additional climate change-induced poverty will claim an increasing part of national budgets. Climate change can also be expected to stimulate efforts to migrate to countries and areas with more resources available for adaptation.

Protection of forests is important for both climate change mitigation and poverty reduction

Many poor populations are dependent on forests for their livelihood. Protecting and enhancing those livelihoods by protecting the forests have been identified as an important part of the response to climate change. The effect of climate on water supplies is another factor with increasing impact on poverty.

Investing in low-carbon and renewable energy provides opportunities for poverty reduction

Conceptually, poverty can be viewed in terms of the skewed pattern of energy consumption by developed and developing countries (Europe's kilowatt-hour consumption per capita per day is at least seven times that of Bangladesh) and within national populations (40 per cent of India's population do not have access to electricity). Promoting more rapid economic growth in developing countries, which is possible only with greater energy availability, would not be consonant with addressing the global climate challenge if this meant permitting developing countries to increase energy consumption by using what are currently the lowest-cost technologies, namely, coal and fossil fuels. The alternative would be for these countries to leapfrog into clean energy and energy-efficient technologies; however, this would in turn require making the investments necessary to lower the cost of renewable energy and facilitating affordable access to the relevant technologies. Introducing green technologies may provide a long-term boost to growth and employment, but at the same time it will also exert increased pressure on the financial capacity of developing countries owing to the large-scale investment requirements.

Food insecurity

A rising world population and the threat of climate change compound the food insecurity problem

The relative neglect of agriculture in many developing countries over the past decades has prevented the food supply from keeping up with the increased food demand that has resulted from a growing world population and the changing consumption patterns associated with rising urban populations. Food insecurity also increased once more countries began to rely on external food supplies. The prices of basic grains and other essential food products have become more volatile not only because of more frequent droughts and floods, but also because of the increasing influence of financial speculation in commodity markets. Policies encouraging the production of biofuels as a response to the threat of climate change have also affected food availability and food prices and have become a new driver of food insecurity for the poor (see, for example, Vos, 2009). A large part of this shift is being driven by public policy of the individual countries acting unilaterally. Poverty eradication objectives thus pose a challenge to achieving an adequate level of international coherence in food and energy policies.

Policy coherence on the basis of a new consensus?

Poverty reduction strategies have to be country-specific

No two countries are alike. A mistake of some of the earlier "overarching" development approaches was to overgeneralize and suggest what was almost a common set of policies for all countries, leaving little room for variation and customization. "One-size-fits-all" straitjackets have not proved very effective.

Development and poverty reduction are ultimately path-dependent processes. Countries cannot escape the effect of their past on their present and can build their future on the basis only of their present. No country can start from scratch and the effectiveness of certain policies or market-induced changes depends on previous events.

Also, it is clear that there are no silver bullets; hence the formulation of an effective development and poverty reduction strategy cannot be compared to solving a puzzle by fitting all the pieces together at once. There are indeed pieces that need to fall into place dynamically over time. The optimal sequence also has to be country-specific and in a highly uncertain world, a good deal of experimentation will be inevitable.

Fitting things together will require a high degree of policy coherence, even if outcomes carry a fair degree of uncertainty. For such coherence to be achieved, it is necessary to see clearly how policies in different areas are linked, both contemporaneously and over time. As noted above, policies regarding initial distribution of assets are related to policies regarding investment in human capital. Further, policies on distribution of assets cannot succeed unless accompanied by suitable policies regarding prices, credit, infrastructure and institution-building. The effectiveness of industrial policies will depend in part on whether macroeconomic policies are supportive and ensure, for instance, that export incentives are not wiped out by real exchange-rate appreciation. Whether there is a need for social assistance policies and targeted poverty reduction programmes will depend crucially on the success of industrial and macroeconomic policies in generating employment and ensuring decent wages. At the same time, social spending can make the carrying out of industrial policies easier by providing a more educated and more healthy labour force. Population ageing, climate change and food insecurity pose further policy challenges to ensuring that economic and social development will be sustainable for all.

National development strategies should serve to achieve coherence in macroeconomic, sectoral, environmental and social policies

National development strategies would need to tailor such coherence to the country context. There are no blueprints on how best to do this, although the lessons learned from past experience can provide a sense of direction, as noted below. Globalization and global rules-setting have limited the space for conducting national development policies; hence greater coherence needs to be sought also between policymaking in the national arena and that conducted in the international arena.

Broadening the approach to macroeconomic policies

Macroeconomic policies in support of reducing economic insecurity and poverty would need to aim at greater social cohesion through productive employment creation, which would require such policies to be counter-cyclical, pro-investment and sensitive to employment objectives. This will require—much more than has been the case in most developing countries over the past decades—a better integration of macroeconomic and development policies. Starting in the 1980s, macroeconomic policies became narrowly focused on controlling inflation, fiscal prudence and promoting export growth, an approach that would bring, so it was believed, economic stability, growth and poverty reduction through trickling down effects. As discussed, this promise was not fulfilled. In contrast, the fast-growing East Asian economies embedded macroeconomic policies in a broader development strategy and did not substitute industrial policies for generalized trade liberalization. The pillars of a broader, more developmental approach to macroeconomic policies could be constructed with the following recommendations clearly in mind:

Fiscal policies should be counter-cyclical and supportive of employment creation and human development

- Fiscal policies would give priority to development spending, including investment in education, health and infrastructure. This would also mean using fiscal instruments such as tax breaks, accelerated depreciation allowances and subsidies to boost productive investment.
- Macroeconomic policies would be conducted on the basis of counter-cyclical rules.[13] These could entail fiscal targets that would be independent of short-term fluctuations in economic growth (so-called structural budget rules) as well as commodity stabilization funds. Such rules have been effectively applied by Chile over the past two decades. The effective management of this counter-cyclical policy stance has been one ingredient in the much stronger growth performance and macroeconomic stability of Chile compared with other Latin American countries (Fiess, 2002; Ffrench-Davis, 2006).

Capital controls may help create more space for conducting counter-cyclical policies

- Where countries have open capital accounts, conducting counter-cyclical monetary policies has become increasingly difficult. The space for doing this can be increased by introducing measures to control and regulate international capital flows as well as the operations of the domestic financial sector. Countries like Chile and Malaysia have managed to follow this course for a certain period of time with some degree of success.
- As in the East Asian experience, monetary policy would be coordinated with financial sector and industrial policies, including directed and subsidized credit schemes and managed interest rates, so as to directly influence investment and savings. The right mix of these policies can be applied deliberately so as to promote investment in specific industries at specific times, and especially in sectors with the greatest potential for upgrading skills, reaping economies of scale and raising productivity growth, thereby increasing the rates of return on investment.
- Such measures can further set the tone for a different kind of competition policy which, instead of promoting competition for its own sake, would look to utilize it to foster diversification and development.

---

13 See Ocampo (2008) and Ocampo and Vos (2008, chap. IV) for more elaborate discussions of this approach; in this regard, see also Cornia, ed. (2006).

Exchange-rate policies should be supportive of industrial policies

- Maintaining competitive exchange rates has been considered essential for encouraging export growth and diversification. A depreciated real exchange rate lowers labour costs and enhances the competitiveness of labour-intensive exports. The empirical evidence suggests, however, that this does not "condemn" countries to permanent specialization in low-tech exports; rather, with consistent policy direction, export diversification into higher-end products will be promoted (Rodrik, 2007a; Cornia, 2006; Ocampo and Vos, 2008). This requires a rethinking of the priority given to inflation targeting[14] which has often resulted in exchange-rate overvaluation, undermining export growth and diversification (United Nations Conference on Trade and Development, 2003).

Agricultural policies should be embedded in the broader development strategy

- Agricultural development policies have been key to successful development strategies in East Asia. Needed would be a broader approach to agricultural development policies, focusing on access to land, extension services, improved inputs, credits and rural infrastructure so as to secure a greater and more predictable marketable surplus and income to farmers and inputs for agro-industrial development. Crop and weather insurance mechanisms, which have recently been introduced in developing countries to provide income protection to farmers, have been analysed and found to be more effective when embedded in a broader agricultural development strategy (United Nations, 2008, chap. III; Linnerooth-Bayer and Mechler, 2007).

Integrating social, labour-market and industrial policy

Successful industrial policy choices not only constituted a coherent set of policies with regard to trade, exchange rates, interest rates, allocation of credit, provision of subsidies, pricing and the provision of infrastructural facilities, but were also embedded in a broader programme of social development. Less successful industrial development processes, such as those of Latin America during the import-substitution era, paid insufficient attention to income inequality, thereby limiting the size of the domestic market and hence expansion of the protected industries.

Incoherence between industrial, labour-market and social policies can hamper long-term growth

In the future, lack of coherence among social, labour-market and industrial development policies could prove a significant millstone weighing down any development effort. The greater technological focus of production and exports requires a more capable labour force and hence ensuring continuous improvements in educational performance and better health outcomes.

National development strategies can be helpful in articulating labour-market policies that serve both economic and social development objectives. Labour-market policy discussions often focus rather narrowly on the possible trade-offs between the degree of labour protection and wage-setting, on the one hand, and industrial competitiveness, on the other. Costly hiring and firing practices and wage rigidity embedded in labour legislation protecting formal sector workers have been seen as impediments to competitiveness and formal sector job creation in developing countries. Such views led to the placing of "labour-market flexibilization" high in the agenda of the Washington Consensus.[15]

14 Multi-country evidence can be found in Epstein and Yeldan, eds. (2009).

15 Labour-market flexibilization had not been put on the "checklist" of the initial agenda of the Washington Consensus (Williamson, 1990) but, becoming of increasing importance during the 1990s, it was listed prominently on the checklist of what is sometimes labelled the "Washington Consensus Plus" agenda (Rodrik, 2007b).

Related labour-market reforms have not been accompanied by stronger employment growth, however—especially in economies where the degree of labour underutilization is high and the degree of informalization and job precariousness is high as well, features common to most developing countries.[16] More generally, maintaining a narrow focus on labour protection and issues of competitiveness is typically not the best way to ensure a balance in outcomes—a balance whereby businesses can win on productivity gains and workers can benefit from greater job opportunities and income security. As indicated, macroeconomic policies can affect employment conditions adversely, while low wages, inadequate social protection and lack of access to education and health services tend to affect labour productivity.

How to strike a better balance will need to be determined in a manner that is specific to each country context; however, the internationally agreed decent work agenda clearly lays out the principles for a coherent policy approach. Furthermore, these principles should help provide a basis for the application of active labour-market policies designed to promote employment generation directly and improve employability and productivity through skills development programmes, as well as of "passive" labour-market policies aimed at providing adequate worker protection (for example, through unemployment insurance, income support policies, establishment of labour standards and adequate wage-setting).

Appropriate labour-market policies can also serve as built-in stabilizers and thus as counter-cyclical policies. For example, decent wages can protect aggregate demand from falling too steeply even when business investment demand falls. Similarly, severance pay and unemployment benefits can protect demand in the face of downturns leading to unemployment.

This counter-cyclical role in combination with policies directed towards enhancing opportunities for retraining and enhancement of skills is particularly critical in today's world of dynamic processes where the spectrum of products in demand in the global market is constantly shifting. In order to survive and achieve success in dynamic world markets, a country needs to constantly diversify and upgrade the range of products that it can produce. However, such diversification and upgrading are not possible without commensurate enhancement of the skills of the workforce.

Furthermore, the demands of sustainable development will need to become a main focus of social and industrial policies. The choice of infrastructure and the setting of industrial priorities (not only in manufacturing but also in agriculture, forestry and energy) will need to be consonant with the task of meeting simultaneously the challenges of climate change adaptation and mitigation and those of improving the livelihoods of the poor.

Improving access to productive assets and finance

Providing low-income households with access to land and credit is vital for poverty reduction

It is already well understood that social policy should encompass increasing the ability of the poor to acquire human capital by increasing public spending on health and education programmes. Mention has already been made above of the potential of cash transfers to mothers, tied to children's school attendance, for enhancing household demand for schooling and for ensuring visits of mothers and children to health centres. However, social policy should also embrace more explicit efforts to ensure access of economically vulnerable households and individuals to land and financial markets. Land reform programmes undertaken in the 1990s in Brazil, Colombia and South Africa are examples of what can be done in this regard, although they have remained small and underfunded.

16 See, for example, Howell, ed. (2005); United Nations, Department of Economic and Social Affairs (2008).

The liberalization of the financial sector has not helped the poor achieve more secure income conditions; those with other assets, including information, education and land or physical capital for providing collateral, have been much better able to exploit the liberalized financial markets. To increase access of the poor to credit would require the implementation of a long list of arcane, technical fixes to the system. Although promoting institutions that make microloans would constitute one step, to date these institutions account for not even 1 per cent of the credits provided by commercial banks in Latin America. As argued in United Nations (2006a), expansion of microcredit schemes critically depends on development of broader networks of institutions, including credit unions, savings banks, development banks and special lending windows of commercial banks. Legal changes that allow the use of movable assets as collateral and of leasing and factoring, creation of credit bureaux, and fiscal incentives that encourage group lending and more timely bankruptcy procedures would all contribute to increasing the supply of conventional bank credits to the poor, thereby creating an inclusive financial system.

Programmes providing the poor with access to credit need to be embedded in broader financial policies

Welfare programmes and social protection

The need for social protection measures arises from several conditions. First of all, employment opportunities, despite their expansion, may not be sufficient to employ all those who are willing to work. Support for the unemployed therefore proves to be important. Second, certain segments of the population may not be, for various reasons, in a position to take part in the labour force and thus benefit from employment expansion and wage income. Third, even the employed may experience the need for extra protection when wages are too low, which creates the problem of the "working poor".

Over time, social protection programmes have taken various forms, ranging from workfare programmes, in place in many countries for a long time, to recently popular cash transfer programmes, as discussed above. While most of these programmes were originally launched and used as ex post measures to help affected people cope with economic downturns, in more recent years, they have been increasingly used ex ante as measures to reduce the exposure of the poor to insecurity.

Welfare programmes can serve as both ex post and ex ante mechanisms for dealing with income insecurity

Many countries in Latin America introduced workfare programmes after having gone through spells of economic crisis. Such programmes would offer jobs to displaced workers, though at wages below the market average (typically about half of the mean wage rates). In most instances, however, such programmes have remained temporary and ex post responses. In contrast, India's Maharashtra Employment Guarantee Scheme, which guarantees 100 days of employment per year to all who wish to participate, is an example of a workfare programme that was transformed from a post-shock temporary arrangement into a semi-formal permanent employment scheme.

A similar transformation of arrangements from ex post to ex ante can be seen in cash transfer programmes used to promote specific development objectives, such as school attendance by children and use of health services. Just as budgetary support has become a more popular form of providing aid at the macrolevel, so has provision of cash become a more popular form of social protection at the household level.

Conditional cash transfer programmes help the poor to invest in human capital

A perennial issue with respect to the design and implementation of various welfare and social protection programmes is whether they are best pitched as universal policies or as policies specifically targeted at the poor. The trend in recent years has been towards the latter approach. However, social protection programmes involving targeting and conditionality have faced various criticisms. In particular, it has been argued that

Universal approaches to social policies are more coherent in respect of providing social protection than multitudes of targeted programmes targeting and conditionality, inter alia, stigmatize the programmes, create and reinforce divisions among the population, create an extra administrative burden and suffer from leakages. In response to these criticisms, it has been suggested that social protection measures should instead be based on the principle of universalism. Accordingly, proposals have been made regarding a "Global Social Floor" (International Labour Organization, 2007, Van Ginneken, 2009) and a "Global Jobs Pact".[17] Social policy needs to be coherent by avoiding a narrow focus on social protection and targeting the poor, while leaning more towards universalism and also addressing issues of redistribution, human capital formation and social reproduction at the level of the family or household (United Nations Research Institute for Social Development, 2006).

Universal social security can facilitate achieving a "Global Social Floor"

An effective way to embody the principle of universalism is to design social protection in the form of social security, whereby all working members of the society contribute from their earnings to a common social fund and draw benefits from this fund, according to pre-specified rules, when they are old and when in need while still of working age. Structured in this way, a universal social security set-up can also facilitate achieving the goal of the Global Social Floor. Achieving the Global Social Floor, which would involve benefit rules guaranteeing such a floor, will likely require resource flows both within and across nations. Also, by promoting employment, the Global Jobs Pact can make it easier to set up the universal social security arrangement.

However, formidable problems lie in the way of setting up universal social security arrangements in many developing countries where vast number of people work in informal sectors. This makes the collection of contributions from their earnings and the effective distribution of benefits daunting tasks at the current stage of those countries' development. Thus, achieving universal social security cannot be separated from achieving a dynamic structural transformation of the economy and conducting active labour-market policies (discussed above), since the latter will facilitate the former by moving more people into the formal sector.

Effective social policies also require capable national States

The kinds of State capabilities needed for effective social programmes are of the same type that would be required for effective industrial policy (Memis and Montes, 2008). Any effort to upgrade the capacity of the State to implement social policy should be seen as part of the overall development effort. Privileging the provision of social and basic services by the private sector or external entities could provide immediate advantages, but would not exempt the State from the obligation to set standards and monitor and regulate such provisioning.

Reshaping policy space

The spread of globalization, economic liberalization and fiscal consolidation programmes has brought about a significant shrinkage of developing-country policy space for poverty reduction. Domestically, recovering domestic policy space will require deploying the broader set of macropolicies, such as that of re-establishing capital-account management, as discussed above.

New global challenges are further eroding policy space

A redrawing of the boundaries between the policy capabilities that should be left to the domestic authorities and those that should be left to international authorities is unavoidable as the international community grapples with the ongoing international

17 See the resolution entitled "Recovering from the crisis: a Global Jobs Pact", adopted on 19 June 2009 by the International Labour Conference of the International Labour Organization at its ninety-eighth session.

economic crisis, which has raised doubts about the sustainability of the previous pattern of growth. Providing global public goods, such as a fair multilateral trading system, and stable and predictable international financial markets, and maintaining a stable global climate, will require the constriction of domestic policy space in exchange for a more stable and sustainable economic environment for each individual country. The crisis has demonstrated the need for coordinated financial regulation, the absence of which had promoted deregulatory competition among financial centres. In the area of trade, the need for uniform international trade disciplines must be balanced against the need to facilitate the increasing participation in trade of economies with more limited capacity. There is also a glaring absence of multilateral mechanisms for more humane and mutually beneficial migration. The international aid system is rife with costly duplication, fragmentation among donors and misalignment with the needs of aid recipients.

A global response to climate change will condition the space for conducting national policies

Multilateral progress on climate change mitigation and adaptation will have an enormous impact on social and economic development in years to come: climate change is already occurring and multilateral disciplines are under development (a wide variety of individual country policies already exist). These disciplines could restrict policy space for trade, finance, technology and social and industrial development in exchange—hopefully—for greater flows of technology and finance consistent with the global community's shared goal of eradicating poverty.

The options available for achieving greater policy coherence at national and international levels will be assessed in the following chapters.

Chapter III
Towards a new aid architecture

Summary

- While the international community has agreed to focus its assistance efforts on poverty eradication, the global aid system has become highly fragmented and its components highly dispersed.
- The mushrooming of aid agencies with diverse objectives, as well as inconsistencies between donors and aid recipients in terms of goals and actions, has contributed to aid volatility and loss of ownership, thereby weakening efforts to reduce poverty and promote development.
- Aid effectiveness is achievable by transitioning to a needs-based aid architecture built on new forms of partnerships among donors and recipients that are aligned with national sustainable development strategies. Resource mobilization for the new architecture would increasingly rely on approaches pioneered in the search for innovative sources of development financing, including internationally coordinated levies.

Introduction

There have been substantial shifts in the system of official development assistance (ODA) over the past 60 years. Shifts in the dominant development ideas and in the relative economic power among countries have induced changes in the mechanisms and modalities of aid. The emergence of significant global economic players from the ranks of developing countries as well as the international philanthropy community is expected to initiate a new realignment which is already putting its stamp on the international aid system. The increased participation of new players, the ongoing deep rethinking of decades-old beliefs held on correct economic management approaches, the challenges facing donors in raising the aid resources required, and emerging development challenges, such as climate change, present both dilemmas and opportunities to those engaged in reshaping the global aid system.

International aid approaches changed when shifts occurred in the dominant development ideas

The present chapter examines these challenges with a view to understanding the strengths and weaknesses of the international aid system. It assesses the effect that aid and its delivery mechanisms have had on the support for economic development and the building of partnerships for development cooperation. The fact that, over time, the aid "architecture" has become increasingly fragmented and its components increasingly dispersed has substantially affected the effectiveness of development assistance. If, moving forward, the aid architecture is to become more effective and live up to the challenges of today, the ways in which resources for development assistance are mobilized and the modalities for providing that assistance will need to be fundamentally reformed.

The aid "architecture" has become increasingly fragmented

Changing views about development assistance

Overlapping donor motivations have been subject to changes over time

The motivations behind donor provision of development assistance may be divided into three categories: developmental, geopolitical and humanitarian. These motivations, which often overlap, have been subject to changes over time. While it is difficult to make across-the-board generalizations about donors, one can argue that the approach to development aid has been strongly influenced by changing views regarding the development process itself.

The scarcity of capital was considered to be the key development bottleneck

During the 1950s and 1960s, the scarcity of capital had been considered to be the key development bottleneck. ODA could play an important role in overcoming this bottleneck, especially in cases where foreign-exchange constraints formed the main obstacle to increasing investment levels. Development assistance focused on providing finance and technical assistance for infrastructure projects, including roads, bridges, ports and energy systems, which by their very nature required investments that were long-term, hence lumpy. Since this was also the era of State leadership in economic development, there was a notable effort by assisting countries to establish economic planning offices through technical cooperation and capacity-building, based on the presumption that Governments in poor countries aspired to be developmental States. It was believed that the role of ODA would be catalytic and temporary in the early stages of development until growth enhanced domestic resource mobilization and eased access to private sources of external finance.

As discussed in chapter I, dissatisfaction with the results of the modern growth strategies of the 1950s and 1960s, whose success had depended on government performance, sparked a paradigm shift in development thinking. Aid flows were perceived to have been poorly managed, and wasted through the "rent-seeking" activities of government functionaries and their favoured allies. Capacity-building often did not take root. Meanwhile, bank lending, in particular, became an attractive external financing option for Governments in many developing countries, especially middle-income countries, compared with aid flows or multilateral bank lending often subject to restrictive policy conditions. As private capital flows proved strongly pro-cyclical and as borrowing conditions abruptly changed at the end of the 1970s, many developing countries ended up saddled with unserviceable debts. The debt crisis that emerged came to be perceived as another failure in the development effort, reflecting unsound fiscal management and failure to create dynamic export sectors which could have kept debt service-to-export ratios within sustainable boundaries. These events also spurred reconsideration of international development cooperation. The multilateral financial institutions introduced structural adjustment programmes which conditioned new development financing to policy adjustments which were to eliminate many of the perceived market distortions introduced by Governments and ensure macroeconomic stability along the lines of the Washington Consensus (see chap. I). Bilateral aid donors often aligned support behind the existence of an International Monetary Fund (IMF) agreement, hence subjecting it to similar policy conditions

The social costs of adjustment under the new paradigm proved to be highly significant

The implied social costs of adjustment under the new paradigm proved to be highly significant. This, together with the influence of earlier concerns raised in the 1970s that growth might not be a sufficient condition for poverty reduction (see chap. II), led to a shift in the focus of aid to more direct support of poverty reduction and social programmes. The lending policies of the multilateral banks underwent the same shift in focus. Support for infrastructure and economic diversification was de-emphasized. In all, aid, in its move away from supporting broader transformative development processes, became much more narrowly focused on poverty and the social sectors. Through the implementation of the agendas of the Millennium Development Goals and the Poverty Reduction Strategy Papers (PRSPs), this constriction was overcome only partially.

The proportion of ODA support for economic infrastructure and production sector development declined

The above-mentioned shift has been visible in the sectoral allocation of aid of the major donor countries united in the Development Assistance Committee (DAC) of the Organization for Economic Cooperation and Development (OECD).[1] As shown in table III.1, the share of ODA allocated to social infrastructure and services increased from an average of 21 per cent during 1970-1979 to 34 per cent in 2000-2008. The shares of debt relief and humanitarian aid also increased. This was at the cost of general programme support as well as support for economic infrastructure and production sector development[2] (including support for agriculture). The combined share of these previously predominant destinations of aid resources fell from 50-60 per cent in the 1970s and the 1980s to about 30 per cent in the 2000s.

Table III.1:
Sectoral allocation of net disbursements of ODA by DAC members, as a proportion of total ODA[a]

Percentage

Sector	*1970-1979*	*1980-1989*	*1990-1999*	*2000-2008*
Social infrastructure and services	21.27	25.22	26.94	33.96
Economic infrastructure and services	12.31	19.05	19.79	13.03
Production sectors (including multisector)	20.18	23.95	16.28	13.31
Commodity support/ general programme assistance	19.52	15.86	9.96	4.59
Debt relief	4.22	2.58	10.31	16.08
Humanitarian aid	0.93	1.72	4.72	6.28
Administrative costs of donors	..	2.32	4.48	5.14
Support to non-governmental organizations	..	1.41	1.31	2.85
Refugees in donor countries	..	..	0.91	2.32
Unallocated/unspecified	21.57	7.88	5.27	2.44

Source: Organization for Economic Cooperation and Development/Development Assistance Committee (OECD/DAC) database.

a Period averages.

1 The Development Assistance Committee is the principal OECD body dealing with issues related to cooperation with developing countries. The DAC donor countries are Australia, Austria, Belgium, Canada, Denmark, Finland, France, Germany, Greece, Ireland, Italy, Japan, Luxembourg, the Netherlands, New Zealand, Norway, Portugal, the Republic of Korea (a member since 1 January 2010), Spain, Sweden, Switzerland, the United Kingdom of Great Britain and Northern Ireland, the United States of America and the Commission of the European Union. Non-DAC donors reporting aid to DAC are Taiwan Province of China, the Czech Republic, Estonia, Hungary, Iceland, Israel, Kuwait, Latvia, Liechtenstein, Lithuania, Poland, the Republic of Korea (prior to 2010), Saudi Arabia, Slovakia, Slovenia, Thailand, Turkey and the United Arab Emirates.

2 For the impact on public investment allocations in the Lao People's Democratic Republic, see Memis, Montes and Weeratunge (2006).

A complex and fragmented aid architecture

Shifting aid objectives and mechanisms have created an increasingly fragmented and highly dispersed aid architecture, which, while it has been responsible for the clear and tangible benefits enjoyed by recipient countries in specific areas, does not appear to be supporting an effective system overall. Aid effectiveness has been found wanting on several counts: while abundant in some contexts, resource flows have fallen short of needs in others; aid delivery has become highly fragmented thereby increasing transaction costs; for many recipient countries, resource flows tend to be volatile, thereby complicating budget processes and development project implementation; and policy conditionality has undermined country ownership and effective use of resources.

Is aid sufficient?

Most donors have not met the long-standing target of 0.7 of gross national income (GNI) for ODA

A proliferation of donors does not necessarily mean more aid. The average size of aid programmes has become smaller (see below). DAC donors, the major providers of ODA, have gradually increased disbursements in absolute terms over the past 50 years. There had been a drop during the 1990s after the fall of the Soviet Union, reflecting the significance of geopolitical influences on aid giving, and a revival during the 2000s. As a proportion of donors' gross national income (GNI), however, aid flows have been on a declining trend since the 1960s, falling from a high of 0.54 per cent in 1961 to a low of 0.22 per cent in the late 1990s (see figure III.1). Over the past 10 years, ODA recovered as a share of donor country GNI and that share is estimated to reach 0.35 per cent in 2010. However, the recovery in aid flows is, to a large extent, attributable to debt relief (Addison, Arndt and

Figure III.1
Trends in ODA disbursements from OECD/DAC members, 1960-2010[a]

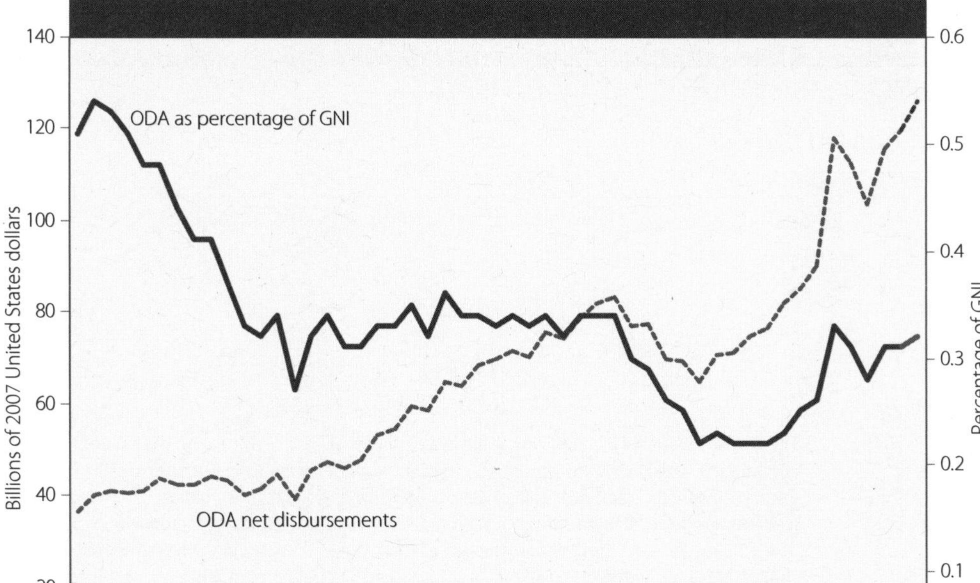

Source: OECD/DAC database.
a Data for 2010 based on OECD/DAC projections.

Tarp, 2010), reflecting a disregard for the principle agreed in the Monterrey Consensus of the International Conference on Financing for Development (United Nations, 2002) that debt relief should be additional to traditional aid (para.51). The recent increases in total aid flows from DAC members have proved far from sufficient to meet the long-standing United Nations target of 0.7 per cent of GNI.

Delivery gaps are largest in aid commitments for Africa

The delivery gap in respect of fulfilling the commitments to support the Millennium Development Goals development agenda has been made all the more glaring by the poignant calls for additional assistance to the poorest countries to enable them to address food security problems and climate change. That delivery gaps are largest in aid commitments for Africa reflects the continued unevenness in the distribution of aid flows, which does not strongly favour populations in low-income countries. Figure III.2 indicates that, excluding India and China, the 10 per cent of the developing world's population that lived in the poorest countries received 14 per cent of bilateral ODA in 2006-2007, slightly up from their share in 2000-2001. Overall, bilateral aid from DAC countries is not strongly concentrated among the poorest countries. In contrast, multilateral aid, which accounts for about one fifth of ODA flows generated by DAC members, shows a stronger bias towards the poorest countries (United Nations, 2009c).

There has been an acceleration of non-DAC aid flows

DAC members contribute about 90 per cent of the total volume of ODA flows. Recently, a number of non-DAC countries, including emerging developing countries like China, Brazil and India, have increased their role as donors. This is not a new phenomenon. Recently, China has expanded its foreign assistance to low-income countries, in particular to Africa, but previously—during the 1960s and 1970s at the height of the cold war—it also provided substantial foreign assistance, including for the financing of infrastructure projects in parts of Africa. Several oil-exporting countries have substantially increased

Figure III.2
Distribution of DAC bilateral ODA for developing countries, by population decile ranked by GDP per capita, 2000-2001 and 2006-2007

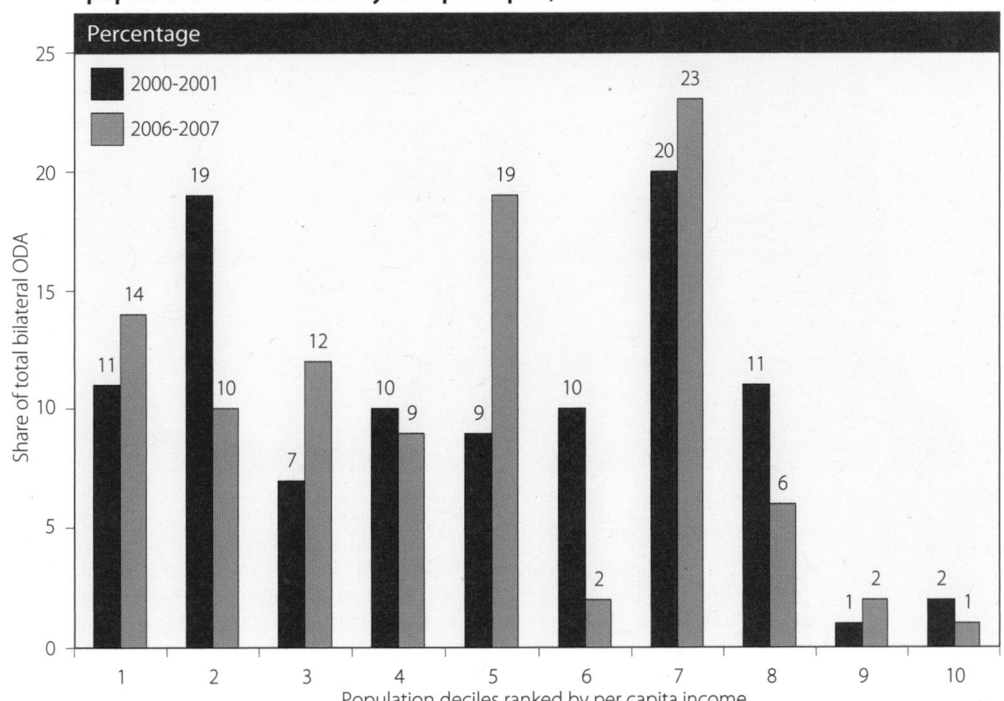

Source: United Nations (2009c, p. 15).

their ODA over the past decade in the wake of higher world oil prices, as they did during the 1970s and 1980s. Figure III.3 shows the recent acceleration of non-DAC aid flows during the 2000s but it also shows that, in real terms, these flows have been well below the amounts of South-South development assistance provided during the 1970s.

China, India, Saudi Arabia and Venezuela (Bolivarian Republic of) are among the most active non-DAC donor countries, but the contributions of Brazil, the Republic of Korea, Thailand and Turkey have also been on the rise. In 2008, the Republic of Korea increased its ODA budget by 31.5 per cent, which in absolute terms thereby surpassed the aid budgets of DAC members Greece, New Zealand and Portugal (United Nations, 2010).[3]

Non-DAC ODA is not necessarily more focused on low-income countries

Countries in Asia and Africa are the main recipients of non-DAC South-South aid flows. Africa's share declined significantly, however, during 2000-2007 as compared with previous decades. The amount of non-DAC ODA directed at low-income countries is no greater than that provided by DAC members (Organization for Economic Coooperation and Development, Development Co-operation Directorate (DCD-DAC), 2010).

Private foundations and international non-governmental organizations have also become prominent development actors

While there is even greater uncertainty regarding private foundations and international non-governmental organizations in respect of their quantitative contribution to development, they have become quite prominent in the area of development assistance, particularly within specific fields such as health services. The 2009 Index of Global Philanthropy and Remittances (Hudson Institute, Center for Global Prosperity, 2009)

Figure III.3
ODA provided by non-DAC countries, 1970-2007

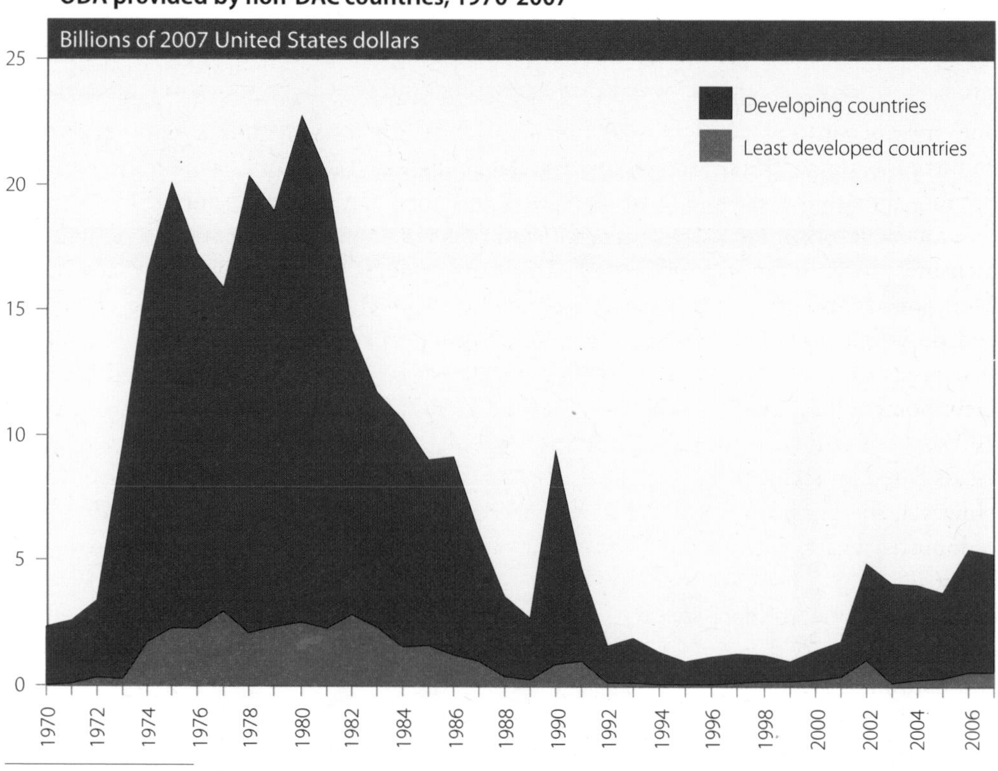

Source: OECD/DAC database.

3 It should be noted that there is some uncertainty about the exact levels of ODA coming from non-DAC members. OECD estimates non-DAC contributions of $5.7 billion for 2006. For the same year, a United Nations-sponsored study estimated that Southern contributors disbursed between $9.5 billion and $12.1 billion, representing 8-10 per cent of total aid flows (United Nations, Economic and Social Council, 2008). The OECD estimates do not include the contributions of China, India and Venezuela (Bolivarian Republic of).

estimates that foreign assistance to developing countries financed from private foundations, non-governmental programmes and individual donations in OECD countries amounted to $49 billion in 2007.

Targeting aid commitments as a percentage of GNI was originally suggested by the World Council of Churches

Even after adding flows from DAC, non-DAC and private sources, total aid would remain far from reaching the OECD target of 0.7 per cent of GNI. Hence, is the level of aid inadequate? When measured against the political commitment, clearly it is. The origins of this target date back more than half a century, however. It was first promoted by the World Council of Churches in 1958 which had argued that only with substantial aid from the advanced countries, could the poorer nations carry out their development plans and "avert the human disasters that follow from their failure".[4] The Council estimated that at least 1 per cent of the national income of the rich countries should be allocated for this purpose, but as it expected that 0.3 per cent of GNI could come from private sources, 0.7 per cent would need to be provided in the form of official grants and concessional loans. The target was subsequently sanctioned by influential economists, including Paul Rosenstein-Rodan and Hollis Chenery, who independently estimated that the foreign exchange needed (calculated as the difference between capital requirements and domestic savings) to reach a target rate of growth of about 5 per cent per year in developing countries would be in the order of $10 billion. This happened to have been equal to 1 per cent of the combined GNI of the advanced countries in 1961.[5] Although it is based on a rather simple estimation made more than 50 years ago and although the nature of global development challenges has changed radically, the target of 0.7 of donor GNI for aid has remained accepted internationally to this day. Such acceptance is probably due to the fact that the target has never been met and the needs of the poorest countries remain so large.

Is a global aid target still relevant today?

However, there are more than enough reasons to rethink the target. First, it does not appear to make much sense to calculate the financing requirements of one set of countries as a fixed share of a largely unrelated aggregate of a different set of countries. Second, the original estimate of the required level of ODA was based on the assumption that all of the aid would support investment and all of the investment would lead to commensurate increases in income growth. The related evidence is not very strong (see below). Moreover, as discussed, the motivations behind disbursing aid have changed over time and the focus is far from exclusively on promoting economic growth. Third, it is likely that needs vary over time and will be context-specific. In a fairly recent United Nations Development Programme (UNDP)-sponsored study (United Nations Millennium Project, 2005), the attempt to estimate the aid flows required to meet the Millennium Development Goals based on recipients' needs resulted in a figure of 0.54 per cent of rich-country GNI. However, these estimates were based on a few country-level needs assessments only and it is doubtful whether, given the diversity in contexts, total aid requirements can be derived by "scaling up" financing needs of a few individual countries. Further, we need to ask the question how to incorporate other recipient needs that, to be addressed, may require additional support through ODA, such as those relating to food security, climate change and natural disaster relief.

In sum, owing to the lack of adequate needs assessments and to the fact that the existing target has in actuality been defined independently of recipients' needs in the current context, it is difficult to assess whether present levels of ODA are sufficient. Hence,

4 World Council of Churches (1958), "Minutes and reports of the eleventh meeting of the Central Committee of the World Council of Churches: Nyborg Strand, Denmark, August 21-29, 1958" (Geneva), appendix XIV, pp. 124-125.

5 See, for instance, Clemens and Moss (2005) for a recounting of the origins of the 0.7 per cent target.

although the ratio of ODA to GNI may still be a relevant indicator of the budget priorities of donor countries and of how much they are capable of contributing to international development, it still does not make clear the absolute size of required aid flows.

Aid fragmentation

As the number of projects has gone up, the average size of aid projects has gone down

The trends in ODA flows just described have caused the aid architecture to become more fragmented, with a largely uncoordinated proliferation of destinations, donors and modalities. This has made the sufficiency of aid even more difficult to determine. The number of donors has risen exponentially while the average size of aid projects has declined considerably. The World Bank (2007) has estimated that, in 2006, donor support for development encompassed over 60,000 ongoing projects, with some partner countries engaging in over 1,000 donor-funded activities, hosting over 1,000 missions each year, and preparing as many as 2,400 progress reports annually. Figure III.4 demonstrates that, in low-income countries, as the number of projects has gone up, the average size of projects have gone down. In this regard, the United Republic of Tanzania manages over 700 externally funded development projects and in 2005 received over 540 donor missions. The average number of official donors—bilateral and multilateral—per country has increased threefold since the 1960s; the number of countries with over 40 active bilateral and multilateral donors has ballooned from zero to over 30 since 1990 (ibid.).

Resurging Southern providers and non-governmental organizations and private foundations have added to this proliferation. Southern bilateral development assistance is virtually all in the form of project loans and grants, each with its own modalities and procedures (see box III.1). Through international philanthropy, historic contributions

Figure III.4
Number and average size of aid projects in low-income countries, 1997-2008

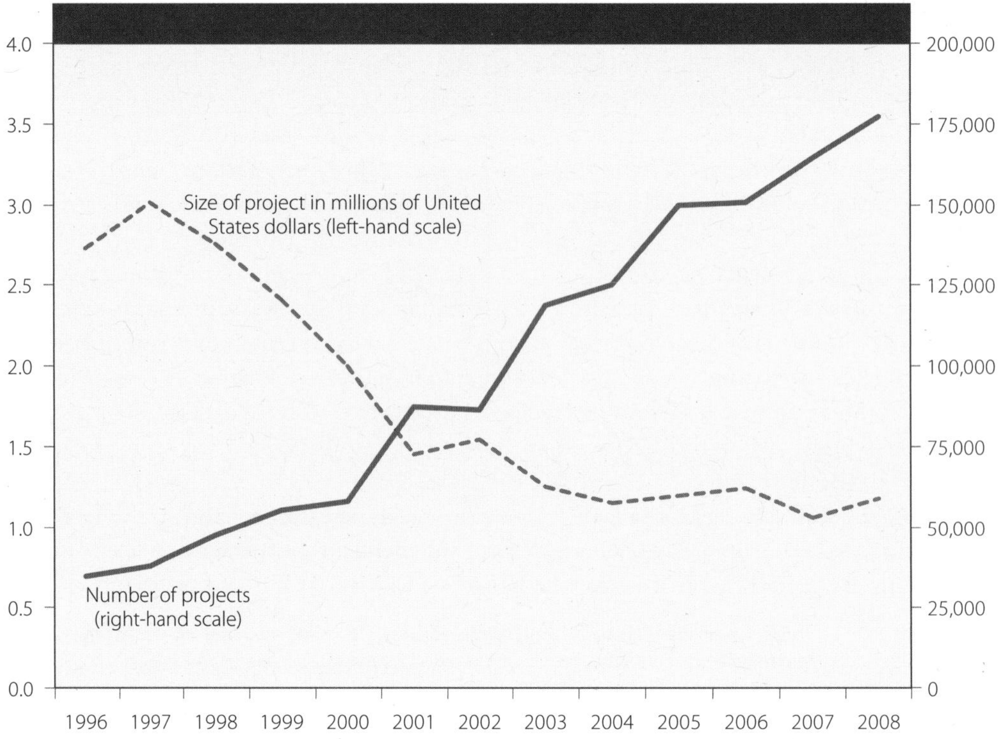

Source: World Bank (2007).

Box III.1

South-South development cooperation

Main trends

South-South cooperation encompasses financial flows, such as loans and grants for social and infrastructure investment projects and programmes, as well as the sharing of experiences, technology and skills transfers, preferential market access and trade-oriented support and investments.

Virtually all Southern bilateral development assistance is in the form of project loans and grants. More specifically, about 90 per cent of South-South development cooperation comes in the form of project finance and technical assistance, with about 10 per cent in balance-of-payments or budget support, although some contributors are planning to move to more programme-based approaches in the future. Many Southern contributors and multilateral creditors have provided debt relief for heavily indebted poor countries (HIPCs), although not all on strictly comparable HIPC terms, with some countries having written off significant sums owed by HIPCs.

Intensified regional cooperation and integration constitute a major catalyst for South-South development cooperation. The bulk of South-South cooperation is undertaken intraregionally to support regional integration initiatives. The African Union, the New Partnership for Africa's Development,[a] Association of Southeast Asian Nations Plus Three cooperation and the Caribbean Community (CARICOM), among others, are important platforms for facilitating South-South exchanges through regional and interregional partnerships while consolidating economic integration. Southern countries can help each other not only financially, but also in many vital areas encompassing, for example, design of development strategies and sharing for mutual benefits of development experiences that have been undergone over the past decades.

Many contributors to South-South development cooperation have programmes that are co-financed by triangular cooperation, whereby Development Assistance Committee (DAC) donors finance projects executed by institutions of the South. As developing countries offering South-South development cooperation programmes are seen as having expertise relevant to meeting developing-country needs, the focus of triangular development cooperation is primarily technical.

Coordination at the country level

Harmonization among contributors on procedures related to the provision of South-South cooperation has not been formalized. An exception is the coordination achieved by Arab institutions (the Abu Dhabi Fund for Development (ADFD), the Arab Bank for Economic Development in Africa (BADEA), the Islamic Development Bank (IsDB), the Kuwait Fund for Arab Economic Development (KFAED), the OPEC Fund for International Development, and the Saudi Fund for Development (SFD)) through the Arab Coordination Group and project co-financing arrangements. The Arab contributors, for example, have adopted common procurement procedures.

There is a certain degree of coordination, on a regional basis, among some Southern providers with Northern donors. For example, Malaysia, Singapore and Thailand coordinate with the Islamic Development Bank, United Nations organizations and Japan through regional initiatives in Cambodia, the Lao People's Democratic Republic, Myanmar and Viet Nam, some of which are related to triangular cooperation arrangements. OECD/DAC is liaising with bilateral Southern contributors with the aim of reaching the stage of agreement on and/or endorsement of good development practices, as formulated by the Development Assistance Committee, which includes soliciting stronger participation of those contributors in the policy formulation process as well as in co-shaping the outcomes. However, in general, few Southern providers engage directly in macroeconomic or social policy dialogue with programme country Governments and rarely participate in national donor coordination meetings, which are usually organized in conjunction with DAC donors.

Challenges of aid effectiveness

There have been repeated calls for Southern providers to bear some of the commitments of donor countries as outlined in the 2005 Paris Declaration on Aid Effectiveness and the 2008 Accra Agenda for Action,[b] the most significant international agreements on aid effectiveness. As of today, 111 non-DAC countries have subscribed to these agreements. However, in spite of the large number of partner country signatories, the Paris Declaration and the Accra Agenda for Action are still perceived as

a Document A/57/304, annex.

b Document A/63/539, annex.

Box III.1 (cont'd)

reflecting an agenda set by Northern donor countries. There is a widespread view that South-South development cooperation took root in a special historical context, with distinct features vis-à-vis official development assistance (ODA). South-South cooperation is recognized as a common endeavour of peoples and countries of the South, born out of shared experiences and sympathies, based on their common objectives and solidarity, and guided by the principles of respect for national sovereignty and ownership, free from any conditionalities. Moving towards the Paris Declaration targets may mean that some of the benefits of Southern development assistance to programme countries will decline; and a move towards more programme-based assistance may mean that there is less direct project funding available for infrastructure projects. Untying development assistance could potentially lead to slower project implementation if the competitive bidding process turns out to be time-consuming.

Yet, some policy orientations of the aid effectiveness agenda are governed by universal values regarding international cooperation for development. These values include respect for national ownership and leadership as well as mutual accountability, whereby providers of cooperation and their partners are accountable to one another for development results. This was recognized collectively by Southern countries during the High-level Conference on South-South cooperation held in Nairobi in December 2009, which stressed the need to enhance the development effectiveness of South-South development cooperation by continuing to increase its mutual accountability and transparency, as well as coordinating its initiatives with other development projects and programmes on the ground, in accordance with national development plans and priorities. Although the indicators of the Paris Declaration cannot be applied in their entirety, some could provide important reference points for South-South development cooperation. In this respect, there is a need for a platform of Southern countries able to take the lead in developing such criteria, taking into account the aid effectiveness agenda.

Support for multilateralism and development

South-South development cooperation funding represents an important complement to ODA flows. Against the backdrop of global economic turbulences, there are clear indications that global development cooperation in the coming years will operate under increasingly stringent aid budgets. At the same time, South-South development cooperation is expected to continue growing. For example, the United Nations system, as an important channel for South-South development cooperation, has witnessed significant growth in contributions from non-DAC countries in recent years. Non-DAC countries contributed $708 million to the United Nations development system in 2007, representing a 220 per cent increase over 2004 and a 57 per cent over 2005. This momentum, if maintained, will contribute to support for the efforts of developing countries to realize the internationally agreed development goals, including the Millennium Development Goals.

In addition to providing additional flows, South-South development cooperation opens up to developing countries an effective avenue for capacity development. Developing-country skills and technological solutions have evolved in an environment of similar factor endowments, such as labour abundance, capital scarcity and poor infrastructure, while expertise of developing countries is likely to be at levels more appropriate to the size of markets in other developing countries. With these comparative advantages, Southern contributors are regarded as competitive providers of more appropriate and cost-effective responses to the needs of their fellow developing countries.

The best practices in South-South development cooperation could inform the aid effectiveness agenda and help to reshape the framework for international development cooperation, for South-South development cooperation has been perceived by programme countries as a modality that is more flexible and predictable as well as more responsive to country priorities. Another hallmark of this modality is its cost-effectiveness and efficient implementation. These merits could provide important lessons for donors involved in redefining the aid effectiveness agenda.

Yet, identification of good practices and learning in South-South cooperation needs to be improved. While some of this work is being done in the context of OECD/DAC, the new Development Cooperation Forum, held by the Economic and Social Council, could play a critical role in engaging developing countries in identifying such good practices and, notably, engage countries offering South-South cooperation programmes on a major scale.

Source: UN/DESA.

have been made to achieving malaria eradication and the goals of other global health programmes and in the area of the discovery and dissemination of high-yielding agricultural crops, among others. At the same time, non-governmental aid mechanisms have contributed to further aid fragmentation, as their operations and disbursements are more difficult to align with national priorities.

Aid fragmentation complicates the pursuit of coherent long-term development policies

Aid fragmentation can be costly: donors undertake identification missions, negotiate the terms of projects to be funded, maintain their own accounting methods, tend to set their own conditions, and prefer to do their own monitoring and evaluation. A European Union (EU) report estimates the costs of delivering EU aid programmes at €2 billion-€3 billion; if all EU aid had been delivered in the form of budget support, transaction costs might have been less than €0.9 billion (European Commission, 2009). Indirect costs may be even much higher, thereby affecting the institutional capacity of developing countries and complicating the pursuit of coherent long-term development policies by Governments, especially when they are highly dependent on aid and are dealing with multiple donors every day.

Earmarking of aid and proliferation of vertical funds

The last two decades have seen the proliferation of special-purpose funds for specific aid objectives. Among the major funding pools are the Global Environment Facility which provides support for a set of multilateral environmental agreements, and the Global Fund to Fight AIDS, Tuberculosis and Malaria. Aid for Trade is a donor facility launched during the Doha Round of the World Trade Organization to help developing countries exploit the market access that they have obtained through trade negotiations.

Special-purpose aid vehicles imposes many dilemmas on the demand side of aid

While the establishment of special-purpose aid vehicles facilitates coherence in particular areas on the supply side of aid, it gives rise to many dilemmas on the demand side because of well-known inflexibilities of earmarked funding. For example, the delivery of health services in response to AIDS is often hampered by inadequate health systems. To achieve the goal of "fighting AIDS", it may be necessary to rebuild the whole health system, but special-purpose funds by their very nature cannot be re-channelled in this way. The administrative demands associated with accessing different special vehicles on the recipient side are high; and the costs of earmarking are just as relevant at the international as at the domestic level. Here lies one argument for providing assistance to countries through the overall budget channel and allowing recipients to use these resources according to their own priorities.

Aid effectiveness

The stable flow of resources is key for aid effectiveness

Aid effectiveness evaluations since the 1970s have generally been undertaken in regard to aid's contribution to overall economic growth, even as its purposes and role in development have been shifting. Addison, Arndt and Tarp (2010) and de Haan (2009) argue that aid has a positive impact on economic growth, albeit with decreasing returns. In general, for each 10 per cent increase in the proportion of ODA to gross national income (GNI), the impact would be an increase of 1 per cent in economic growth (Tarp, 2010). Successful post-war European reconstruction (see the discussion below on the Marshall Plan approach) and other "economic miracles" in the second part of the twentieth century demonstrate that carefully designed development objectives, appropriate institutional settings, and a stable flow of resources are key for aid effectiveness. Easterly (2006), in contrast, argues that while aid has been successful in a number of specific programme cases, failure has been the norm, owing mainly to both donor fragmentation and the diversion by recipients of fungible aid resources towards unproductive uses. Bhagwati (2010) also underlines absorptive capacity and fungibility problems as key factors undermining aid's effectiveness. From different analytical perspectives, other studies have stressed the risks of becoming aid-dependent and experiencing few incentives for economic development (Reinert, 2005).

Greater coherence among aid objectives is critical

Donors have been trying to mend the situation. The 2005 Paris Declaration and the 2008 Accra Agenda for Action have called for greater coherence among aid objectives and for the acceleration of the implementation of the agreed principles therein. The Paris Declaration provides new codes of conduct for donors which aim to reduce fragmentation, including through target-setting for greater harmonization in aid provisioning, alignment behind recipient country development programmes, coordination of donor missions and diminishing the use of project implementation units. The quality of aid is to be enhanced by more predictable aid flows programmed at the country level. Strengthening mutual accountability of donors and recipients, an additional aim set out in the Paris Declaration, should help reduce transactions costs and strengthen State capacity. An example is the joint Economic Commission for Africa (ECA)-OECD project discussed in box III.2.

Box III.2

The Mutual Review of Development Effectiveness (MRDE) in Africa

Pursuant to the Millennium Summit, held in 2000, at which the Millennium Development Goals were agreed, both African Governments and their development partners entered into a series of mutual commitments designed to promote the achievement of the Goals in Africa. These commitments were embodied in the New Partnership for Africa's Development (NEPAD)[a] launched by African leaders in 2001, and in subsequent declarations by the African Union Commission, and in the responses from development partners that followed.

Coordinated review of commitments

The New Partnership for Africa's Development proposed the establishment of a system enabling African countries and their development partners to discuss development effectiveness and aid management issues. At their meeting on 3 November 2002, the NEPAD Heads of State and Government Implementation Committee (HSGIC) underscored the need for mutual review of development partners in terms of their commitments to Africa. To this end, the Economic Commission for Africa (ECA) and the Development Assistance Committee (DAC) of the Organization for Economic Cooperation and Development (OECD) developed a framework within which "Joint reviews of development effectiveness", could be carried out for African countries and their development partners.

The joint mutual reviews involve objective evaluations of performance by African countries and external development partners based on an agreed set of commitments and indicators that are monitored through the review process. In this sense, the 2005[b] and 2009[c] reports reviewed the commitments made, actions taken to deliver on those commitments, results, and priority actions. Building on the first report, the 2009 report covers four main topics: sustainable economic growth, investment in people, good governance and development finance. It treats capacity development and policy coherence as key cross-cutting issues together with regional integration and international systemic issues.

a Document A/57/304, annex.

b ECA and OECD, "Development effectiveness in Africa: promise and performance—applying mutual accountability" (October 2005).

c ECA and OECD, "The mutual review of development effectiveness in Africa, 2009: promise and performance" (April 2010).

Box III.2 (cont'd)

Progress on economic growth and climate change commitments

Africa has made good progress with respect to its commitments on promoting growth, investing in the health and education of its people, improving governance and mobilizing resources. Development partners have scaled up their financial and technical assistance.

Positive results that have been achieved in Africa include strong and sustained economic growth, outpacing global per capita growth since 2001 after lagging behind for two decades, and helping to reduce poverty. Multiparty democracy has taken a stronger hold, and the number of State-based armed conflicts has been reduced. There has been significant progress towards the Millennium Development Goal of achieving universal primary education by 2015. However, the picture with respect to other Millennium Development Goals, particularly that of reducing the maternal mortality ratio by three quarters is troubling, and based on present trends, no country in Africa will meet all the Goals by 2015.

African Governments have made commitments to promote environmental sustainability and to integrate climate change adaptation strategies into national and regional development policies. The key future policy priorities with regard to climate change and environmental sustainability entail mainstreaming environmental and climate adaptation issues into economic planning. In this regard, twenty-seven African countries have identified their priority adaptation needs through the development of National Adaptation Programmes of Action (NAPAs); the Conference of African Heads of State and Government on Climate Change (CAHOSCC) was established to represent Africa at the fifteenth session of the Conference of the Parties to the United Nations Framework Convention on Climate Change;[d] and under their Climate for Development in Africa Programme, the African Union Commission, ECA and the African Development Bank jointly established the African Climate Policy Centre (ACPC). Moreover, climate change adaptation has been integrated into national development programme design and implementation. Along the same lines, development partners have made commitments to undertake enhanced action on mitigation, support for adaptation, technology transfer and financial resources. The key policy effort that needs to be pursued by development partners is therefore increasing financial and technical support to help Africa adapt to climate change and to develop clean energy.

Challenges remain ahead

Although much has been done on both sides of the partnership – for example, regarding external debt policies – more needs to be done on both sides to meet commitments. For example, in respect of policy coherence for development, there is a need to align trade, climate change, financial regulation, tax policy, corruption, peace and security, and development finance policies of African Governments and their development partners. There are remaining challenges that arise from the need to improve the coherence of climate change, trade and aid policies of OECD member countries and from the need for African Governments to direct the benefits of economic growth and larger Government revenue towards the achievement of the Millennium Development Goals and to enhance efforts to promote collective regional action on key political and economic issues, together with accelerated regional economic integration. Development partners and the wider international community need to respond positively to Africa's call for stronger representation in international institutions tackling wider systemic issues and to deliver on existing commitments to increase the volume and improve the effectiveness of official development assistance (ODA).

The above-mentioned mutual review of development effectiveness (MDRE) outcome reports have become important mutual accountability mechanisms for African countries and their development partners. They also serve as a basis for dialogue on Africa's development agenda within G-8 Africa[e] and other critical international forums. The MDRE reports make policy recommendations on what needs to be done to close any implementation gaps, highlighting best practices and how these can be replicated, as well as avoidable bad practices.

d United Nations, *Treaty Series*, vol. 1771, No. 30822.

e A process of dialogue between the Group of Eight (G-8) and African countries.

Source: UN/DESA based on ECA, "The mutual review of development effectiveness in Africa" (22 March 2010).

Reconciling national priorities with the taxpayer-approved objectives of donor countries has been difficult

Nonetheless, putting these principles into practice has not proved to be easy. Despite the targets agreed by the signatories of the Paris Declaration who had endorsed the principles contained therein, "only 15 per cent of donor missions are undertaken jointly with other donors, well below the 40 per cent target set for this indicator, and only 9 per cent of partner countries undertake mutual assessments of progress in implementing agreed commitments and more broadly their development partnerships, against a target of 100" (World Bank, 2006b, p. 79). Reconciling national development priorities with the taxpayer-approved objectives of donor countries has been difficult. Even now, less than a quarter of aid flows from DAC donors is provided in the form of budget support and in a few instances aid flows are part of multi-annual programmes. While one of the objectives of the Poverty Reduction Strategy Paper (PRSP) agenda was to give recipient countries more of an opportunity to occupy the driver's seat so that donors would then be aligned behind nationally defined development strategies, in practice the PRSPs have been found to come with too many strings attached and to be excessively donor-driven (see below and chap. II; and United Nations, 2009a). And in fact they did prove in many instances to be ineffective in improving ownership and donor alignment (Wood and others, 2008).

Additional donor channels could set back efforts to reduce transaction costs

The newfound prominence of South-South cooperation has emerged amidst the abovementioned efforts of traditional donors, who are applying mainly the lessons learned from the poverty reduction strategy effort of the 1990s. Some DAC members have expressed concern that the aid provided by non-DAC donor countries (many of whom do not report their ODA figures and are not bound by the principles of the Paris Declaration and existing conventions on the provision and use of aid) may undermine progress on jointly agreed commitments to improve aid effectiveness. The presence of additional donor channels in an already crowded field increases the risk of duplication of activities and could lead to a setback for DAC donors who have the intention to reduce transaction costs for aid recipient countries by rationalizing reporting and accountability obligations. Yet, South-South cooperation partners have also expressed their own concern that the "aid effectiveness" process is being driven too much by OECD, and that project aid—the preferred modality of South-South cooperation—could become a casualty of the preference for programme aid as governed by the principles set out in the Paris Declaration. There is still no international venue where these issues can be addressed, except possibly the Development Cooperation Forum held by the Economic and Social Council (see box III.1 above).

Aid volatility

Aid volatility has compounded macroeconomic instability

In countries where aid flows are a large driver of their economy, aid volatility has compounded macroeconomic instability, affecting private and public investment spending and long-term growth. One study (Kharas, 2008) found that for the average recipient country, ODA flows are five times more volatile than gross domestic product (GDP) and three times more volatile than exports earnings.[6] ODA thus could magnify real business cycles in recipient countries. Measured volatility cannot be associated with donor actions alone: using their own procedures, donors often have to respond—by halting aid disbursements, for example, if the prior year's resources were unutilized—to unexpected and unfortunate economic and political events beyond their control in recipient countries. Figure III.5 suggests that, for a sample of 65 recipient countries, higher levels of aid volatility is associated

6 Volatility is measured as the coefficient of variation against a long-term trend.

Figure III.5
Aid volatility and economic growth in 65 recipient countries, 1970-2007

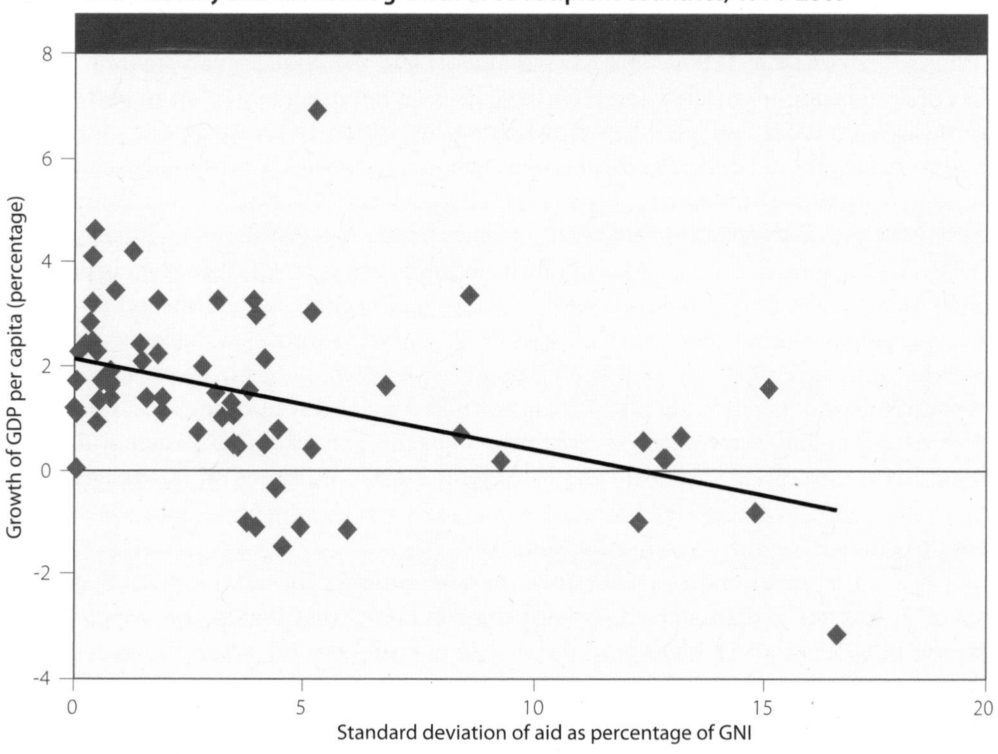

Source: UN/DESA, based on World Development Indicators Online.

with lower long-term rates of growth of GDP per capita. Least developed countries and small island developing States are among the aid-dependent countries facing the highest levels of volatility in ODA inflows.

The deadweight losses associated with aid volatility can be as large as 15-20 per cent of the total value of aid, which, at the current aid levels, would amount to welfare losses of about $16 billion (Kharas, 2008).[7] To an average recipient, the deadweight loss of aid volatility is about 1.9 per cent of GDP. Per dollar of aid provided, the cost would lie between 7 and 28 cents, depending on the donor. In the same study, the degree of aid volatility varies across donors and losses due to aid volatility are largest in cases where the United States is the major donor, with losses from volatility for every dollar disbursed being more than double those associated with Japan, the next most "volatile" donor.

Conditionality and country ownership

Developing-country "ownership" must be meaningful

Political considerations and concerns about accountability to their own taxpayers have led donors to attach conditions regarding how aid is to be spent. As indicated, funds have often been rigidly earmarked for particular purposes. Determining the role and the mechanisms of conditionality in foreign assistance projects depends very much on establishing a practical and effective characterization of "ownership". The concept of ownership held a prominent place in attempts within the donor community to explain shortfalls in country performance within the context of programme conditionalities: while programme conditionalities were

7 In economics, a deadweight loss is a loss of economic efficiency. In the present case, the efficiency loss is associated with the unpredictability of aid flows.

regarded as sovereign commitments, the recipient Government's insufficient ownership of those commitments was deemed one reason why, in certain cases, they had not been met. Ownership in practice therefore became a criterion for programme success.

Through the Poverty Reduction Strategy Papers, which have often not really been country-owned, the donor community shifted the focus of its aid more towards poverty reduction

By the late 1990s, donor Governments and aid agencies had come to realize that their differing approaches and requirements were imposing high costs on developing countries and making aid less effective (Mkandawire, 2010). In an attempt to address the need to reduce the aid delivery costs being generated, recipient countries sought access to funding "earmarked" for particular purposes. Through the PRSPs, the donor community shifted the focus of its aid more towards poverty reduction. As discussed in chapter II, PRSPs were supposed to generate comprehensive long-term strategies for reducing poverty, while being at the same time sufficiently operational to guide aid efforts and to ensure that their focus was reflected in the allocations of annual Government budgets. Based on a review of how PRSPs had been designed and implemented, a study by Dijkstra (2010) concludes that, in practice, the PRSPs tended to be weakly linked to the actual processes of formulation and approval of Government budgets. Part of the explanation is to be found in the perception that there was too strong a donor influence on the design of the poverty strategy, which eroded the sense of Government ownership of both the strategy and the external funding mobilized in support of it.

True ownership would require that countries have control over their own policies

The question then comes down to determining how to achieve country ownership in practice and reconcile this with the conditions that donors feel compelled to impose in order to justify the use of the money of their own taxpayers. True ownership would require that countries have control over their own policies, yet this often comes into conflict with the mechanism of donor conditionality (Dijkstra, 2010).

Towards a needs-oriented international aid system

Effective partnerships are based on the recognition of national leadership and ownership of development plans

Incoherence in the international aid system has been built up by a process of accretion of elements derived from various sources. The existing system is the product of changing fashions in concepts of development, the responses of donors to the challenge of redeploying their resources more effectively, and well-intentioned, and mostly unilateral, efforts to reform the system. The overarching principles of reform were identified in the Monterrey Consensus of the International Conference on Financing for Development (United Nations, 2002), which called for "[e]ffective partnerships among donors and recipients ... based on the recognition of national leadership and ownership of development plans and, within that framework, sound policies and good governance at all levels" (para. 40). The process initiated by OECD under the rubric of aid effectiveness encompasses most of the details associated with successful pursuit of this goal. It is therefore agreed that this reform process must be completed and its promise fulfilled.

Addressing the system's key weaknesses, as highlighted above—namely, fragmentation, instability and unpredictability of aid flows, lack of flexibility and alignment with recipients' priorities, long-term dependence on external aid, and deficient partnership and country leadership/ownership, as well as recipient country problems of absorptive capacity and misuse of funds—will require even more good intentions and political will than has already been demonstrated.

Putting recipient countries in the driver's seat

What is required is a much stronger commitment by donors to accepting the principle of needs-based allocations and alignment of aid flows behind national development strategies, as is consistent with the principles of the Paris Declaration. Rather than such attempts to make gradual improvements as are currently being deployed, what seems to be needed is a more radical shift towards full adherence so as to overcome the continued fragmentation and problems of country ownership which undermine aid effectiveness. Based on this approach:

A much stronger commitment by donors to accepting the principle of needs-based allocations is required

- Sustainable development strategies would provide the framework for policy coherence at the national level and also articulate the nature of the financing gaps that aid flows can fill and the timing of those flows
- Bilateral and multilateral as well as non-governmental donors would be aligned and asked to respond to needs through multi-year commitments
- Alignment with other sources of development financing could be achieved as part of the same process (see below)
- Earmarking of aid funds by donors would become less relevant, although still possible if it served specific purposes (such as rallying private sector support through vertical global health funds), but always with the requirement of coherence with the priorities and financing needs of the development strategy
- Monitoring, evaluation, accountability processes and the updating of funding requirements would be the responsibility of a joint standing committee of donors but one chaired by the recipient country
- Ex ante conditionality would be restricted to recipient countries that had elaborated national development strategies, although donors would not attach further policy conditions to their support; instead, continued support would be decided upon based on monitored progress and outcomes of the implemented strategy

Certain successful past experiences can guide the way towards making such an approach work in practice. In fact, the successful Marshall Plan for post-war reconstruction and development in Western Europe was built on principles similar to those suggested above (see box III.3; and United Nations, 2008, chap. IV). Even though the environment in which developing countries exist today is quite different from that of post-war Europe, the Marshall Plan principles can help provide a coherent framework for coordinating national development strategies with international assistance. Without the provision of an articulate account of a Government's macroeconomic objectives and their relation to detailed programmes for infrastructure investment, sustainable development of the agriculture, energy and industrial sectors, productive job creation, education, health and social protection, among others, it is difficult to see how limited supplies of foreign assistance, financial and technical, could be really effective.

Certain principles derived from the Marshall Plan can help provide a coherent framework

Mkandawire (2010) suggests that far more than contributing resources to rapid economic recovery after the Second World War, the Marshall Plan embodied ideas that took root and shaped the European Union's subsequently effective economic cooperation with Ireland, Portugal and Spain through needs-oriented assistance programmes. The Marshall Plan achieved a coherent framework for coordinating economic recovery and development plans. It relied on domestically generated planning and configured both its time frame and grant-to-loan proportion to meet the problem at hand. At the time, the

Essentially, the Marshall Plan intervened to ease shortages, bottlenecks and other constraints on growth and structural change

Box III.3

Seven virtues of the Marshall Plan

The Marshall Plan was the assistance framework established by the United States of America for the economic recovery of Western European countries in the post-war period (1947-1951). The seven principles under which the Plan operated are summarized below.

1. **Realistic time frame.** The post-war adjustment applied a more realistic time frame than that normally envisaged by the United States Treasury or by an International Monetary Fund (IMF) programme. Instead of 18 months, the timescale was from 4-5 years.

2. **Alignment with an overall economic programme.** The architect of the plan, United States Secretary of State George Marshall, made it clear that there was to be an end to piecemeal assistance, which had suffered from a lack of coordination and had had less impact than expected in stimulating economic recovery. A key requirement, therefore, was that each State recipient of aid had to produce a four-year outline plan for recovery, setting out targets for the main economic variables and providing an account of how the Government intended to achieve its objectives.

3. **Genuinely domestic programming.** Marshall insisted that these plans, together with estimates of the need for assistance, had to be drawn up by the Western Europeans themselves: "It would be neither fitting nor efficacious for (the United States) to undertake to draw up unilaterally a program designed to place Europe on its feet economically. This is the business of Europeans … The role of this country should consist of friendly aid in the drafting of a European program and of later support of such a program…" Marshall thus acknowledged the existence of national sensibilities, admitted that the recipient countries were better informed about the facts of their situation than outsiders, and generally showed a deference towards European traditions and preferences that has subsequently been conspicuously absent from the attitudes of the rich countries and international institutions towards the rest of the world.

4. **Flexible intermediate targets.** A fourth feature of the Marshall Plan was the release of aid in tranches that depended on the countries' intermediate targets' being met. Marshall Plan conditions were different from those established in recent practice and more flexible and were to be met over a longer period than that allowed by IMF rules, for example.

5. **Gradual and asymmetric international integration.** The Marshall Plan acknowledged that the damage to European productive capacities and the great disparity in economic strength between the United States and Europe meant that rapid liberalization of trade and payments would quickly lead to European payments-related crises. It was accepted that Europe would gradually dismantle a wide range of direct and indirect controls on its trade between 1950 and 1958 according to an agreed timetable within the framework of the European Payments Union. This gradual liberalization of trade provided European producers with protection against competition from the United States and gave them time for, and encouragement in, the reconstruction of enterprises capable of producing competitive substitutes for dollar imports. At the same time, the United States agreed to a more rapid improvement in access to its own market for European exports, a policy of asymmetric liberalization which stands in marked contrast to the present approach of the European Union and the United States, which insists on a rapid opening of developing countries' markets and on restricting the range of policy options available for their development.

6. **Significant grant component.** Marshall Aid consisted largely of grants and the small proportion of loans had a large grant component: they were usually offered for 35 years at 2.5 per cent interest with repayments starting in 1953. It is worth emphasizing this structuring of financial help at a time when the terms "aid" and "assistance" are used loosely to cover everything from gifts to loans at market (or above-market) rates of interest. The wisdom of adding to the debts of already heavily indebted economies is highly questionable—all the more so when they are grappling with economic restructuring and institution-building, which is typically the case for countries trying to accelerate their development or to recover from the chaos that normally follows the end of violent conflict. A

Box III.3 (cont'd)

generous supply of grants, monitored within and conditional on a coherent economic programme along the lines of the Marshall Plan, can be more effective than loans in lifting countries out of a "stagnation trap" where heavy debt-servicing obligations hold back the domestic and foreign investment that could improve the longer-run performance of the economy, including its capacity to service debt. Another advantage of grants is that they are not usually subject to the long and complex negotiations, legal and financial, associated with the provision of loans. This is important inasmuch as one of the lessons of the Marshall Plan is that prompt assistance at the start of a promised programme can help to sustain positive expectations, which most likely will have been raised by politicians, and generate a momentum for change that will stand a chance of becoming self-reinforcing.

7. **Coordination among recipients.** Finally, yet another virtue of the Marshall Plan that is still relevant to attempts to tackle current problems is its insistence that there should be a degree of united and cooperative effort among the Europeans themselves, and that the plans of the 16 recipient countries and the allocation of aid should be coordinated within a regional body. This requirement partly reflected United States foreign-policy objectives with regard to a more integrated Europe, and also provided a structure for cooperation in areas where there are significant externalities, economies of scale and other transboundary issues. The peer review of national programmes provided national policymakers with a regional perspective on their own policies and encouraged a culture of regular contact and cooperation among national bureaucracies which is today taken for granted in Europe.

Source: Adapted from United Nations (2008, chap IV, pp. 143-145).

Marshall Plan essentially intervened to ease shortages, bottlenecks and other constraints on growth and structural change.

The currently prevailing view is that programme failures are due to a weak commitment to reform (or a lack of ownership) and a slackening of discipline through postponement of necessary adjustment. In contrast, Marshall Plan resources were seen as investments in social cohesion and structural change and as providing Governments with the breathing space required to make difficult and often painful policies successful (United Nations, 2008). When such policies threatened to cause social upheaval on a scale that might upset the adjustment process, as was the case in post-war Italy at one point, Marshall Aid was available to cushion the social costs through support to the Government budget.

With a multiplicity of donors, there is a need to establish mechanisms of coordination

European recipients of Marshall Plan resources had the advantage of dealing with only one donor (Mkandawire, 2010). In the currently fragmented aid system, with its multiplicity of donors, there is a need to establish mechanisms of coordination, a need that has also been recognized in the "aid effectiveness" process. Operational since 1995, the panel on donor coordination in the United Republic of Tanzania is one example of a country-led approach to improving coordination and making donors accountable for their activities (Helleiner, 2005). (Not all donors agreed, however, to participate in the effort initially.) In the United Republic of Tanzania, formal public expenditure reviews and the application of the medium-term expenditure framework appear to have been effective in fostering wide participation of stakeholders in the budget process. Ngowi (2005) has indicated how these mechanisms have in turn strengthened the links between sector policies and resource allocation, by providing valuable analyses and feedback on budget execution which has improved resource use. However, he also notes that the impact on poverty reduction appears to be weak, though the efforts will perhaps bear fruit in the long term.

A key aspect of the experience of the United Republic of Tanzania has been the role played by a broader macroeconomic framework in relating to donors. To achieve such an arrangement was also the intention of the PRSP approach; this was stymied, however, by the fact that in practice the estimation for the maximum resource envelope was undertaken mainly by IMF. Ngowi (2005) reports that the United Republic of Tanzania

Revenue Authority consistently met its revenue targets and collections reached an average of 12.5 per cent of GDP in the past 10 years compared with a figure of less than 8 per cent in the previous decade.

Recipient countries can take the initiative in rationalizing the operations of donors in their economy

The aid effectiveness principle of country ownership/leadership itself suggests that, in a situation where there is an interest in engagement on the part of both DAC and non-DAC donors, nothing should prevent a recipient country from taking the initiative in rationalizing the operations of those donors in its economy. An example of recipient country donor management is provided by India which allows only donors whose funding exceeds a minimum level to operate in the country. If donor competition is so harnessed as to be in the interest of a recipient country's national strategy, expanding South-South cooperation could play an "anti-trust" role in engaging the donor community. Private foundations must also accept country leadership in their operations in developing countries, which would entail aligning programmes with the domestic development priorities included within recipients' national regulatory frameworks (a course those foundations often espouse) .

Space for experimentation and the possibility of failure should be incorporated in aid evaluation

Country leadership in consolidating all aid flows could minimize the costs arising from earmarking restrictions. Countries would access these funds only if they fit the overall national sustainable development strategy. The United Nations Development Assistance Framework (UNDAF) process of integrating all donor projects into one overall programme aligned with a national development strategy could serve as a model approach for the future if the Framework can manage to further distance itself from the existing practice of acting essentially as a collection box for individual donor project financing. The PRSP experience, governed by the attempt to "plan everything" and obtain agreement from all parties, should be instructive. Because of the high level of uncertainty associated with development programmes, space for experimentation and the possibility of failure should be incorporated in evaluation. Entire responsibility for policy choices should be lodged fully with aid recipients, as is the case, at least in formal terms, at the present time. If aid recipients are to be fully in command of the policy choices they make, however, then outcome evaluation instead of policy conditionality should eventually become the norm for all aid projects and programmes.

As addressing capacity weaknesses by the implementing Government is part of the development effort and of learning, upgraded capabilities need to be looked upon favourably in the context of outcome evaluation. Programmes should be deemed "good enough" if they reflect a broad relationship between means and ends. Embedding the identification of external funding gaps within an overall national strategy will require the determination of the multi-year progress that must be made in domestic resource mobilization and consequent reduction in aid and external debt dependency.

It is donor accountability for which there are no existing sanctions

While there are unavoidable geopolitical considerations that exert pressure on donors to continue support for poorly performing recipients, accountability of the recipient countries is usually inherent in what is in fact a "repeated game" situation: donors can always withdraw in the next funding iteration. It is donor accountability, instead, for which there are no existing sanctions.

Consequently, the proposed aid process requires some ancillary mechanisms to strengthen aid effectiveness. As these suggestions would be desirable even in the absence of a fundamental reorientation towards national strategies as suggested above, progress should be made along these lines irrespective of a fundamental restructuring. Among the key elements are the following:

- All aid flows should eventually be disbursed through general budget support
- Reducing the number of special global funds is in the interest of both donors and recipients, although one would expect that a few large funding pools, such as, potentially, one for climate change, would continue to exist
- Donors should begin progressively to budget aid flows in cycles of two or more years at a time, which will necessitate difficult adjustments in donor country political decision-making
- Some special delivery mechanisms, such as through trust funds (see below), can be established consistent with the overall approach of country leadership

Resources will still be needed for global responses to "natural" disasters and to climate change

It is also important to note that, even with the reorientation of the aid system towards country programmes, there will still be requirements for global responses to "natural" disasters and humanitarian emergencies and to climate change which must be provided for by the international community. Special global funds with specific modalities could be devoted to natural disasters, as discussed in *World Economic and Social Survey 2008* (United Nations, 2008). The climate change response remains more complex: it still awaits agreement on a global climate regime, which can integrate aid, trade, finance and technology. The challenges in this regard were explored in *World Economic and Social Survey 2009* (United Nations, 2009a) and will be discussed further in chapter V.

Reforming channels and resource mobilization for development assistance

As the country needs-based system evolves, most ODA requirements would be defined increasingly through a bottom-up approach

While the present target of 0.7 per cent of GNI of OECD/DAC countries, set on the basis of the estimated foreign-exchange needs of developing countries in the 1960s, has remained unfulfilled in the aggregate, a needs-oriented aid system would probably redefine the amount of aid needing to be mobilized. However, in the transition to the new system, the target might still serve as a benchmark to rally political support to address development deficits in the poorest countries, as much as additional targets may need to be set to ensure sufficient resource mobilization for supporting climate change mitigation and adaptation efforts in developing countries, aid for trade and the delivery of global public goods. There will also be continued need for separate pools of funds for disaster relief and humanitarian aid efforts.

On the way forward, two further fundamental changes should be considered. The first would aim at a better alignment of aid flows with other domestic and external sources of development financing through the use of trust fund mechanisms. The second change would entail increased use of funding sources encompassing innovative forms of international levies and leveraging of international liquidity for development purposes.

Enhancing aid predictability and aligning all sources of development financing

Individual country trust fund mechanisms could facilitate the alignment of donor funding

The use of trust fund mechanisms to support individual countries or groups of countries could further facilitate the alignment of donor funding with country priorities, ensure long-term financing and align traditional ODA resource mobilization with innovative forms of development financing. Bilateral donors and existing global funds would contribute to trust funds which would disburse resources in accordance with programmatic and budgetary needs of recipient countries. The trust funds could also be allowed to purchase Government securities of developing countries with a view to tying aid to future domestic resource mobilization efforts. Experience in this area does in fact exist: in a number of cases, multi-year aid commitments have been converted into bond purchases to fund and front-load resources for research on tropical medicines. Recipient countries, in turn, could also be allowed, periodically, to deposit budgetary savings earned during economic upswings into the trust funds as insurance against external shocks, and to draw upon them in response to shocks.

In sum, the advantages of pooling aid resources into a trust fund are simplification and harmonization of procedures, and better support for national goals, priorities and strategies. It can avoid duplication and overlapping efforts, and minimize the burden of integrating externally supported projects into national development strategies. However, the ownership and management mechanisms of trust funds need to be carefully worked out so that the country ownership is not undermined. Pledges of contributions to trust funds should in principle be neither conditional nor earmarked.

New funding sources to underpin the aid architecture

New forms of international taxation could play an increasing role

New forms of international taxation (such as a small levy on international financial transactions) could play an increasing role in providing the resources needed to create a new development finance architecture. The new tax revenues could be channelled through a global fund into country-based trust funds. Mobilizing resources for development assistance through such innovative forms of financing would reduce volatility in available aid flows and vulnerability to political expediency.

A key innovation is the partnership "modality" in resource mobilization established between developed and developing countries

These new approaches which aim at raising the resources needed for a type of development cooperation—dependent on individual country funding—have been piloted, relatively successfully, under the rubric of "innovative sources of finance". The effort, inspired by the 2002 Monterrey Consensus, has spawned a far-ranging worldwide effort to mobilize aid resources from countries at different levels of development and to pilot them towards meeting the internationally agreed Millennium Development Goals. The Leading Group on Innovative Financing for Development (which was founded following the Paris Ministerial Conference on Innovative Development Financing Mechanisms held in 2006 and whose action stems from the New York Declaration on action against hunger and poverty issued in New York on 20 September 2004) promotes discussion on these issues. The Leading Group currently comprises 55 member countries, 4 observer countries, 15 international organizations and more than 20 non-governmental organizations. A key distinguishing feature of this approach is the partnership "modality" in resource mobilization established between developed and developing countries (United Nations, General Assembly, 2009a).

Innovative funding sources of aid hold the promise of less volatility and vulnerability to political expediency

Based on the pilot projects in place, innovative funding sources of aid hold the promise of less volatility, greater sustainability in the long run, reduced vulnerability to decisions that are based on political expediency, and potentially broader participation in fund generation—participation extending beyond Governments to include, for example, citizens (through direct collection) and the private sector (through the utilization of Web-based checkboxes). Actual innovative sources of finance explored so far include currency transaction taxes, taxes on the arms trade, taxes on carbon emissions, an international financial facility, advance market commitments, "solidarity levies" on items such as international airplane tickets, enhanced efforts to combat tax evasion and illicit financial transfers, and a world lottery (Atkinson, ed., 2005).

An early pilot entailed an international levy on air transport. The level of taxation on air transport is lower than on other means of transport, since aviation fuel is tax-exempt in most countries. One report (United Nations, 2005, chap. IV) estimated that a

5 per cent rate applied to airfares would yield $8 billion per annum and that an indirect tax on passenger transportation could reach $20 billion per annum. Estimates of revenue from a currency transaction tax differ widely because of differences in proposed tax rates. Realistically, a currency transaction tax set at two basis points of market currency transactions can raise revenues in the range of US$ 33 billion-US$ 35 billion per annum; other estimations (Clunies-Ross, 2004) yield higher revenues, namely, US$ 60 billion per annum.

The feasibility of re-channelling the provision of global liquidity for development purposes has increased

The original Monterrey innovative financing proposal that referred to the use of special drawing rights (SDRs) for development purposes is expected to draw renewed interest as a result of recent new SDR allocations. Re-channelling the provision of global liquidity managed on an equitable basis, in reserves and payments, to fund poverty reduction and investment in clean energy becomes a more feasible option, given these recent increased allocations of SDRs.

International tax cooperation could triple the resources available for development

The possibility of improving, through international cooperation, collection of taxes currently evaded has received extensive consideration in the Leading Group. Conservative estimates of the scale of the annual resources potentially available for developing countries from the tax lost on the illicit outflow of profits (profits of both foreign companies and domestic residents) and the tax lost due to the income arising abroad from the accumulated assets owned by residents is, for the mid-2000s, of the order of $200 billion-$250 billion,[8] half of which would be attributable to Asia (FitzGerald, 2010). This estimate, which is more than double the level of ODA from DAC members, suggests that the total amount of international fiscal transfers (aid plus tax) available for development finance could be tripled. All developing countries would be in receipt of these resources, except those developing countries that were themselves tax havens. FitzGerald suggests that, since the tax jurisdictions concerned are all closely connected with financial centres in advanced economies, it would be possible to reallocate a portion of the increase in tax income to maintaining the incomes of inhabitants of tax havens and providing them with an alternative economic future. The logical (but perhaps still politically farfetched) implication is that external assistance financing mechanisms could be based on principles of fiscal federalism applied at the global level rather than on principles of humanitarian charity.

All of the mechanisms utilized by innovative financing can be applied to meeting climate change-related needs

In the Copenhagen Accord,[9] agreed at the fifteenth session of the Conference of the Parties to the United Nations Framework Convention on Climate Change,[10] held in Copenhagen from 7 to 19 December 2009, developed countries committed to a goal of mobilizing jointly $100 billion dollars per year by 2020 to address the needs of developing countries, with the funding to come from a wide variety of sources, "including alternative sources of finance" (para. 8). The implication is that all the mechanisms in the innovative financing agenda are on the table in terms of achieving the announced target. A global carbon tax is often mentioned (Addison, Arndt and Tarp, 2010); however, because of the potential costs required to compensate for its distributive and environmental effects, a concerted carbon tax mechanism would be most suitable for and effective in developed countries but less so in developing ones (United Nations, 2009a, chap. VI). Bredenkamp and Pattillo (2010) have set out the mechanics by which special drawing rights can be used to raise the required flow of $100 billion. The recent international discussion concerning a multilateral financial transactions tax sheds new light on a long-standing proposal to apply a currency transactions tax in order to fund climate change-related efforts.

8 Other studies, using different methods, arrive at larger estimates, in the order of $850 billion-$1.0 trillion per year (see Kar and Cartwright-Smith, 2008).

9 See FCCC/CP/2009/11/Add.1, decision 2/CP.15.

10 United Nations, *Treaty Series*, vol. 1771, No. 30822.

Existing mechanisms rely heavily on "earmarking" towards specific ends

Progress has been most visible in international responses to tropical diseases, through initiatives utilizing the air-ticket solidarity levy, the Advance Market Commitment (AMC) and the International Financial Facility for Immunisation (IFF), among others. Existing mechanisms rely heavily on "earmarking" towards specific ends. The feasibility of a more general development-oriented levy mechanism, one more in line with a needs-oriented international aid system, needs to be tested.

Governing the aid system globally

There is a need to upgrade aid coordination and accountability at the international level

A coherent aid system centred on putting recipients in the driver's seat would need to be matched and facilitated by upgrading coordination and accountability at the international level. There is a need, too, for a global process for setting standards, monitoring progress, and learning from experience that would be broader than that possible under OECD. A larger set of contributor and recipient countries, meeting on a more politically symmetric partnership basis, can build upon the achievements of the process launched pursuant to the principles set out in the Paris Declaration. The Development Cooperation Forum launched by the Economic and Social Council in 2007 has the potential to serve as the kind of venue in which DAC and non-DAC donors can be brought together to promote mutual accountability and aid effectiveness. The Forum has the mandate to facilitate co-operation among countries receiving aid, multilateral institutions, parliamentarians, local governments and a range of civil society and private sector entities.

Progress is necessary in enhancing policy coherence in other areas

Progress in enhancing coherence in the trade, finance and climate change regimes will facilitate the progress of efforts to achieve greater coherence within the international aid regime. Rebalancing towards a focus on "differentiated" responsibilities in the trade system, after decades of emphasis on the "common" ones will allow developing countries to reduce their dependence on external finance which is often necessitated by a too abrupt international integration. This kind of problem was already well known at the time of, and addressed in, the Marshall Plan (see box III.3; and Reinert, 2005). Ensuring that the international aid system provides long-term development finance, and the policy space needed by countries to progressively improve their domestic resource mobilization, is certainly the best way to mark out a path towards the most robust country ownership and, in addition, it offers the best insurance against aid volatility. Chapter V presents suggestions on how to establish a more sustainable and development-friendly global financial regime, one that would be capable of facilitating the flows of financing needed to actualize the trust fund concept presented above. The *World Economic and Social Survey 2009* (United Nations, 2009a) proposed recasting the international climate change "game" as a win-win strategy to be implemented by the orienting of activities towards solving the problem of energy poverty through clean energy investments in developing countries. This approach is congruent with the poverty reduction objectives of the aid system.

Aligning all aid with national development strategies is an approach based on a concept that has already been generally agreed in principle

Aid has always been perceived as having a "catalytic" role in development. It is considered to be time-bound and only supplementary to much larger flows arising from domestic resource mobilization and foreign investment. Nevertheless, a giant step in upgrading the aid system could be achieved by aligning all aid with national development strategies, an approach based on a concept that has already been generally agreed in principle and has been shown to be feasible in pilot situations. Even if this approach continues to give rise to a host of implementation issues, it is without a doubt preferable to the alternative—the current disorganized, cluttered, bureaucratized and politics-dependent aid system which is still struggling to prove its effectiveness in promoting poverty reduction and development.

Chapter IV
Retooling global trade

Summary

- In recent decades, the approach to trade liberalization, both unilaterally and multilaterally, has followed a pattern of advancing countries' *common* responsibilities, while paying insufficient attention to the *differentiated* responsibilities of economies with more limited capabilities for gainfully integrating in the global trading system.
- The design and application of multilateral trade rules should be adjusted to allow developing countries, especially low-income countries, greater space for conducting active production sector and export promotion policies to meet sustainable development objectives.
- Coherence in global governance requires rethinking the scope of World Trade Organization disciplines. For instance, needs for strengthening financial regulation in the aftermath of the global financial crisis create tensions with the General Agreement on Trade in Services which aims at easing cross-border financial services flows. Such conflicts can be averted by defining multilateral rules for trade in financial services as part of a reformed international financial regulatory framework. A more focused agenda may also facilitate completing the Doha Round negotiations and establishing a more development-oriented multilateral trading system.

Introduction

Export-led growth emerged as a pillar of development strategies in the last three decades. The progressive reduction of tariff and non-tariff barriers to trade between countries has been instrumental in generating a fivefold expansion of the volume of world exports since 1980. Paradoxically, economic growth in most developing countries has not matched the rates of economic progress achieved in the first decades after the Second World War when many followed import-substitution strategies. Exceptions to this pattern—notably China and the newly industrializing countries in East Asia—have systematically followed a pragmatic approach that combines a gradual exposure to external markets with an effective collaboration between the private and the public sector towards building dynamic long-term competitiveness. Their experiences suggest that neither protectionism nor abrupt liberalization is the best strategy for achieving high and sustained rates of economic growth.

A fivefold expansion of world exports did not result in accelerated global economic growth rates

A significant portion of the measured rise in trade volumes is accounted for by increasing trade in intermediate goods (World Trade Organization, 2009a), in line with the worldwide trend towards delivering goods and services through global value chains (GVCs). Inside global chains, unfinished goods cross borders several times during the assembly process. Since each border crossing of a product (intermediate or final) is recorded as an international transaction, the same product gets counted more than once in international trade statistics, thereby inflating the recorded volume.

Capital-account and trade liberalization were promoted as part of market-oriented reforms in developing countries in the 1980s and 1990s. Capital-account opening constrained the use of exchange rates to promote trade competitiveness as exchange rates became increasingly determined by volatile capital flows and inflation-related considerations. Trade liberalization, in turn, limited the scope of trade protection and incentives, such as tariffs and subsidies, for promoting economic diversification as well as supporting domestic activities through business cycles. The proliferation of international agreements on subsidies, intellectual property rights, trade-related investment measures and services has set further limits to national policy space.

Global value chains have diminished the relevance of traditional trade policy instruments

Traditional instruments of trade policy are also losing relevance in a world where trade is increasingly taking place through global value chains and transnational corporations engaged in international production. New policy approaches will be needed to provide incentives to foreign investors if countries are to "buy into" these chains.

The present chapter aims to identify how interactions between the current multilateral trade rules and national development policy space can be so reconfigured as to promote a fairer trading system, one more congruent with development objectives.

The recent crisis and trade

The global recession of 2008-2009 has been the deepest and most disruptive in the last quarter-century. What started as a crisis in financial markets in major economies quickly spread to the rest of the world, through the international financial system to other developed economies and mainly through trade channels to developing countries. Starting in the last quarter of 2008, world trade entered into a free fall which lasted until the second quarter of 2009. Simultaneously, there was a collapse in world commodity prices.

The sharp fluctuations in exports from Asia reflect the importance of global value chains

Exporters from Asia were among those most affected by the drop in global aggregate demand, associated mainly with the decline in imports from developed countries (United Nations, 2010). The sharp decline and recovery of Asian exports reflect the impact of the value chain-dominated production structure, where changes in orders and inventories are transmitted rapidly from one market to another (Escaith, 2009). As much of export production depends on suppliers of intermediate inputs, many of which are also located in Asia, the demand shock triggered in developed economies spread out quickly, but with a strong regional concentration, through abrupt declines in orders inside the global value chains.

The seizing up of world financial markets has also negatively affected trade volumes through higher spreads on developing-country debt and reduced availability of trade credits. Commodity prices collapsed. Oil and metal prices were the most affected, dropping by about 70-80 per cent from their peak levels reached in 2008. Although a recovery from these trends began in the first quarter of 2009, the close link between commodity prices and financial markets, including through the United States dollar exchange rate, suggests the presence of highly volatile prices in the near future (United Nations, 2010).

Crisis responses have included "low-intensity" trade protectionism

The magnitude of the crisis, and the fact that it originated in and first affected the advanced industrialized economies, led to policy responses—including financial sector bail-outs, wage subsidies, cheap credits and direct interventions to rescue industries—that have affected trade competitiveness. Notably, the responses in rich countries relied more on subsidies, while poor countries used mainly duties to restrict imports (Gamberoni and Newfarmer, 2009). Besides other traditional trade policies (such as anti-dumping measures), many fiscal and financial packages have included elements—like direct support from the government to industries, bail-outs, subsidies and actions associated to "buy/

lend/invest/hire" locally—that favour the consumption of domestic goods and services. These measures have broken the pattern imposed by the market discipline and laissez-faire hegemony that dominated the economic thinking in the last quarter-century. As discussed below, crisis responses have brought back to the centre of the debate the role of policy space in mitigating the effects of economic downturns.

Data for 2008 show that in the face of recession in the global economy, the use of trade remedies increased significantly. The World Trade Organization Secretariat reported that there had been a 28 per cent increase in anti-dumping investigations in 2008 compared with 2007. The measures taken so far can be characterized as exemplifying "low-intensity" trade protectionism in contrast with the "beggar thy neighbour" measures of the 1930s (Drache, 2010). During the interwar years, Governments had responded to the recession by introducing high and escalating tariffs on imports, competitive currency devaluations and discriminatory trading blocs which paralysed international trade flows almost entirely. This prolonged the global recession and fed into trade conflicts among countries, adding to the factors that built up to the Second World War. This experience led international leaders to conclude that economic cooperation was the only way to achieve both peace and prosperity, at home and abroad. This awareness led to the signing of the General Agreement on Tariffs and Trade (GATT) less than a month before the commencement of the United Nations Conference on Trade and Employment in 1947, held in Havana from 21 November 1947 to 24 March 1948.[1] Under the new multilateral system, trade and economic growth prospered, giving birth to what is now often referred to as the economic "golden age" of the 1950s and 1960s.

Changing global production and trade

Current-account liberalization triggered an important expansion in global trade flows. Global exports of goods and services grew at a real average rate of 6.3 per cent starting in 1980 until 2008, while gross domestic product (GDP) growth averaged 2.9 per cent during the same period (see figure IV.1).

Developing countries have expanded their market shares in low- and high-tech manufactures

Developing countries played an important role in the expansion of trade. As shown in figure IV.2, although developed economies continue to dominate world markets, developing countries expanded their market shares, especially in both low- and high-technology manufactures,[2] which both reached about 40 per cent of global exports by 2005-2008. The developing-country share in global exports of primary commodities had decreased from an average of 50 per cent during the period 1976-1979 to 40 per cent during the period 1985-1999. During the 2000s, however, this share increased again to about 45 per cent. Trends in terms of trade that had showed declining prices for primary commodities relative to those for manufactures in the 1980s and 1990s were reversed in the 2000s and this influenced trade shares (Ocampo and Parra-Lancourt, 2010).

1 The General Agreement on Tariffs and Trade lasted until 1994, when it was succeeded by the World Trade Organization. The original text of the GATT (available from http://www.wto.org/english/docs_e/legal_e/gatt47_01_e.htm) is still in effect through the World Trade Organization framework, subject to the modifications embodied in GATT 1994.

2 Traditional trade statistics and classifications like the one used here have not yet incorporated distinctions regarding the value added incorporated in each country, as they continue to measure only products crossing borders. For this reason, assembly-line and labour-intensive products, which in reality have very little technological impact in a particular country, end up being classified as high-tech. Several institutional processes are being launched to update these and other analytical instruments (Escaith, 2008).

Figure IV.1
Growth of real world gross product (WGP) and of the volume of world exports of goods and services, 1971-2009

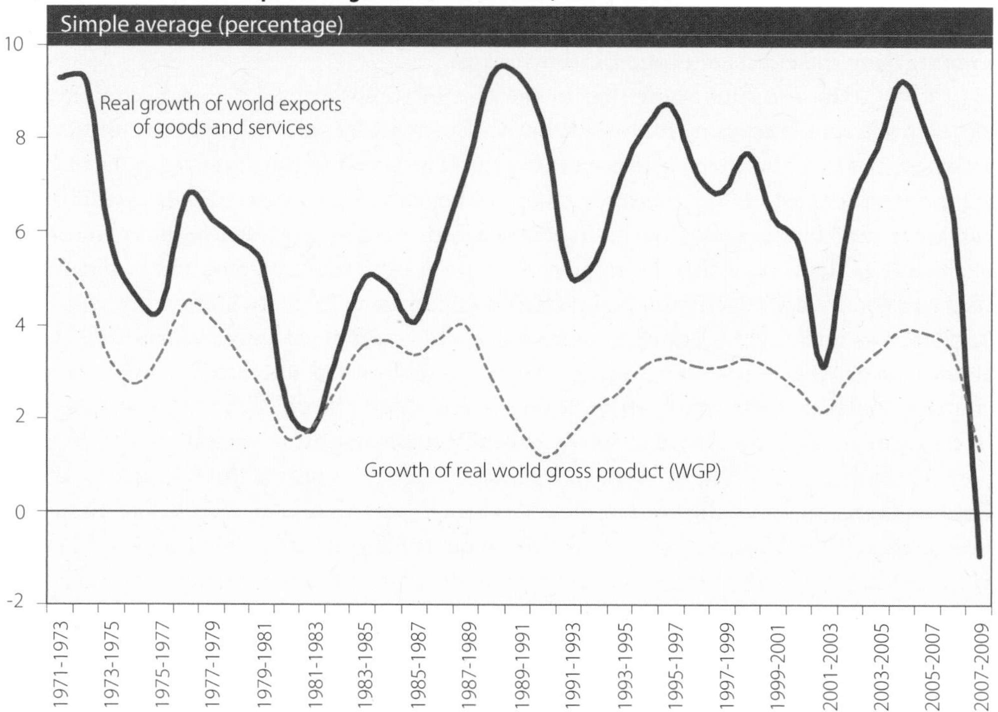

Source: UN/DESA estimates, based on United Nations National Accounts Main Aggregates Database.

Figure IV.2
Share of exports of developing countries, by technology content, in world trade, 1976-2008

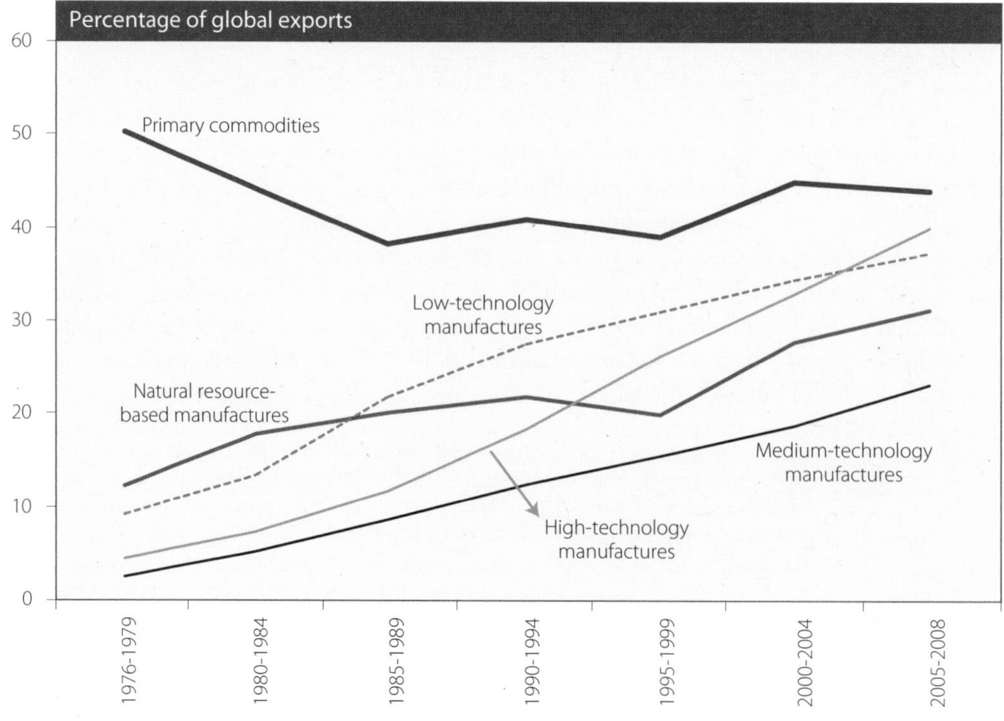

Source: UN/DESA calculations, based on UN Comtrade.

Note: For methodology, see United Nations (2006b, chap. III, appendix).

The share of primary commodities in total non-fuel exports from developing countries also declined: from more than 50 per cent around 1980 to less than 30 per cent in the 2000s. Developing countries as a group also managed to substantially increase their share of exports of high-tech manufactures, which reached 25 per cent of their total exports during the 2000s (figure IV.3).

Traditional export patterns continue to prevail in some regions

However, traditional export patterns continue to prevail in regions where export growth was not rooted in dynamic structural transformation. In South America, for example, the share of primary commodities and natural resource-based manufactures in total non-fuel exports even increased slightly in the period from the 1990s to the 2000s, reflecting the incentives that the laissez-faire trading system provides towards maintaining static comparative advantages (see figure IV.4A). A similar, although more dramatic pattern can be observed in sub-Saharan Africa (see figure IV.4B).

The increase in exports of high-tech manufactures has been highly concentrated

As illustrated in *World Economic and Social Survey 2006* (United Nations, 2006b), the increase in exports of high-tech manufactures has been highly concentrated, partly as result of the so-called flying-geese pattern in East Asia, which had entailed the diffusion to other Asian countries of the more labour-intensive components of production from Japan that were destined for other industrialized countries (Memis and Montes, 2006). The opening of China to the world economy was the next manifestation of this pattern in which production is transferred to neighbouring countries with lower real wages (Memis, 2009). Other emerging economies, like Mexico and small countries in Central America and the Caribbean, came to play a role in assembly (maquila) industries and other mostly low- and medium-tech industries, following duty-free market access granted by the United States of America (see figure IV.5).

Figure IV.3
Exports of developing countries, by technological intensity, as a share of their total non-fuel exports, 1976-2008

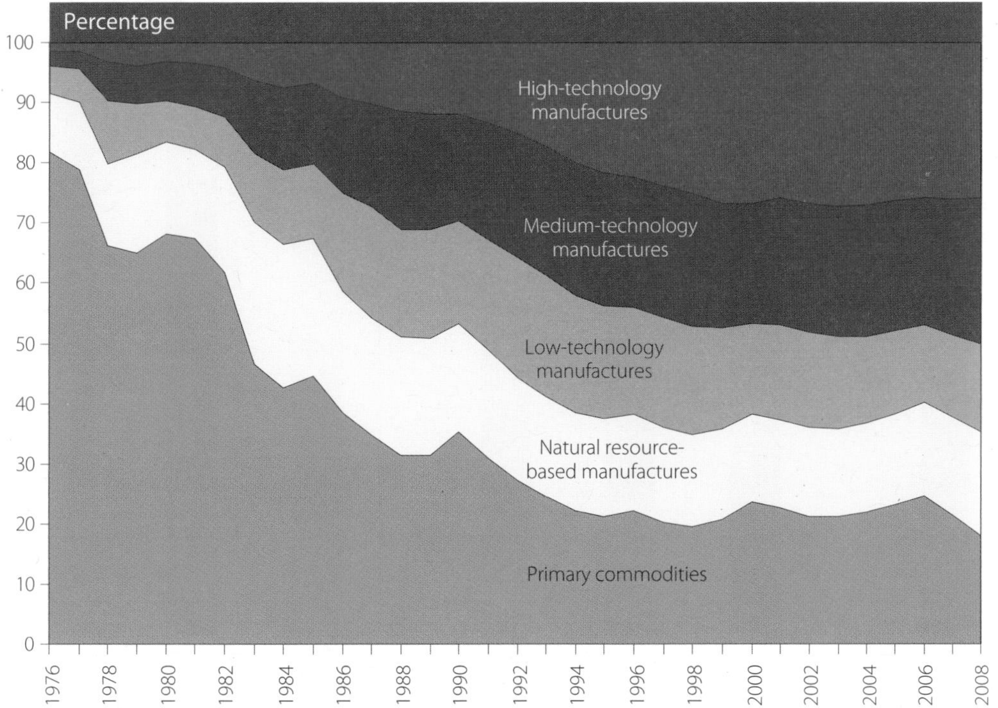

Source: UN/DESA calculations, based on UN Comtrade.

Note: For methodology, see United Nations (2006b, chap. III, appendix).

Figure IV.4
Share of exports, by technology content of commodities, in total non-fuel exports, South America and sub-Saharan Africa, excluding Nigeria and South Africa, 1980-2008

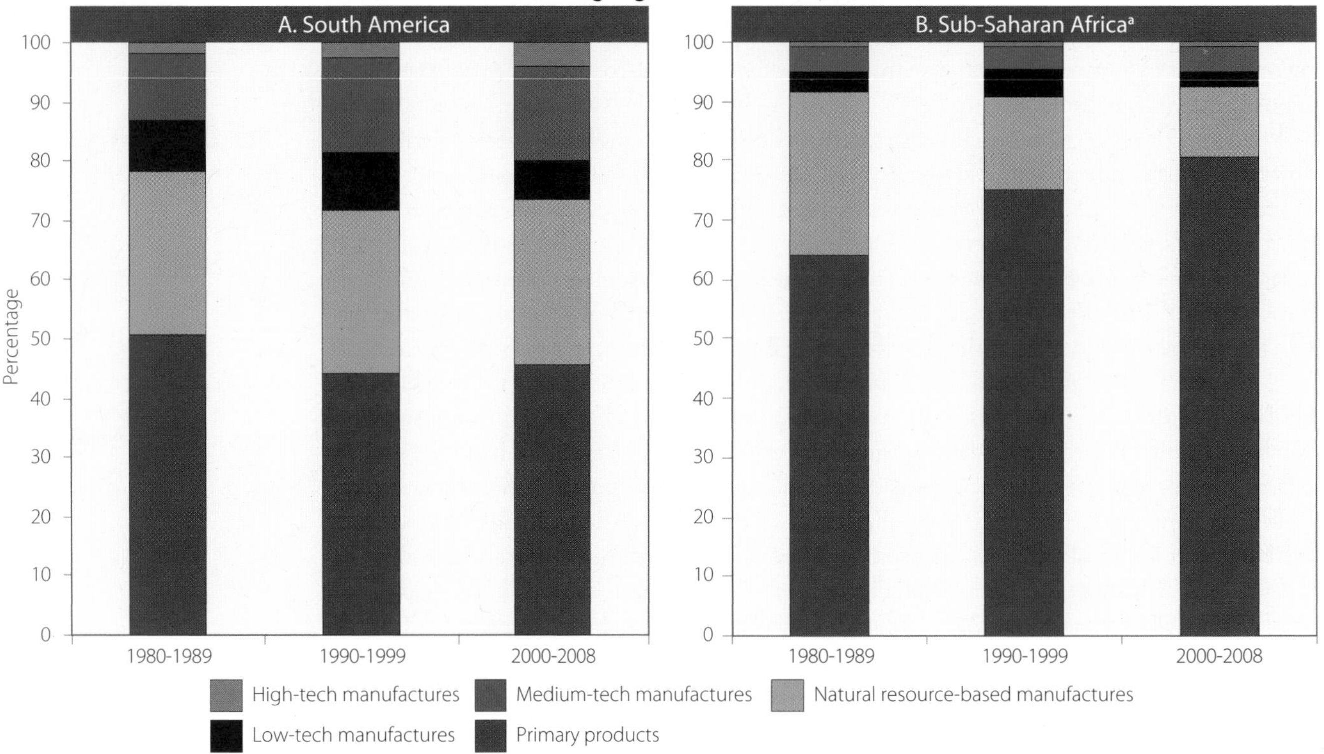

Source: UN/DESA calculations, based on UN Comtrade.

Note: For methodology, see United Nations (2006b, chap. III, appendix).

a This figure excludes Nigeria and South Africa because of their size and distinct productive structure, as compared to the rest of the region.

Figure IV.5
Selected regional patterns of exports, by technological intensity, 1980-2008

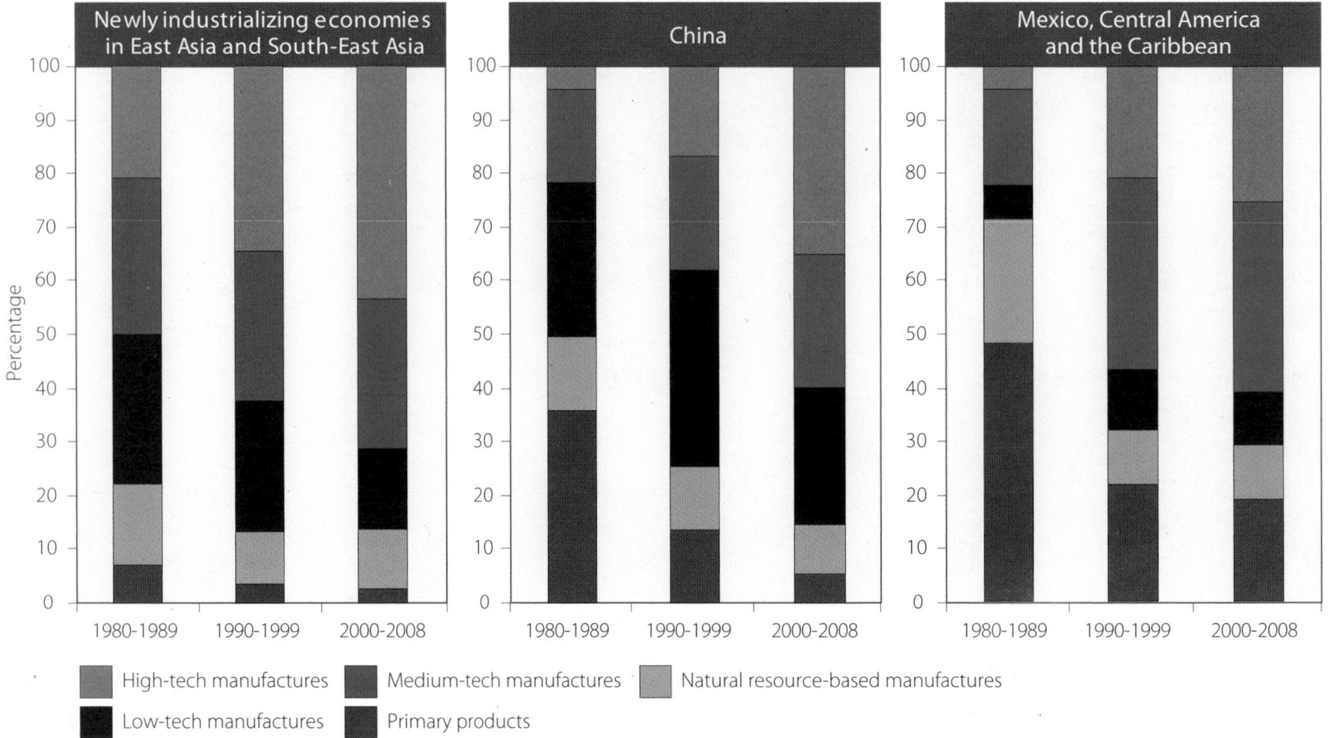

Source: UN/DESA calculations, based on UN Comtrade.

Note: For methodology, see United Nations (2006b, chap. III, appendix).

Transnational corporations play a major and growing role in the world economy

This increase in developing countries' participation in exports of manufactures can be explained to a large extent by the increased dominance of transnational corporations and global value or supply chains. Today, there are some 82,000 transnational corporations worldwide, with 810,000 foreign affiliates. These companies play a major and growing role in the world economy. For example, exports by foreign affiliates of transnational corporations are estimated to account for about one third of total world exports of goods and services, and the number of people employed by transnational corporations worldwide totalled about 77 million in 2008 (United Nations Conference on Trade and Development, 2009a).

There has been greater geographical fragmentation of production processes

However, as stated in the introduction, the internationalization of production goes beyond the expansion of transnational corporations. In effect, over the past 40 years, the world has seen an accelerated geographical fragmentation of components production processes within networks of firms connected through contractual or informal arrangements forming global value or supply chains (GVCs).[3] This shift coincided with the increasing importance of branding in the markets of industrialized economies and with the pursuit of low-cost labour by private companies seeking to maximize the value of their shares in highly speculative financial markets. Nowadays, specific industrial operations, from the conception stage to the assembly of final products, are no longer undertaken by a single establishment but are increasingly outsourced within these global value chains, which has resulted in what is known as "trade in tasks".

Global value chains profit from the revolution in information and communications technology

Two main types of value chain systems have emerged: one demand-driven and the other supply-driven. In the first type, retailers in advanced countries in sectors like textiles and other consumption goods focus only on coordination and distribution. They delegate production to outside firms, exploiting the opportunity to maximize their profits by fostering competition among external suppliers. In the second system, companies distribute their production processes, optimizing costs by producing and assembling different parts of a product in different countries. Both systems profit from the advances in information and communications technology and from the simultaneous formation of productive clusters, initially in East Asian countries and, more recently, in other developing-country regions.

Evaluating the share of intermediate goods and services in total exports is not an easy task. The most recent estimates of the World Trade Organization (2009a) suggest a share of intermediate manufactured products in non-fuel world trade of about 40 per cent in 2008. A study combining trade statistics and input-output tables produced estimates of the shares of trade in intermediates in trade in goods of about 56.2 per cent and in trade in services of about 73.2 per cent for Organization for Economic Cooperation and Development (OECD) countries in 2006 (Miroudot, Lanz and Ragoussis, 2009). According to the study, trade in intermediates represented more than half of total trade in every region in 2006 (table IV.1).

The value of trade in services experienced a fivefold increase

Another factor behind the observed expansion of world trade (ninefold in nominal terms) has been the increase in international outsourcing and offshoring of services. As in the case of trade in goods mentioned above, this was facilitated by radical innovations in communications technology. These innovations have allowed companies to transfer their customer services to other locations where technicians speak English and other relevant international languages but where salaries are lower. As observed in figure IV.6, trade in services rose from 0.5 billion United States dollars in the 1980s to an average

3 This phenomenon, which began as so-called components trade, was in its early stages referred to as the "new" international division of labour. Subsequently, as components production fragmented further, it evolved into trade in "tasks".

Table IV.1:
Trade in intermediates as a percentage of total trade, by region, 2006

	Manufacturing	*Services*
Asia	49	57
Commonwealth of Independent States	82	55
Europe	52	64
Latin America	62	66
Middle East and North Africa	70	72
North America	55	50
Oceania	59	60
Sub-Saharan Africa	70	73

Source: Miroudot, Lanz and Ragoussis (2009), table 10.

Figure IV.6
Total exports of services, developed and developing economies, 1980-2008

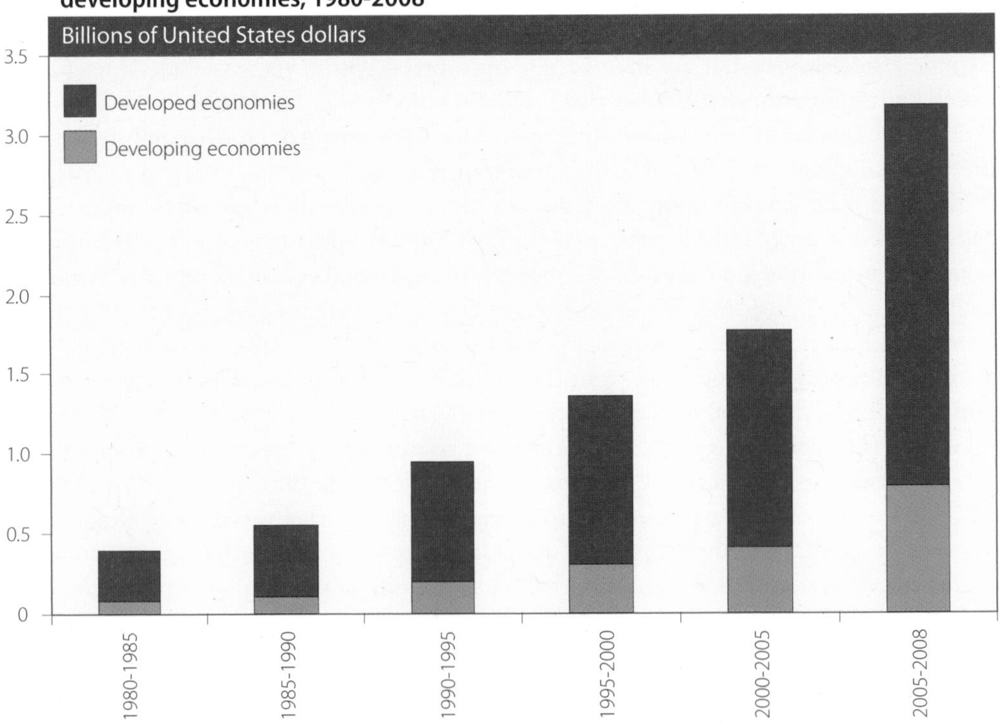

Source: UN/DESA calculations, based on *UNCTAD Handbook of Trade Statistics* online.

of $2.5 billion in the 2000s. The participation of developing countries in global services trade rose from 19 to 24 per cent during the same period.

As table IV.2 shows, financial services, services that entail the receipt of royalties and licence fees, communications, and computer and information services increased substantially, constituting collectively almost 20 per cent of total services exported in the period 2005-2007, with countries like India profiting from this new development.

In summary, trade patterns have moved from country specialization in terms of goods (manufactures for the North; primary commodities for the South) to intra-firm/network specialization in terms of tasks, with the South gaining considerable advantage in the production of manufactures. Despite these important changes in trade specialization patterns and production processes, however, much of the attention, when developing-country interests are addressed in trade negotiations, remains focused on gaining market access for agricultural products, as discussed further below. Although many developing countries, especially the poorest among them, still depend on exporting primary commodities (see figure IV.7), a narrow focus in trade negotiations on market access for primary products might be costly for long-term development. In the present context of the negotiations, it

Table IV.2:
Global services exports, by sector, as a percentage of total global services exports, 1980-2007

	1980-1985	*1985-1990*	*1990-1995*	*1995-2000*	*2000-2005*	*2005-2007*
Transport	34.9	30.2	26.5	24.1	22.5	23.0
Travel	28.5	33.1	33.6	32.8	29.9	26.9
Other services	36.6	36.6	39.9	43.2	47.5	50.1
Other business services	27.7	23.4	24.3	23.6	24.2	24.8
Financial services	1.1	3.1	3.9	5.0	6.3	7.7
Royalties, licence fees	2.9	3.1	4.1	4.8	5.3	5.3
Computer and information	0.0	0.3	0.6	1.6	3.8	4.4
Communications	0.7	1.4	1.5	2.1	2.3	2.4
Construction	2.2	2.0	2.4	2.9	2.0	2.2
Insurance	1.9	2.8	2.5	2.0	2.4	2.2
Personal, cultural, recreation	0.1	0.5	0.7	1.1	1.4	1.2

Source: UN/DESA calculations, based on *UNCTAD Handbook of Trade Statistics* online.

Figure IV.7
Continued reliance of least developed countries on exports of primary products, 1980-2008

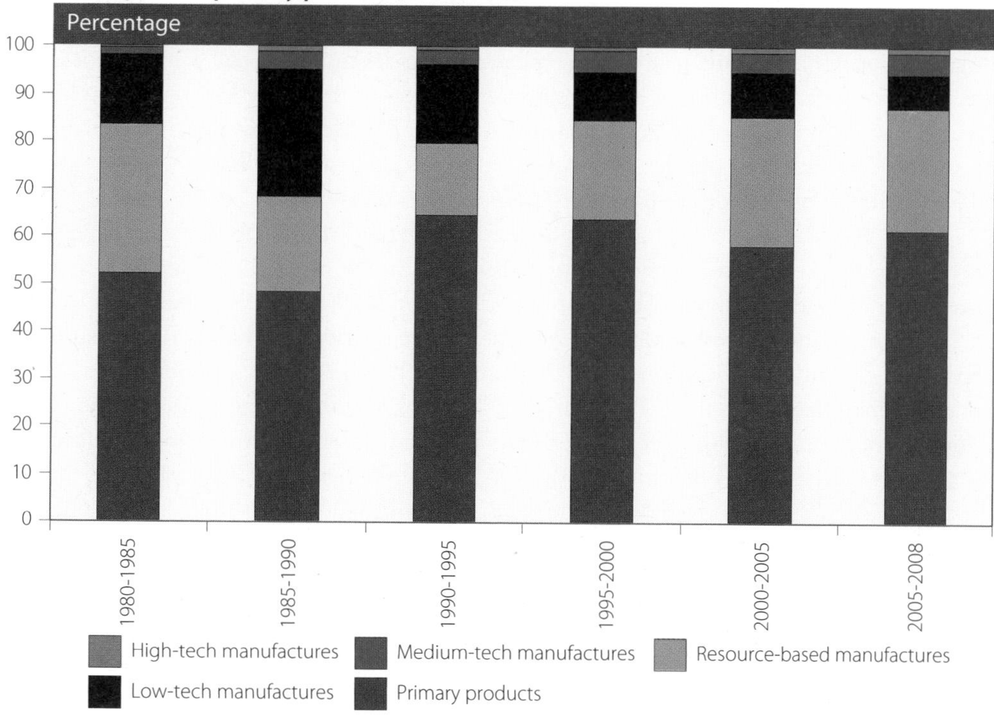

Source: UN/DESA calculations, based on UN Comtrade.

Note: For methodology, see United Nations (2006b, chap. III, appendix).

would imply giving up substantial policy space for promoting industrial diversification, needed to generate dynamic gains from trade, in exchange for greater market access based on existing static comparative advantages. For many of the low-income countries, the latter would reinforce reliance on traditional exports and a weaker impetus towards effecting the structural change needed for dynamic productivity growth (see chap. II).

The multilateral trading system and economic development

Reconciling national development strategies with multilateral trade rules

When a Government joins with other Governments in complying with certain rules, it has the objective of securing benefits (often referred to as international public goods) that are not to be had when market forces operate unimpeded (Toye, 2010). Multilateral trade rules help to limit the discriminatory or exploitative trade behaviour of economically powerful nations. Ex ante, the expectation is that limiting national sovereignty by accepting some self-imposed constraints on and limits to policy space will increase total national welfare.

Rules have been modified several times over the years to deal with development issues

Given the differences in the level of national development among its members, since the creation of the GATT there has been an ongoing internal conflict regarding how to deal with developing countries' aspirations towards securing development policy space within a multilateral trading system that upholds non-discrimination as a core principle. This has been evidenced by the fact that the rules had to be modified several times over the years to handle development issues (Laird, 2007). The original GATT was conceived not as a development institution, but as part of the International Trade Organization (ITO) to be established under the Havana Charter for an International Trade Organization, signed on 24 March 1948. After the effort to bring about the ratification of the International Trade Organization Charter failed, it became necessary to amend the GATT by introducing special provisions for dealing with development issues. In 1955, for example, developing countries were granted special treatment in the GATT, which allowed them, contrary to normal GATT rules, to protect particular industries and to plead balance-of-payments-related justification for adding to quantitative restrictions on trade.

Earlier on, there had been less pressure on developing countries to make burdensome commitments

Part IV of the GATT, introduced in 1964, did recognize the special needs of developing countries within the trading system, but much of the language was couched in terms of "best endeavours". The Enabling Clause of 1979, officially called the Decision on Differential and More Favourable Treatment, Reciprocity and Fuller Participation of Developing Countries (decision of 28 November 1979 (L/4903)), provided legal cover for the Generalized System of Preferences (GSP), for regional arrangements among developing countries, and for special treatment in favour of the least developed countries. As a result of these modifications to the GATT rules, there was little pressure put on the developing countries to make burdensome commitments, but this changed with the Uruguay Round.

The Uruguay Round

Partly because of the pressure from developed countries, partly because of their own reforms, and partly because of some disillusionment regarding the value of special and differentiated treatment (S&D), developing countries participated actively in the Uruguay Round. The bargain behind the creation of the World Trade Organization was that developed countries would allow agriculture to be subject to trade disciplines and would dismantle the quota system on textiles and clothing (two areas in which developing countries are thought to enjoy a comparative advantage) in exchange for some important concessions regarding opening of markets and the acceptance of a wide range of concrete obligations (Laird, 2007). Up to the present day, the treatment of agriculture by developed countries continues to be the subject of negotiations, previous promises not having been followed by their concrete realization.

Initially, certain specific subsidies, for example, for research and development, were defined as non-actionable

The first of these obligations was the severe curtailment of subsidies for local industries, under the World Trade Organization Agreement on Subsidies and Countervailing Measures (World Trade Organization, 1994). Article 8 of the Agreement defined certain specific subsidies as non-actionable (that is, non liable to a lawsuit) (United Nations Conference on Trade and Development, 2006). Subsidies extended to research fell in this category, as did subsidies provided in the pursuit of regional or environmental objectives. The subsidies permitted for research and development (R&D) included the financing of venture capital funds and the transfer to the private sector of technologies and innovations developed in government research laboratories. Also included in this category was public procurement policy in support of the proliferation of domestically defined standards for particular technologies. Moreover, activities in support of a shift in economic activity to new products or the use of new technologies could be subsidized as long as they were in the pre-competitive phase (that is, before they resulted in the production of goods that were exported or subject to significant import competition).

However, it is important to note that the provision that classified those subsidies as non-actionable had come up for review in 2000, when no agreement over its extension could be reached. Thus, the subsidies concerned became actionable. The Fourth Ministerial Conference of the World Trade Organization, held in Doha from 9 to 14 November 2001, revisited this issue along with the proposal of some countries to allow certain subsidies for development.[4] In practice, this has meant that the subsidies referred to above are tacitly allowed, with neither developed nor developing countries challenging them.

Prohibiting subsidies conditional on export performance severely constricts domestic policy space

Probably the most serious drawback of the Agreement on Subsidies and Countervailing Measures for development is that it prohibits making subsidies conditional on export performance. In other words, the Agreement withdraws a major monitoring

4 More specifically, the Fourth Ministerial Conference took note of the proposal to treat measures implemented by developing countries with a view to achieving legitimate development goals, such as regional growth, technology research and development funding, production diversification and development and implementation of environmentally sound methods of production, as non-actionable subsidies, and agreed that that issue should be addressed as an outstanding implementation issue. During the course of the negotiations, members were urged to exercise due restraint with respect to challenging such measures (World Trade Organization, 2001a, para.10.2). According to Aguayo Ayala and Gallagher (2005), this call for restraint has been respected, and developed and developing countries alike continue to utilize such subsidies under a tacit agreement not to challenge them under the dispute settlement mechanism.

standard that outward-oriented sectoral strategies in East Asia utilized successfully to ensure that support was given only to those enterprises that were able to compete in international markets. It is still possible to establish other performance standards under a reciprocal control mechanism (such as the percentage of technology personnel employed, the percentage of sales contributed by new products and the allocation of retained earnings); but none of these alternatives enable a performance-based incentive policy that directly relates to international competitiveness and minimizes the risk of abuse and rent-seeking.

A flexible tariff policy is still possible for many developing countries

In any case, it is clear that fiscal cost is a major constraint on many developing countries' use of such subsidies. In addition, although a flexible tariff policy is still possible for many developing countries, this potential has remained largely unexploited. Further, additional constraints on flexible tariff policies potentially resulting from the Doha Round negotiations on agricultural and non-agricultural market access could reduce policy space in the future.

As the World Trade Organization system has the ability to restrict discriminatory policies of large market economies, non-members seek accession even under the costly conditions imposed by existing members. Additionally, the World Trade Organization has a dispute resolution process which constitutes the only effective international economic enforcement mechanism. This has stimulated the expansion of the World Trade Organization's purview to include the so-called trade-related areas, namely, investment, property rights and services.

At present, it is difficult to link investment support to export-related disciplines

The second obligation developing countries accepted came into effect through the Agreement on Trade-Related Investment Measures (TRIMS), (World Trade Organization, 1994). This Agreement limits regulations on foreign investment, such as local-content requirements, technology transfer and local employment requirements (critical in efforts to improve linkages to the local economy), and makes it difficult to link investment support to export-related disciplines aimed at withdrawing support from producers that do not achieve international competitiveness within a predefined period of time. Nonetheless, foreign direct investment (FDI) regulating measures that do not violate national treatment[5] or impose quantitative restrictions continue to be consistent with World Trade Organization rules.

The third concession was reflected in the Agreement on Trade-Related Aspects of Intellectual Property Rights (TRIPS), (World Trade Organization, 1994) which established restrictions on the use of intellectual property. The Agreement reduced developing countries' ability to develop domestic technological capabilities, as they can no longer profit from freely copying and replicating technologies from abroad, a privilege (reverse engineering) that all developed countries and others had profited from successfully in earlier periods. In practice, the Agreement poses serious challenges in the areas of public health (see box IV.1) and climate change policies. Yet, the TRIPS Agreement does allow some flexibility through the mechanisms of compulsory licensing and parallel imports.

The General Agreement on Trade in Services is also an investment agreement

Last, but not least, there is the General Agreement on Trade in Services (World Trade Organization, 1994), through which World Trade Organization rules (the most-favoured-nation and national treatment principles), applicable only to trade in products, were extended to trade in services—encompassing a variety of areas ranging from banking,

5 Foreign investors must be treated as well as domestic investors. Treating foreign investors better than domestic investors does not violate this principle.

Box IV.1

The TRIPS Agreement and public health

Many developing countries are coming under pressure from richer countries and private corporations—through trade-related technical assistance and bilateral trade agreements—to implement the Agreement on Trade-Related Aspects of Intellectual Property Rights (TRIPS) in a way that goes beyond the requirements of World Trade Organization rules and gives strict protection to intellectual property. By making medicines more expensive, strict intellectual property rules can undermine a State's obligation to respect, protect and fulfil its commitment to the right to health and the right to life. When trade-related intellectual property restrictions undermine the ability of the State to fulfil its human rights obligations, countries must then attempt to exploit the flexibilities provided by the TRIPS Agreement (as reaffirmed in the Doha Ministerial Declaration[a]), which might in the end still prove insufficient.

The question whether a State is in violation of an obligation that it has assumed in regard to, say, the right to health for all citizens is often resolved through legal proceedings if that State is reluctant, including for budgetary reasons, to use normal legislative and administrative processes to fulfil that obligation. The 2004 case involving two Thai living with HIV/AIDS and Bristol-Myers Squibb concerned its patent for didanosine, which had made the cost of using the drug prohibitive. In this case, recourse to legal proceedings was necessitated by budgetary factors, by the Government's desire to convey the message that Thailand welcomed foreign investment, and by the threatened imposition of trade sanctions by the United States of America.

Implementing the TRIPS Agreement itself has been a difficult and costly process for many developing countries, particularly those that did not provide patent protection previously. Setting up a governmental intellectual property office is expensive, with high costs involved, for instance, in training patent examiners. Members do, however, have access to mechanisms designed to ensure that the cost of drugs remains low, the main ones being compulsory licensing and parallel imports. These function as follows:

- A compulsory licence removes the exclusive right of a patent owner. It allows a Government to issue a licence permitting the manufacture, use or sale of a drug without the consent of the patent owner, as long as the patent owner is paid for the use of his or her patent. By permitting equivalent generic versions of patented drugs to be made available, a compulsory licence can have the effect of reducing the price of drugs overall.
- The parallel imports mechanism can achieve a similar result by allowing the Government to grant a licence for the import of cheaper versions of a patented drug. This mechanism is not explicitly mentioned in the TRIPS Agreement: the absence of regulation thus gives countries the freedom to establish their own regimes.

By permitting different brands of the same drug to be available in the same market, both compulsory licensing and the parallel imports mechanism create competition, which usually leads to a reduction of prices.

a See document A/C.2/56/7, annex, para. 17.

Sources: Dommen and Kamoltrakul, eds. (2004); and Ford and others (2004).

education and rubbish collection, to tourism, health delivery, water supply and sanitation. Inasmuch as the General Agreement on Trade in Services covers the case of companies that establish themselves in a foreign country to provide services there, it is also an investment agreement (Wade, 2005). In that sense, it restricts the scope for competition policies for FDI coming under Mode 3 (so-called commercial presence) in each subsector listed by a nation in its commitments under the General Agreement on Trade in Services.

Although the General Agreement on Trade in Services permits a considerable range of exemptions, since Governments can specify limitations on some of the commitments in particular sectors, such reservations must be signalled at the beginning, because it is difficult from a legal point of view for Governments to introduce them later.

The broader multilateral trade agenda has increased its influence over national policies

Because of the complexity of regulatory needs in many services, developing countries are at a disadvantage in identifying what limitations should be included in advance.[6]

As a result of the introduction of this substantial new agenda, the multilateral trading system has become more restrictive at the same time that its influence over national policies has expanded. The World Trade Organization requires countries to change existing domestic laws that conflict with their membership obligations,[7] while the Trade Policy Review Mechanism requires members to give regular public accounts of the state of their compliance with those obligations; the World Trade Organization has also strengthened its dispute settlement mechanism. These institutional innovations, taken together, have had two general effects. They have made considerable inroads on what, before the coming into force of the Uruguay Round agreements, were traditionally matters of domestic governance; and they have further "judicialized" the process of trade cooperation. This has given rise to the temptation to use the World Trade Organization as a forum for consideration of other global issues, like climate change, that could be used to justify protectionism, as explored below.

In various instances, provisions were added to particular World Trade Organization agreements that meant that developed countries, in their application of the terms of those agreements, would have to take special account of the needs of developing countries. Nevertheless, the cost and administrative difficulties faced by the latter in implementing their commitments were greater than anticipated, while many of the gains promised by the developed countries did not materialize.

The Doha Round

The Doha Round was launched in 2001 with the express intention of establishing more development-oriented multilateral trading rules. In the Doha Ministerial Declaration of the Fourth Ministerial Conference of the World Trade Organization, the determination was expressed to place the needs and interests of developing countries at the heart of the Doha Work Programme.[8] Positive efforts were to be made "to ensure that developing countries, and especially the least developed among them, secure a share in the growth of world trade commensurate with the needs of their economic development".

The Hong Kong Ministerial Declaration provided specific measures for least developed countries

The Hong Kong Ministerial Declaration, adopted on 18 December 2005 (World Trade Organization, 2005), included a limited package for the least developed countries, comprising five specific proposals (annex F). The Ministerial Declaration also expressed its support for developments regarding the TRIPS Agreement and public health (see box IV.1), the extension of the TRIPS Agreement transition period for least developed

6 United States action could find itself subject to dispute should current proposals to re-regulate the financial sector become law. In the additional protocol under the General Agreement on Trade in Services entitled "Understanding on Commitments in Financial Services", which the United States signed with other countries, the United States carved out only trading in onion derivatives under the World Trade Organization category "Trading of securities and derivative products and services related thereto". It is thus subject to complaint on additional regulation on all derivatives except those related to onion futures. (The Onion Futures Act is a 1958 United States law banning the trading of futures contracts on onions and constitutes the first and only ban in United States history on the trading of futures contracts of a specific commodity). Moreover, the United States signed on to a standstill provision on regulatory changes applicable to the World Trade Organization financial services list which is still in effect (Public Citizen, 2009).

7 The TRIPS Agreement, for example, requires the introduction of minimum standards, border controls and domestic enforcement procedures along with the setting up of the respective authorities. Although it came into force on 1 January 1995, together with the other World Trade Organization Agreements, it gave all members a transition period within which to effect the necessary changes in legislation and practice.

8 See document A/C.2/56/7, annex, para. 2.

countries, and an enhanced Integrated Framework (EIF).[9] In respect of trade in services, it was decided (para. 26) that the least developed countries would not be expected to undertake new commitments (this paralleling the wording of the draft text on non-agricultural market access), while there was a "best endeavours" agreement to give priority to the sectors and modes of supply of export interest to least developed countries, particularly under Mode 4 (temporary movement of labour (para. 47)).

At the Pittsburgh Summit, held on 24 and 25 September 2009, leaders from the Group of Twenty (G-20) called for significant progress on the Doha Round in 2010. This should constitute an integral part of the concerted efforts directed towards establishing a rebalance of the global economy. However, the additional progress urged has not materialized. There is still an important gap in terms of providing developing countries, especially the least developed among them, with duty-free and quota-free market access for their products. Most of the progress in this area has been due to the elimination of tariffs through most-favoured nation agreements (see United Nations, 2009c, pp. 27-28; and box IV.2). Agricultural subsidies in advanced countries remain high and continue to reduce income opportunities for farmers in developing countries.

Box IV.2

The least developed countries in the World Trade Organization

There have been notable improvements in market access for least developed countries. Twenty-eight World Trade Organization members have pledged expanded market access. Many of them have actually agreed to drop all barriers and provide "duty-free and quota-free" treatment to all least developed country exports. They thereby join a number of other countries that already provide open markets. The average non-weighted tariff applied by major trading partners to exports of least developed countries fell from 10.6 per cent in 1997 to 6 per cent in the first quarter of 2001.

Technical assistance to enable least developed countries to make the most of their rights and perform based on their obligations under World Trade Organization Agreements is also being provided. For instance, under the Joint Initiative on Technical Cooperation for Least Developed Countries, launched by the World Intellectual Property Organization and the World Trade Organization, assistance is being offered to enable these countries to bring their intellectual property system up to standard while fully utilizing World Trade Organization flexibilities. Members of the World Trade Organization are currently looking at means to assist least developed countries in the process of joining, since least developed countries acceding to the World Trade Organization have to learn how it works. They also need to draft domestic laws that comply with World Trade Organization rules, to establish mechanisms for enforcing those rules, and to negotiate with existing members suitable conditions for entry into the World Trade Organization.

Finally, the World Trade Organization provides a forum where least developed countries can and do raise particular issues relating to food safety and quality standards; indeed, least developed countries may find it difficult to ensure that their exports comply with developed countries' sanitary standards. In this regard, World Trade Organization Agreements limit importing countries' capacity to impose arbitrary requirements on exports of least developed countries, and encourage the use of internationally developed standards.

Source: World Trade Organization (2001b).

9 The Integrated Framework For Trade-related Technical Assistance to Least Developed Countries, also known as the Integrated Framework (IF), was established at the High-level Meeting on Least Developed Countries' Trade Development, held at the World Trade Organization in October 1997, to support least developed countries in trade capacity-building and integrating trade issues into overall national development strategies. The IF has been redesigned and is in operation on a pilot basis in Cambodia, Madagascar and Mauritania. It will help least developed countries mainstream trade into their national development plans and strategies for poverty reduction.

However, even if the limitations introduced by the multilateral framework and its application at the national level are overcome, this does not imply that developing countries will automatically be able to reap much higher gains from trade. Historical evidence indicates that for this to happen it is essential for countries to have built up adequate production and trading capacities so that trade can be an engine for growth. Aid for Trade, as well as space for implementation of industrial and productive policies, is key in this respect.

Aid for Trade

The Aid for Trade initiative recognizes the need to enhance production and trading capacities for trade to become an engine for growth

The Aid for Trade initiative (AfT) recognizes that the trading and production capacity of developing countries, especially the poorest ones, needs to be strengthened. The case made for Aid for Trade is based, generally, on the belief that, while trade can be a tool for development, countries need, inter alia, infrastructure, institutions, technical capacity and investment, particularly in order to take advantage of the market access-related concessions that they have obtained under the World Trade Organization (Page, 2007). To some extent, then, the debate presents a challenge to the call for "Trade, not aid", through recognition of the fact that there is a need for assistance to developing countries so as to enable them to expand and diversify their trade in a manner that deepens the development impact. Put another way: aid can help develop trade, to the point where trade eventually replaces aid.

As table IV.3 shows, lower middle income countries and low-income countries that are not least developed countries have together received the highest share of Aid for Trade-related funds over the period 2001-2008. Least developed countries have received the lowest level of trade-related assistance spending relative to total aid among the large aid recipients. These figures are a cause for concern as least developed countries and African countries are among the most likely to need support for trade.

Table IV.3:
Destination of Aid for Trade commitments to countries, by income group, 2001-2008

	Percentage					*Millions of United States dollars*
	Least developed	*Other low- income*	*Lower middle income*	*Upper middle income*	*Unallocated by income*	*Total Aid for Trade*
2001	24	20	43	7	5	15 437
2002	23	18	46	9	4	15 666
2003	31	13	42	7	6	17 523
2004	27	15	51	4	4	23 531
2005	31	15	40	10	4	22 578
2006	28	13	44	5	10	22 234
2007	35	18	34	6	7	26 526
2008	27	13	42	11	7	38 548
2001-2008	28	15	43	7	6	182 044

Source: UN/DESA calculations, based on Organization for Economic Cooperation and Developnment, Query Wizard for International Development Statistics (QWIDS).

The benefits of an Aid for Trade programme can be categorized first in terms of assistance to help developing countries generate supply-side responses, as removal of tariffs on agricultural products in the developed world, for example, might not trigger a strong export response given the large shares of small-scale farming and a general lack of infrastructure (Laird, 2007). Furthermore, developed countries are increasingly tightening import restrictions through the application of (sanitary and phyto-sanitary) standards, with which poor countries are often unable to comply. Second, assistance may be provided for microtrade adjustment, designed to help developing countries cope with undesirable outcomes in particular industries due to the factor redeployment effects of trade liberalization. Macro adjustment assistance could include compensation for preference erosion and lost tariff revenue; compensation for the latter could play a substantial role in repairing the loss of fiscal space of small developing countries.

Several disagreements persist concerning the practical implementation of Aid for Trade

Despite general agreement that these are important issues for all developing countries, there is no consensus on the relative importance of what is essentially infrastructure development assistance—both hard and soft—and support for responding to adverse external shocks. Equally important, there is no defined mechanism for the collection, allocation and disbursement of Aid for Trade funds. When this was a subject of negotiations, there was pressure to define a new structure for trade aid, one that was outside normal aid mechanisms and parallel to the structures created to deal with other international concerns such as health and the environment. For the purpose of sidestepping the necessity of securing developing countries' support within the framework of the trade agreement being negotiated, Aid for Trade has been absorbed into normal country aid programmes.

Although there may be increased funding for trade-related purposes, it will be difficult to ensure that the actual use of funds is in accord with the objective of expanding global trade or is aligned with national trade and development priorities. This can be explained, first, by the fact that, given its distinct area of influence, the World Trade Organization as an organization is not inclined to challenge traditional aid agencies. Second, aid agencies are generally reluctant to subject their allocation or mechanisms to external criteria. Finally, Aid for Trade had been carved out of the trade negotiations with the effect that developing countries lost the ability to have a direct influence on deciding modalities. Inevitably, the question also arises to what extent Aid for Trade would be additional to existing aid commitments or merely a re-categorization[10] of existing funding directed towards trade and related activities, which, in some countries, could well be of lower priority in terms of development.

Policy space and regional trade agreements

Bilateral or regional trade agreements may further erode national policy space

Under the World Trade Organization's multilateral framework, countries can still use certain types of subsidies, and flexible tariffs policies, particularly FDI regulating measures and flexible compulsory licensing. However, the rise of bilateral and regional trade agreements has the effect of restricting some of these flexibilities and, in fact, eroding the policy space available to developing countries (Haque, 2007).

In effect, slow progress in the Doha negotiations combined with their bilateral negotiating advantage has spurred developed countries, in particular, to aggressively pursue

10 Most of the reporting on Aid for Trade concerns commitments. However, in the case of least developed countries, there have been some attempts within the enhanced Integrated Framework to match the supply (offers of assistance) to the demand (recipient country requirements).

bilateral and regional trade agreements. Indeed, the surge in regional trade agreements (RTAs), bilateral free trade agreements (FTAs) and, more recently, economic partnership agreements (EPAs), has continued unabated since the early 1990s. As can be seen in table IV.4, there were 271 regional trade agreements in force in March 2010.[11]

Economic partnership agreements, regional trade agreements and free trade agreements are drawn up overwhelmingly by parties of vastly different trade capacities.[12] What motivates the establishment of those agreements is the promise of preferential treatment. They seem, in fact, to generate a domino effect: non-members are tempted to join existing North-South preferential agreements so as not to lose out on access to sizeable export markets and sources of FDI (Baldwin, 1997). Hence, while to engage in international commitments may be a "sovereign" decision, there is often little alternative.

Table IV.4:
Regional trade agreements as of March 2010

	Goods agreements				
Regions concerned	*Preferential arrangements*	*Free trade agreements*	*Customs unions*	*Services agreements*	*Total*
OECD-OECD	0	15	9	10	34
OECD-LAC	0	13	0	11	24
OECD-Asia Pacific	0	26	1	12	39
OECD-Africa	0	12	0	1	13
OECD-EiT	0	8	0	3	11
LAC-LAC	1	13	4	14	32
LAC-Asia Pacific	2	9	0	9	20
LAC-Africa	0	0	0	0	0
LAC-EiT	0	0	0	0	0
Asia Pacific-Asia Pacific	8	26	1	16	51
Asia Pacific-Africa	0	3	0	0	3
Asia Pacific-EiT	1	12	0	0	13
Africa-Africa	0	2	5	0	7
Africa-EiT	0	0	0	0	0
EiT-EiT	0	21	1	0	22
Developing-Developing	2	0	0	0	2
Total	14	160	21	76	271

Source: World Trade Organization Regional Trade Agreements Information System (RTA-IS).

Abbreviations: LAC, Latin America and the Caribbean; OECD, Organization for Economic Cooperation and Development; EiT, Economies in Transition.

11 Some 462 RTAs had been notified to the GATT/World Trade Organization as of February 2010. Of these, 345 RTAs were notified under article XXIV of GATT 1947 or GATT 1994; 31 under the Enabling Clause; and 86 under article V of the General Agreement on Trade in Services. World Trade Organization statistics on RTAs are based on notification requirements rather than on physical numbers of RTAs. Thus, for an RTA that includes both goods and services, two notifications are counted.

12 The ongoing economic partnership agreement negotiations between European countries and the 79 countries members of the African, Caribbean and Pacific (ACP) Group of States (mostly former colonies) are necessitated by the fact that existing preferential arrangements are in violation of World Trade Organization rules. The trend in these negotiations, in respect of responsibilities, has been towards the "common" as opposed to the "differentiated" side of the balance.

Many regional agreements curb government policies that favour local firms

The issue is whether there is a net benefit accruing to developing countries from bilateral or regional North-South agreements. In many cases, industrialized countries have succeeded through these agreements in extracting the compliance of developing countries in areas where they failed to secure consent in the World Trade Organization. In effect, many regional trade agreements impose binding obligations on the contracting parties with regard to investment liberalization and protection, as well as competition policy and government procurement (the so-called Singapore issues or "WTO plus"), thus expanding the rights and access of foreign firms and their products in developing-country markets, and further curbing or prohibiting government policies that encourage or favour local firms and the domestic economy (Shadlen, 2005).[13]

Some regional agreements limit the capacity to regulate capital flows and impose capital controls

Additionally, many North-South bilateral free trade agreements and bilateral investment treaties (BITs) have provisions requiring all transfers relating to investment from the other party (including contributions to capital, profits, dividends, capital gains, interest and loan repayment) to be allowed without delay into and out of a country's territory, which severely limits the capacity to regulate capital flows and impose capital controls (to be explored further below as well as in chap. V).

In summary, resolving the conflict between economic development and the principle of non-discrimination in the trading system has been difficult. However, some progress has been made in terms of more policy space given to the least developed countries, specifically in terms of longer adjustment periods (see also box IV.2). On the other hand, low-income countries that are not least developed countries, as well as many middle-income countries, have seen their options constrained by their acceptance of World Trade Organization terms and limitations emerging from other policy areas, such as those encompassing bilateral trade agreements and other measures discussed below.

Many developing countries have agreed to assume obligations beyond those imposed by membership in the World Trade Organization

In practice, the international system has placed great value on the rapid convergence of developing countries' trade policies with those of developed countries. In fact, through regional and bilateral agreements, many developing countries have even agreed to assume obligations that extend beyond those imposed by membership in the World Trade Organization, through bilateral commitments on tariff levels, for example. This is explained by the fact that poorer countries typically have limited fiscal resources, which constrains their capacity to support large-scale enterprise and sectoral economic development programmes. Moreover, the volatility of private capital flows has made exchange-rate management in support of international competitiveness difficult.

These limitations to national policy space have been compounded by changing global trade patterns. Together with the revolutions in information and communications technology, trade liberalization has further stimulated the expansion of trade, which is being driven by the fragmentation of production and the unprecedented growth of global value chains. In general, countries that had managed early on to jump on the global value chains bandwagon, while at the same time strengthening linkages with their domestic economies, had better growth performance, as discussed in chapter II. However, successive iterations in trade negotiations have led to constraints on the space available for conducting the policies that create such linkages.

13 See Gallagher (2005) for a description of the main contentious issues associated with several regional agreements.

The way forward

Although it was evident early on that GATT mechanisms fell short in regard to development orientation, and despite several attempts to provide a special and differentiated space to developing countries in the World Trade Organization, effective implementation of this promise has yet to occur. Although the Doha Round has been labelled a "development round", its limitations with respect to providing enough policy space for development have been evident, which helps to explain its stalled status. The World Trade Organization's single-undertaking approach compounds the difficulties of achieving agreement. Special treatment now applies mainly to least developed countries even as their market access remains limited.

Policy incoherence in several areas underlies important limitations of the multilateral trading regime

Behind these limitations lies policy incoherence in a number of areas: (a) between multilateral and regional rule-setting and space for counter-cyclical policies; (b) between multilateral and regional rule-setting and space for national development policies; (c) between national and international regulation of global value chains and transnational corporations; (d) between trade and environmental objectives; (e) between trade rules and finance regulations; (f) between the facilitation of labour mobility and national policies, particularly of receiving countries; (g) between the multilateral system and regional agreements; and (h) within the World Trade Organization rules themselves. These inconsistencies are explained below, with a view to suggesting how to retool national development efforts.

Retooling counter-cyclical policies

Because downturns have proved more costly in terms of unemployment and lost opportunities (see chap. II), there is a strong economic case to be made for managing aggregate demand and reducing the impact of business cycles on investment, employment and incomes. Trade policies, as an important complement to monetary, exchange-rate and fiscal policies, were formerly used for this purpose. Members of the World Trade Organization have an unchallenged right to use contingency measures that are consistent with its rules. In fact, protectionism has always been a structural element of the free trade system—an institutional safety net in the liberal trading order. In effect, trade agreements foresee a range of measures, commonly referred to as contingency measures, or safety valves, that countries may use to manage adverse circumstances. These rules must strike a balance between commitments and flexibility. Too much flexibility may undermine the value of commitments, but too little flexibility may render the rules politically unsustainable (World Trade Organization, 2009b). The design of contingency measures is frequently a central element of negotiations.[14] Such measures include safeguards, dumping and anti-dumping measures, subsidies and countervailing duties, as well as others like renegotiation of provisions. Developed economies have the advantage of possessing the greater fiscal resources needed to offer the kind of business subsidies that are still allowed under the World Trade Organization rules to handle economic downturns. For developing countries, trade liberalization has restricted the range over which tariffs can be applied for counter-cyclical policy.

In response to the current global crisis, countries all over the world are using a variety of available means to protect their industries from the devastating consequences

14 A categorization of the circumstances warranting, and the arguments for, a temporary increase in protection is presented in World Trade Organization, 2009b, chap II.B, table 1.

of a contracting world economy and rising mass unemployment (Drache, 2010). As mentioned above, the multilateral framework has been instrumental in preventing an escalation of beggar-thy-neighbour measures. While it is a comparatively straightforward matter to detect the use of contingency measures, it is more difficult to identify trade-restrictive measures and subsidies embedded in financial rescue and fiscal stimulus packages that might have adverse trade effects (see table IV.5).

Table IV.5:
A selected list of modern protection(ist) practices

Difficult but acceptable	*Legal but contentious*	*Distorting and controversial*
Stimulus packages	Anti-dumping duties	Import quotas
Wage subsidies	Countervailing duties	Customs and barriers
Packaging/labelling	Industrial policy	Beggar-thy-neighbour tariff walls
Technology licensing restrictions	Currency devaluation	Voluntary export restraints
Industry rescue packages	State aid/subsidies	Export bans
Food/health standards	Unilateral safeguard action	
Bail-outs	"Buy local"	

Source: Drache (2010).

The global recession has uncovered what could be considered a coordination problem. A single country's use of a contingency measure within a trade agreement, triggered by unexpected import competition or a downturn in its domestic industry, gives the industry the opportunity and time to recover. However, such a reprieve will be difficult to procure in the midst of a generalized recession, particularly when all other countries are imposing trade contingency measures. The Great Depression of the 1930s demonstrated that protectionism in the face of a global crisis can deepen and lengthen a crisis. At the same time, the "Great Recession" has shown that recourse to the other extreme—free markets and market discipline—is not enough to maintain sustainable and stable rates of growth. In this regard, these counter-cyclical efforts can be seen as reflecting the search for a new and necessary balance between State interventions and market efficiency in a demand-constrained world.

Restoring coherence between trade and development policies

At a time when developing countries must industrialize to meet their development goals even as they strive to achieve climate change-related goals, it is difficult to imagine an integrated approach that does not take industrial policy seriously. Stronger intellectual property rights and efforts to attract FDI are no substitute for sound industrial policies in developing countries (United Nations, 2009a).

As has been documented in the literature[15] and discussed in chapter II, accelerated rates of growth have generally been accompanied by strategic interventions and collaboration between a developmentally oriented State and the private sector. The capability-building requirements are both direct—to put infant-industry enterprises on

15 See Gallagher, ed., 2005.

a learning curve for mastering new technologies without incurring enormous and unpredictable losses; and indirect—to ensure that skill, capital, technology and infrastructure markets support these efforts. There is also a need to coordinate learning across enterprises and activities (Lall, 2005).

The most effective industrial policies were selective, temporary and performance-related

Because what a country produces and exports does indeed matter (Rodrik, 2004; Hausmann and Klinger, 2006; United Nations, 2006b) industrial policies involving infant-industry protection, export subsidies, directed credit schemes and local content rules have proved to be a key ingredient of successful development, particularly in East Asia (Memis and Montes, 2008). The record of East Asia confirms that the most effective subsidies for infant industries have been selective (not across the board), temporary (not open-ended) and performance-related (not unconditional). One key instrument will be recalibration of the use of subsidies and other mechanisms in support of export industries in developing countries, so as to ensure that they feature: (a) targeted incentives; (b) regulation; (c) coordination of investment decisions; (d) control mechanisms; and (e) environment-friendly characteristics (see below). These elements can be implemented through diverse instruments, according to the particular characteristics of the sector and country (United Nations, 2009a).

As discussed in chapter II, economic diversification and structural change are critical to self-sustaining poverty reduction; and integrating social, labour-market and industrial policies can be an effective approach to achieving these goals. How to reorder priorities in industrial policy so as to promote social objectives will depend on the country context. In many countries, this will require a return to public investment in rural areas and agriculture in order to develop the livelihoods of the poor. It will also entail supporting the expansion of the domestic production of the goods required in the education and health sectors, possibly by taking advantage of government procurement policies. Also important will be reviving domestic support for export industries offering the best opportunities for backward integration instead of promoting industrial policy focused implicitly on maquila-type production (Memis and Montes, 2008). For example, in Viet Nam, State support in expanding rice and (in the nation's hinterland) coffee production improved household incomes and created new export capabilities.

In the context of implementing a national strategy, the State should play the role of facilitator by helping the business sector choose a path that achieves an optimal balance between the economy's deviation from comparative advantage and its growth rate (Chang, 2009). If it deviates too little, it may be efficient in the short run, but its long-term growth may be slowed down, inasmuch as it is not upgrading. On the other hand, too much deviation may accelerate industrialization in the short run, but after a point, the negative effects of protection (for example, excessive learning costs and rent-seeking) may overwhelm the acceleration in productivity growth generated by the infant industries, resulting in negative growth overall.

The changing patterns of trade and production described above have important implications for the formulation of trade and industrial policies in the context of broader development strategies. The rapid spread of information technology, the shrinking of economic distance and the skill requirements and institutional needs of new technologies have made the competitive environment more demanding (Lall, 2005). The fact that minimum entry levels in terms of skill, competence, infrastructure and connectivity are higher, creates the need for the provision of support to local enterprises for learning. This is even more important in the context of global value chains, as discussed below.

It is no longer sufficient for a developing country that wishes to export, to produce goods efficiently and competitively. In order to actually export, developing-country suppliers of labour-intensive products now must not only overcome the traditional trade barriers—which remain high for certain developing-country exports—but also become part of some trade network. Managing to get "picked up on this dance floor" covered by the many competitors worldwide is due as much to luck as to productive efficiency (Mayer, 2008).

It has become crucial for developing-country suppliers of labour-intensive products to become part of trade networks

Based as they were on the low labour cost advantage, the kind of "outward-oriented" strategies pursued, for example, by the Republic of Korea and Taiwan Province of China at the stage of their early industrialization, would not be as feasible or effective or as easy to implement in today's environment. This points to a catch-22-type situation: a developing-country producer needs to secure a major sales order to get started in business, at the same time that corporate buyers in industrialized countries look for firms with a proved track record.

The relationship between the large international firms and small producers in developing countries is fundamentally unequal. The rise of supply chains, as drivers of international trade, has resulted in what are basically monopsony situations, where foreign buyers more or less dictate the prices that they pay to developing-country producers. It is the former that decide where to buy, invest and situate industrial activity and that by and large determine the return received by a developing-country producer. This is because in industries with high sales costs, advertisement expenditures or R&D expenses, large firms enjoy a distinct competitive advantage over small producers.

In supply chains, foreign buyers more or less dictate the prices they pay to developing-country producers

In such trading networks, there is little commitment on the part of buyers to their suppliers, which can be easily replaced by others (Mayer, 2008). If a developing-country producer succeeds in joining a trade network, there is no assurance that such an arrangement will be durable, as new and more attractive sources of supplies are constantly emerging. Thanks to the universal appeal of the mantra of export-led growth, simple labour-intensive manufacturing has become fiercely competitive, with suppliers struggling to contain costs and remain attractive to foreign buyers. Activist policies in support of domestic firms in one country are either promptly challenged in the World Trade Organization or quickly matched by similar actions in other countries. Passive responses to these constraints by countries can compel them to join in a race to the bottom, a condition characterized by compressed wages, stagnant or falling living standards, and the neglect of environmental consequences.

Simple labour-intensive manufacturing has become fiercely competitive

Successful cases like Costa Rica, which attracted Intel to its export processing zone (EPZ) as a major investor and which helped crowd in foreign investments in other sectors, show that prior domestic investments in infrastructure and human capital and export subsidy schemes were key to dynamizing and diversifying export sectors with strong linkages to the domestic economy. In the case of East Asian newly industrializing economies, although some level of labour repression was present (and often justified for national security reasons), this did not reflect a deliberate policy action designed to attract foreign investment (Chowdhury and Islam, 1993).

Prior domestic investments, linkages and export subsidy schemes have been key in successful cases

The inability of individual countries to avoid being swept up into self-defeating competition with others points to a global governance gap in the area of oversight mechanisms covering the operations of global value chains and transnational corporations. In domestic contexts, by contrast, private companies are subject to national laws. There is no legal framework specific to intra-GVC relations, including contractual obligations applicable to GVC operations. Similarly, there is no international dispute settlement mechanism applicable to relations between small and medium-sized enterprises (SMEs) and transnational corporations (in current GVC practice, legal contract enforcement is seldom an option for small and medium-sized enterprises because a dispute usually signals the end of a contractual relationship) (Dembinski, 2007).

Proposals like that on establishing an international competition authority or national trading companies are worthy of consideration

Developing countries need to cooperate and adopt a collective approach on this issue. Interesting proposals which merit consideration have been put forward. Singh (2002) proposes the establishment of an international competition authority, which would aim "to control the anti-competitive conduct of the world's large multinational corporations ... as well as to control their propensity to grow by takeovers and mergers". Absent an international competition mechanism, it would be advisable for individual countries to design their own domestic competition policies which would permit the emergence of larger domestic companies able to compete internationally.[16] This could require abrogation of some World Trade Organization commitments regarding national treatment of foreign firms, as discussed above.

Pack and Saggi (2001) propose the establishment of national trading companies like those set up by some East Asian countries. They note: "Governments could attempt to encourage the development of trading companies as there may be a market failure given the characteristic that setup costs for such companies may be significant but marginal costs of adding firms to the network may be small. Such trading firms could operate across clusters of manufacturing firms."

For countries hosting transnational corporations or participating in global value chains, tax coordination is a key issue

From the point of view of countries hosting transnational corporations or participating in global value chains, tax coordination is another key issue. By the end of 2008, the total number of double taxation treaties had reached 2,827 and the network of international investment agreements (IIAs) continues to expand: there were a total of 2,278 bilateral investment treaties by the end of 2007 (see table IV.6).

It has become increasingly evident that it is better cooperation—not unbridled competition among countries through tax incentives and decreases in regulatory requirements—that is in the interest of all countries. For one thing, transnational corporations or value chains typically do not decide to move to one country rather than another mainly on the basis of tax incentives. Progress in establishing mechanisms of coordination, cooperation and exchange of information is necessary to fill yet another gap in international governance.

Developing countries suffer a disadvantage in terms of negotiating and enforcement capacity

The number of other international agreements with investment provisions had reached 273 by the end of 2008. These agreements established rules, standards and mechanisms for managing tax and investment-related treatment of cross-country business activities. As regards these agreements, developing countries, as in the World Trade Organization, suffer a disadvantage in terms of negotiating and enforcement capacity. Bilateral investment treaties, which have been proliferating since the early 1990s (see figure IV.8), take the obligations of host Governments under the TRIPS Agreement, the Agreement on Trade-Related Investment Measures (World Trade Organization, 1994) and the General Agreement on Trade in Services as a mere starting point (Wade, 2005). They require the host Government to lift even more restrictions on the foreign firms hoping to operate in their territory, and to make even more concessions, in return for better market access.

16 The emergence of the "too big to fail" problem is a recent example of the exercise of competitive forbearance by developed countries in respect of the establishment of large companies in the financial sector at the same time that these countries were pushing World Trade Organization disciplines directed at forcing increased competition in domestic sectors in developing countries.

Table IV.6:
Number of bilateral investment treaties (BITs) and double taxation treaties (DTTs), by country groups involved, 1959-2007 and 1928-2008

Country groups concerned	*BITs, 1959-2007*	*DTTs, 1928-2008*
Developed-developed	233	708
Developed-developing	900	1 053
Developed-least developed	172	86
Developed-transition economies	259	285
Developing-developing	371	390
Developing-least developed	107	89
Developing-transition economies	181	167
Least developed-least developed	1	3
Least developed-transition economies	5	1
Transition economies-transition economies	49	45
Total	2 278	2 827

Sources: International Centre for Settlement of Investment Disputes Database of Bilateral Investment Treaties (http://icsid.worldbank.org/ICSID); and United Nations Conference on Trade and Development data on double taxation treaties (http://www.unctad.org).

Figure IV.8
Number of bilateral investment treaties (BITs) and double taxation treaties (DTTs) signed per decade, 1960-2008

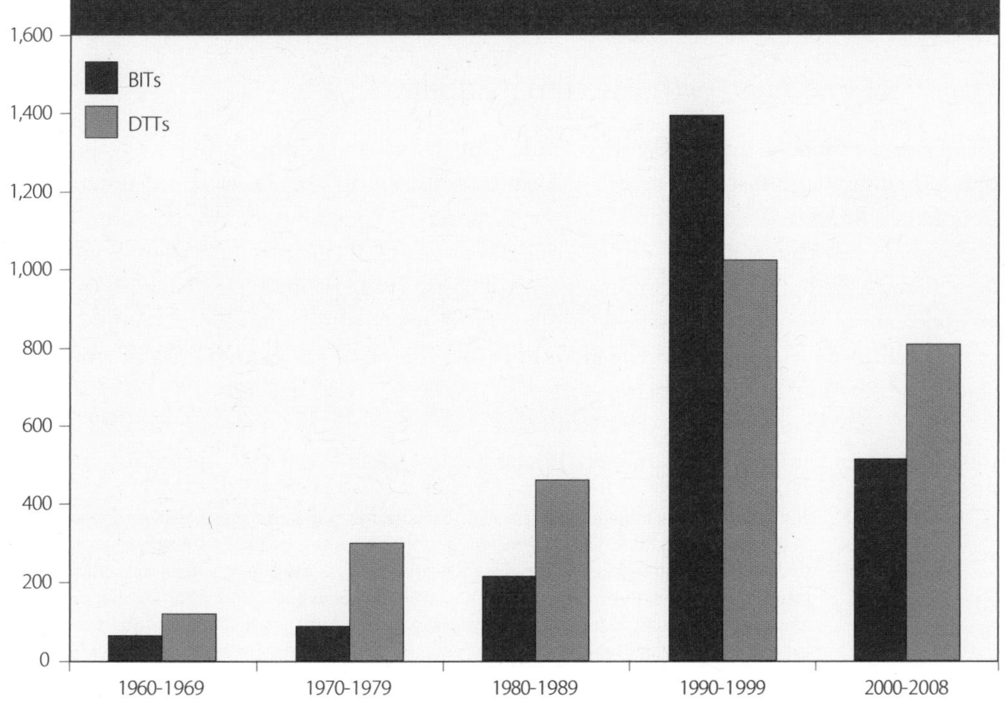

Sources: International Centre for Settlement of Investment Disputes Database of Bilateral Investment Treaties (http://icsid.worldbank.org/ICSID); and United Nations Conference on Trade and Development data on double taxation treaties (http://www.unctad.org).

To deal with disagreements between foreign investors and host country Governments, firm-State arbitration boards are established as components of bilateral investment treaties. These boards allow a private firm to take a Government to arbitration that is conducted by a body dominated by private sector adjudicators who are, more often than not, sympathetic to the needs of the firm. The boards operate using private contract law rather than public law and allow damages against the Government to be levied retroactively. The fact that the World Trade Organization dispute settlement mechanism, where States deal with States under public law, looks evenly balanced by comparison should be a cause for concern.

Another major concern is transfer pricing on within-firm cross-border transactions

Obtaining the proper level of tax revenues from resident foreign companies is often constrained by the ability of multinationals to set transfer prices on within-firm cross-border transactions so as to minimize domestic tax liabilities. Although there are discrepancies in the specifics of each country's laws concerning the application of the "arm's-length principle", many countries have based their transfer pricing laws and regulations on the OECD Transfer Pricing Guidelines for Multinational Enterprises and Tax Administrations (Organization for Economic Cooperation and Development, 2009), which are quite difficult to enforce in actuality.

High informational requirements needed to control transfer pricing tend to put developing countries at a disadvantage

Most of the double-taxation treaties contain provisions that force both taxing authorities to resolve transfer-pricing disputes on the basis of the arm's-length principle. Developing-country authorities tend to be at more of a disadvantage because of the high informational requirements needed to control transfer pricing.[17] Progress is needed on achieving improved, automatic exchanges of information among countries. Such improvements would be in the interest of advanced countries as well by helping them bridge information gaps when enforcing financial regulations. The international community should also consider mandatory country-by-country reporting by transnational corporations as a means of filling this international governance gap.

Coherence with the climate agenda

Climate policy must take priority, since trade is not an end in itself, but is supposed to enhance human welfare

The Director-General of the World Trade Organization (Lamy, 2009) has suggested that climate policy must take priority, since trade is not an end in itself but is supposed to enhance human welfare, which in turn is heavily dependent on climatic conditions. Consistency between trade and climate policies must entail the internalization of environmental costs, including of greenhouse gas emissions. Trade is important because environmental technologies and know-how are generated primarily in developed countries and transferred to developing countries mainly through embodied technologies in imported goods and services, FDI or licensing.

Border adjustment measures have been shown to be relatively ineffective and counterproductive

Given the lack of detail in, and the status of, the Copenhagen Accord,[18] some countries that are prime movers in the field of greenhouse gas mitigation may try

17 The informational requirements are high because the standard for establishing the existence of transfer pricing is the OECD "arm's-length principle", which treats the subsidiaries engaged in trade in goods and services as if they were separate companies. Disentangling the complications associated with the issue of price among subsidiaries requires both information about transactions among hypothetically independent companies and the kind of highly specialized international tax expertise that is practically absent in developing countries. Developing countries could, instead, consider using the simpler approach of setting reasonably wide price range benchmarks (say, within the 80th percentile range of historically observed prices) beyond which the price of an international transaction would be considered a transfer price.

18 See document FCCC/CP/2009/11/Add.1, decision 2/CP.15.

to neutralize the competitive disadvantage that their industries would face at home if they applied unilateral climate policies, for instance, through border adjustment measures (BAMs) such as duties on imports from countries not undertaking comparable mitigation efforts based on carbon-content of products or production methods, or through climate-related standards (Opschoor, 2010). It has been shown (Pew Center on Global Climate Change, 2009) that unilateral border adjustment measures might be relatively ineffective (in terms of their emission reduction effects) and, in fact, counterproductive in terms of achieving climate objectives (owing, for example, to their impacts on the negotiation environment).

Process and production methods should not be used as grounds for the application of trade-related environmental measures

Additionally, border adjustment measures could put developing countries at a disadvantage, as those countries do not have the technologies required to engage in production with higher carbon efficiency. As with other issues, there is a risk that climate objectives would be translated into, or used as the basis for, protectionism. Generally, process and production methods (PPMs) should not be used as grounds for the application of trade-related environmental measures. If they were so used, it would become necessary to address more generally the unresolved issue of how to treat them (United Nations, 2009a).

Because subsidies are and will continue to be used to support the development of alternative energies, the issue of determining how to handle those subsidies under the rules of the World Trade Organization will also have to be dealt with. The issue would be addressed at least in part by having schemes in place for compensating incremental costs of any cleaner or leaner technology in developing countries.

Technology transfer should be a priority

Multilateral trading rules are also posing hurdles to transfers of technologies to developing countries, thereby making the TRIPS Agreement an area of continued controversy (United Nations, 2009a). It has been argued that "commodified knowledge, protected by private property rights" reduces economies' dynamic efficiency, as this leads to underutilization of knowledge and a slowdown of innovation (Stiglitz, 2006). Resolution of this issue is particularly crucial if those technologies are to be effective against the danger of climate change. In the World Trade Organization system, there are several flexibilities available within the framework of the TRIPS Agreement such as compulsory licences, exceptions to patent rights, regulation of voluntary licences, and strict application of patentability criteria. However, although these measures may enable access to technologies to a certain extent, they are usually more difficult to operationalize in developing countries and their use would be limited to specific (mostly emergency and humanitarian) circumstances.

Exclusion of critical sectors from patenting, and a global technology pool for climate change, merit serious consideration

Options such as allowing developing countries to exclude critical sectors from patenting, and establishing a global technology pool for climate change, merit serious consideration, as these options would provide certainty and predictability in accessing technologies and further enable much-needed research and development for local adaptation and diffusion, which would further reduce the cost of the technologies. In addition, modalities for access to publicly funded technologies by developing-country firms need to be explored.

Coherence with the financial architecture

Maintaining a competitive exchange rate has been a common strategy in most developing countries that successfully diversified exports and moved onto a path of sustained economic growth. However, this policy target may be in jeopardy within a context of capital flow volatility. Private international asset flows are by now the most decisive determinants of foreign-exchange rates for most economies. Successful exporters also tend to attract higher private capital inflows since these tend to move in pro-cyclical fashion.[19] This puts upward pressure on real exchange rates which in turn would lead to conflict with trade promotion objectives. Countries also facing domestic inflationary pressures often have opted to allow the exchange rate to appreciate under such circumstances. Such inflation targeting often undermines export competitiveness. During downward cycles in international capital flows, pressures towards currency depreciation would emerge. Governments often try to limit the degree of exchange-rate devaluation by letting macroeconomic stability targets prevail, which then may jeopardize trade policy objectives.[20]

Increased capability in managing the capital account is critical

Restructuring the international financial system so that it sustains exchange-rate values consistent with real sector growth is imperative. To restore coherence between the trade and financial policy arenas, increased capability in managing the capital account, particularly the capacity to control the volume, maturity and currencies of inflows, is critical. Promoting strengthened regional cooperation in monetary and financial matters, particularly to the extent of enhancing intraregional trade, may also be a feasible alternative and could facilitate global cooperation. Both these solutions would bring about greater coherence between the international trading and financial systems to the point where they reinforced, rather than undermined and destabilized, each other.

The Bretton Woods institutions should focus more on their areas of competency

The Bretton Woods institutions have been active in both trade and financial liberalization. The cornerstone of the policy coherence behind these efforts had been the proposition that international private financial markets are the best judge of national economic policies. The integrity of this proposition was shattered with the outbreak of the global crisis in the developed-country financial markets, which has led to many suggestions that the focus of the operations of these institutions should be sharpened and concentrated more on their areas of competence—effective global payments and reserve mechanisms in the case of the International Monetary Fund (IMF) and development project finance in the case of the World Bank—and that they should leave to national policymakers and the outcomes of international negotiations the determination of the overall structure of developing-country trade regimes.

The current Doha Round involves plurilateral-type negotiations on specific services sectors, including financial services. In the financial services group, developed countries and their financial institutions are pressing a group of developing countries to open up their financial services markets by allowing the establishment of foreign financial institutions (under Mode 3) and by allowing freedom of cross-border financial flows, instruments and services (under Modes 1 and 2). If negotiations conclude along the proposed lines, the developing countries could be subject to the type of financial liberalization that would reduce the regulatory capacity they need to minimize financial vulnerability.

---

19 This dynamic was particularly applicable to South-East Asia before the 1997 financial crisis (Montes, 1998) but it also applies to other countries that were seen as having "sound" macroeconomic policies, such as Mexico before its 1994 crisis and Argentina before its 1999 crisis. Recently, the International Monetary Fund (see Ostry and others, 2010) brought attention to this seeming paradox.

20 Currency devaluation tends to increase domestic inflationary pressures and may lead to a widening of budget deficits, especially in a context where Governments have large outstanding external debts.

Policy coherence in matters of international labour mobility

Labour migration could enhance global growth and welfare

The trend among World Trade Organization disciplines towards encompassing services has led to the creation of areas such as "consumption abroad" (tourism, for example, comprises services consumed abroad) and "movement of natural persons" (referring to the migration of people for the purpose of working abroad temporarily). As noted in chapter II, population ageing trends raise the possibility that increasing the flow of the younger workers to rich countries could help reduce poverty in developing countries. The potential of labour migration to enhance global growth and welfare is associated, by some, with the fact that wage differentials across countries of the world remain very high.

As Rodrik (2002) observes, after several decades of liberalization, price differentials of goods, services and capital across countries of the world have narrowed significantly. As a result, the welfare effects of the liberalization of labour flows currently have the potential to be 25 times greater than the further liberalization of flows of goods, services and capital. However, as Rodrik's finding is based on a back-of-the-envelope calculation, studies of greater rigour are necessary to determine more satisfactorily the relative benefits to be derived from further liberalization along different dimensions.

Issues of labour migration might be better addressed in a specialized global forum

It is unlikely, however, that much progress will be made in liberalizing labour movements within the context of the multilateral trade regime. Given the complexity of the matter, the issue of the movements of workers, and people in general, might be better addressed in a global forum capable of dealing more broadly with issues of migration and development.

As pointed out in chapter II, labour migration involves not just the question of filling vacant jobs in developed countries but also the matter of the difficult social adjustments required in receiving and sending countries. In the case of the receiving countries, it must be recognized that temporary labour migration involves the movement of (natural) persons, which often requires addressing issues of family and other social support structures. Moreover, the setting of labour migration policies will require difficult political decisions regarding migrants' access to social services, including health, education, pensions and unemployment benefits. Finally, receiving societies must often wrestle with and manage the social and cultural dissimilarities between labour migrants and the long-term resident population.

Unless the global community is content to retain the present untidy and often inhumane migration modalities, these difficult issues should be addressed, most preferably under a specialized international migration regime equipped to deal with the complex contractual, coordination and social mechanisms involved.

Coherence between the multilateral and regional trading systems

Bilateral agreements are intrinsically more difficult to evaluate than either multilateral or unilateral liberalizations because of their second-best nature, that is, the net benefits tend to be uncertain and difficult to assess (Rollo, 2007). Economic analysis deals with this difficulty by utilizing concepts of trade creation and trade diversion; but measurement of these effects, even for relatively simple trade barriers such as tariffs, is not always straightforward and requires a relatively specialized set of economic analytical skills. This problem of measurement is further complicated by the fact that, increasingly, regional trade agreements extend their compass beyond the simple dismantling of border barriers to trade in goods. As mentioned before, such agreements now include within their purview services and other elements of deep integration for which data are poorer, analytical tools are less developed and the domestic legal implications of any consensus are complex and potentially substantial.

The difficulty with World Trade Organization rules on regional agreements is that they apply ex post

Given that, historically, preferential integration has been a major policy instrument of the World Trade Organization membership—most notably of the members of EU and the parties to the North American Free Trade Agreement (NAFTA)—and that the notifications of preferential agreements have increased since the formation of the World Trade Organization[21]—it is not surprising that negotiations on procedures and disciplines for regional trade agreements were included in the Doha mandate. The new transparency mechanism agreed (albeit provisionally) in December 2006 is the first product of those negotiations. The difficulty with World Trade Organization rules on regional trade agreements is, however, that they apply ex post, after countries have already ratified their commitments, at which point little can be done to establish more development-oriented agreements. Even the transparency mechanism asks only that countries engaged in new negotiations on regional trade agreements endeavour to notify the WTO thereof and of the provisions of any signed agreement when they are made public.

As the number of these agreements is likely to keep increasing, especially while the Doha negotiations remain stalled, fostering developing countries' awareness of exactly what they are signing and the consequences thereof is of fundamental importance. Negotiators of regional trade agreements face important challenges, because of the second-best nature of these arrangements. The bureaucratic stresses for developed countries with relatively well-resourced administrations can be substantial. For administrations in developing countries, where human capital is often the binding constraint, the resource demands of negotiating one or more regional trade agreements alongside multilateral and unilateral trade-related policymaking are potentially much greater. This could lead to serious misunderstandings about the implications, in particular for economic and social development, of specific policy changes demanded by an agreement. The situation is further complicated by the possibility that a regional trade agreement negotiated by a given country could differ markedly from other regional trade agreements under negotiation or in operation by or in that country. Such interactions could mask possibly serious economic and developmental costs.

An advisory centre on regional agreements could be part of a solution

Given the factors of international negative spillovers from regional trade agreements and asymmetric information, there is a case to be made for public provision of the needed analytical frameworks free or at low cost to developing countries. An interesting proposal that could be considered is that for the creation of a new international organization, an advisory centre on RTAs (ACORTA), closely modelled on the Advisory Centre on WTO Law (ACWL) set up to help developing countries involved in trade disputes (Rollo, 2007).

Rebalancing World Trade Organization processes

Expanding developing-country participation in trade rule-making, even in the World Trade Organization where countries are formally equal, is a necessary step in reforming

21 The database on World Trade Organization notifications is available from http://www.wto.org/english/tratop_e/region_e/region_e.htm.

the trade system so as to enable it to support development. There are two main sources of inequality: (a) differential access to information regarding which features of an agreement will benefit one's country; and (b) differential power to influence the outcome of negotiations (Toye, 2010). Countries whose resources are inadequate need assistance; but trade-related technical assistance continues to be inadequate and needs further expansion.

Enforcement mechanisms for trade commitments have to be made more equitable. Unfortunately, it is still true that, in this regard, serious deficiencies remain at every stage of the World Trade Organization dispute settlement process, from inception through judgement and granting remedy to enforcement (Toye, 2010). These deficiencies arise from the interaction of the standard features of a legal process—its cost, absorption of time and uncertainty of outcome—with the inadequacies of the international legal machinery and the huge inequalities of wealth and power that currently exist between nations. Given the substantial cost of bringing a case before the World Trade Organization, in terms of legal and diplomatic person time, poor countries are deterred disproportionately from engaging in a dispute. Poor Governments will also be disproportionately deterred from bringing a case to the dispute settlement mechanism by the prospect of antagonizing more powerful countries, on which they depend in many areas not connected with trade, such as foreign assistance.

Enforcement mechanisms for trade commitments have to be made more equitable

The fact that by convention, the loser pays no compensation for a violation (after a process that can still take over two years to complete) bears more heavily on poor States than on rich ones. There is no centralized sanction for a country that does not take measures to comply with its World Trade Organization obligations. The only sanction is retaliation. Since all economic sanctions are costly to the initiator, a poor country has a much more limited ability than a rich one to impose a sanction. Thus, even if developed and developing countries violate World Trade Organization rules to the same extent, and dispute panels render perfect formal justice, developing countries will win fewer cases than they lose, and will be less sure of a remedy in the cases that they do win.

When a country does not take measures to comply with its World Trade Organization obligations, the only sanction is retaliation

Toye (2010) argues that it should be possible to tilt the system in ways that counteract its existing biases. In domestic litigation, legal aid is used to give the poor better access to costly justice; the injured party is awarded its costs by the court; and centrally organized sanctions prevent it from having to bear all the costs of punishing the violator. Progress along these lines could be made in the international sphere as well, given sufficient imagination and willingness to cooperate. An interesting example is the ILEAP initiative (International Lawyers and Economists against Poverty), a not-for-profit non-governmental initiative to provide timely, responsive and practical legal and economic expertise to developing countries so as to assist them in achieving trade-related development and poverty reduction.

The use of legal aid should be considered in order to give poor countries better access to trade remedies

The key problem is the non-existence in the international sphere of a central sanctioning mechanism. Although there is a mechanism in place through which countries band together in pursuing a dispute, this still imposes heavy costs of coordination on poor countries and does not guarantee attention to the kind of disputes that are particular to very small economies. Still, an improved dispute settlement mechanism in the World Trade Organization would be capable of furthering the interests of the developing countries.

Conclusions

Rebalancing the trade system through a strengthening of the pillar that supports "differentiated" responsibilities, after decades of emphasizing the pillar that supports the "common" ones, is critical to ensuring that trade can play a positive developmental role. Greater coherence between trade policies and the international trade regime, on the one hand, and sustainable development, on the other, requires new flexibilities in the multilateral regime to enable the marking out of a domestic policy space for:

- Counter-cyclical policies designed to stabilize growth and diversify exports
- The development of economic sectors through interventions that are truly selective (not across the board), temporary (not open-ended) and performance-related (not unconditional) and consonant with the decent work and environmental objectives.

Creating these capabilities will entail reducing the inconsistencies subsisting among the areas of trade, finance and macroeconomic policy coordination at the international level. Overcoming such inconsistencies will require strengthening of domestic capacity in managing capital inflows; reforms of the international financial architecture that will reduce capital flow and exchange-rate volatility; and an alignment of implicit financial rule-setting through the General Agreement on Trade in Services with a new framework for international financial regulation. These issues are taken up in chapter V.

Greater policy coherence can be further achieved by rationalizing the international trade agenda which has expanded its scope to include other areas such as intellectual property, international finance and labour services. Inasmuch as the World Trade Organization appears at present to be overseeing issues in areas for which there are missing global regimes, its agenda is overloaded. It might therefore be more effective to address such issues through more specialized agencies. There are missing or weak regimes of global governance not only for financial services, migration, and intellectual property but also for:

- International competition policy and oversight over the operations and impact of global value chains and transnational corporations
- Tax coordination, exchange of information and cooperation in the collection of tax debt
- Climate change, where a regime is needed that directs and expands cooperation in aid, trade, investment and technology

Greater coherence in the global trading regime will also require strengthening multilateral disciplines over regional trade agreements, bilateral trade agreements and investment agreements. Such coherence can be achieved fairly only if, at the same time, equity in the negotiation processes and enforcement of World Trade Organization rules are improved, particularly through providing developing countries with the necessary resources to participate more actively and more fully in international trade rule-making.

Chapter V
Reforming the international financial architecture

Summary

- Instead of increasing investment and growth, capital and financial market liberalization had the opposite effect by increasing volatility and uncertainty, which negatively impacted the long-term investment that is critical for structural transformation and development.
- The emergence of global imbalances and the consequent global economic crisis are key symptoms of financial system incoherence. Rebuilding and reforming the global financial system are necessary coherence with national investment and poverty reduction imperatives is to be achieved.
- Reforming global rules in order to re-establish the capacity of public authorities both globally and nationally to curb excessive private risk-taking and ensure that finance serves the real sector, instead of the other way around, is an urgent priority. Because national authorities are the first line of defence against financial market volatility, their capacities for controlling volatile capital flows must be backed by international institutions.
- It is necessary to end the competition over foreign investment using regulatory and tax policies that characterized individual country policies in the past three decades. Competition practised through other means must be backstopped with well-coordinated macroeconomic and financial regulatory mechanisms.

Introduction

There is general agreement that weaknesses in the system of international financial cooperation played a key role in the current global economic crisis. These weaknesses also played a role in the fuel and food crises.

International financial system weaknesses played a key role in the current crisis

Ensuring that developing countries are able to increase their rate of investment continues to be as big a challenge today, perhaps, as it was in the early days of development thinking. During the 1980s and 1990s, structural adjustment programmes coupled with the liberalization of private capital flows had been expected to increase the rate of investment in developing countries. Instead, the rate of fixed investment stagnated in most parts of the world, despite a significantly higher level of international financial flows (see figure V.1). As will be discussed below, a qualitative improvement must accompany a quantitative increase in investment if sustainable development objectives are to be met; this will require an investment regime that is capable of underpinning private risk-taking by virtue of having sufficient stability and sufficient signalling from States as regards general directions.

Greater capital mobility made macroeconomic policy making more difficult

Greater capital mobility has given developing countries ostensibly greater access to financial resources, but owing to the volatile and boom-bust pattern of financial flows in deregulated markets, it has also made macroeconomic policy management more challenging.

Figure V.1
Rapid financial growth but stagnant fixed investment, 1970-2009

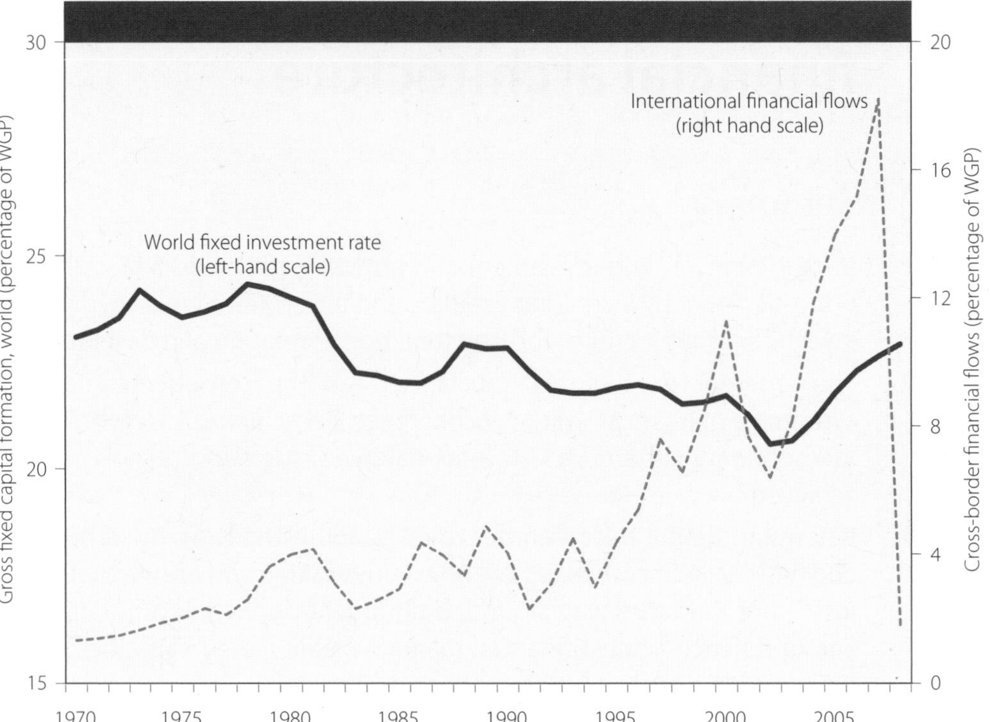

Source: UN/DESA, based on United Nations Statistics Division, National Accounts Main Aggregates Database; and International Monetary Fund, *International Financial Statistics*.

Note: Fixed investment refers to the world total of gross fixed capital formation, according to definitions used in national accounts. Financial flows are measured as the sum of changes in cross-border debt security assets, direct investment abroad, changes in other cross-border investment assets, and net errors and omissions, according to definitions used in balance-of-payments statistics.

Capital mobility has also stimulated regulatory and tax competition among public authorities. Before the global financial crisis, competition associated with expanding financial centres had become a race to deregulate finance—a race that, in the end, had no winners.

In today's world of increased economic and political interdependence, achieving broad-based, rapid and sustained growth in incomes and employment involves policy challenges that are even more complex than those of the past. The fact that pension funds, for example, are now invested internationally has led to the creation of a channel through which a weakness in one financial market can be transmitted to other financial centres and to the real sector.

The gaps and traps left by financial liberalization

Global financial deregulation placed too much confidence in the power of financial markets to self-regulate

The past several decades have seen a push towards global financial deregulation based on a misplaced confidence in the power of financial markets to self-regulate, despite the evidence derived from earlier crises that deregulated financial markets are prone to crises and instability. In developed markets, policymakers seemingly lacked the will to develop a new regulatory framework to deal with significant changes in risk-taking stemming from the growth of credit default swaps, securitizations and other derivative products. To the contrary, some of the crucial mechanisms to protect the financial system that had been put into place in the aftermath of the Great Depression were dismantled. Regulatory and tax competition among expanding financial centres led to a race to the bottom, compounding the problem. In this environment, the "shadow banking system" outside the regulatory umbrella grew enormously, introducing significant risks into the global financial system.

In developing countries, the counterpart of this phenomenon was the deregulation of domestic financial and capital markets, often undertaken as part of structural adjustment programmes. In particular, countries, experiencing marked pressure from the international community, removed capital controls on external private capital flows in an attempt to increase the rate of inflows to support domestic investment. This was part of the decades-long evolution to place financial markets at the centre of economic decisions, yoking economic policy coherence to the notion that whatever projects financial markets deigned to finance would be in line with strong growth and development. However, instead of attracting long-term sustainable investment to achieve structural transformation for development, the move to open capital markets led to short-term inflows and increased volatility, while limiting the macroeconomic policy space necessary for responding to the boom-and-bust behaviour of capital flows.

Structural adjustment programmes often required the deregulation of domestic financial and capital markets

Following the Latin American and Asian crises of the 1990s, many emerging and developing countries used the boom period 2003-2007 to strengthen their internal and external balance sheets to better avoid or manage crises. As part of this strategy, public authorities accelerated their purchases of liquid low-earning developed-country financial assets as a form of self-insurance. This policy was also congenial to countries that had robust export sectors and were concerned with protecting international competitiveness. The end result was a flow of financing from developing countries to developed economies and an increase in global risk, as the accumulation of reserves contributed to growing imbalances, with the potential to destabilize the global economy.

During the boom in 2003-2007, many developing countries attempted to carve out policy space by strengthening balance sheets

Financial market crises

The period of global financial deregulation, which, arguably, started in the 1980s, was characterized by a series of market crises. The savings and loan crisis in the United States of America in the late 1980s was followed by the Mexican "tequila" crisis in 1994, the Asian financial crisis in 1997-1998, payments and currency crises in the Russian Federation, Brazil, Turkey and Argentina between 1998 and 2001 and the bursting of the "dot-com" bubble in United States financial markets in 2000. As shown in figure V.2, the banking crises of the early 1900s and the recent wave exhibited similar periodic patterns, marked by severe real-sector collapses following banking sector crashes.[1]

The period of global financial deregulation was characterized by a series of market crises

The frequency of crises subsided after the 1930s, once regulations devised to limit runs on banks and protect depositors had been put into place, and increased again only in the deregulatory period of the 1980s (see table V.1). It should be noted that the decades between the spikes were the heyday of the global Bretton Woods capital regime, a period of stable and relatively high growth.

Although the recent global crisis was unique in terms of its size and systemic reach, compared with other post-1930s crises, it still resembled them. Those crises were generally characterized by bubbles induced by excess liquidity which subsequently burst when the liquidity was withdrawn; similarly, the period of the mid-2000s build-up to the recent crisis was one of massive global liquidity. Growing global imbalances, with developing countries saving huge amounts in the form of dollar reserves, allowed the United States to borrow cheaply from abroad, keeping long-term interest rates low and increasing leverage in the system (United Nations, 2006b).

1 Reinhart and Rogoff (2008) document the international banking and financial crises that occurred over eight centuries.

Figure V.2
Proportion of countries[a] in the world economy with banking crises, 1900-2008

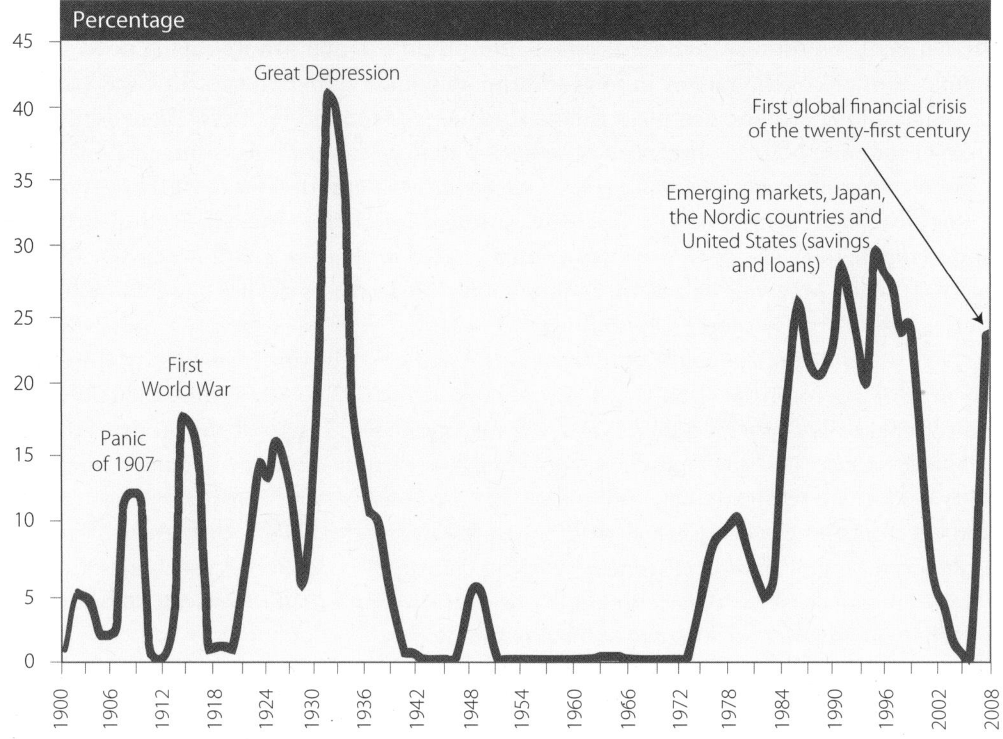

Source: Reinhart and Rogoff, 2008, figure 1.

Note: The figure presents the (three-year moving averages of the) proportion of countries with banking crises weighted by their economic size. Three sets of GDP weights have been used: 1913 weights for the period 1800-1913; 1990 for the period 1914-1990; and 2003 weights for the period 1991-2006. For the period 2007-2008, Austria, Belgium, Germany, Hungary, Japan, the Netherlands, Spain, the United Kingdom of Great Britain and Northern Ireland and the United States of America are included as crisis-ridden countries.

a Countries weighted by their share of world income.

Table V.1:
Frequency of banking crises

	Developed countries	*Developing countries*
1947-1979	3	17
1980-2007	17	127

Source: UN/DESA, based on data in Reinhart and Rogoff (2008), table A.3.

Contrary to the original presumption, the majority of the inflows went to finance consumption and real estate bubbles

In the emerging market crises, excess liquidity became manifest through large international capital flows which were pro-cyclical in nature, increasing during boom periods and quickly turning into outflows during economic contractions. During the boom periods, domestic agents took advantage of the inflows by borrowing relatively cheaply, often in the form of foreign currency loans. Contrary to the original assumption that capital market liberalization would increase long-term investment in poor countries, the majority of the inflows (which were generally short-term in nature) went to finance consumption and real estate bubbles, which burst when the inflows turned into outflows. The capital outflows often led to a devaluation of the domestic currency and a spike in domestic interest rates, leading to widespread defaults (including some sovereign defaults), banking crises, lost wealth and increased poverty, as discussed in chapter II. Instead of increasing investment, capital and financial market liberalization had the opposite effect of increasing volatility and uncertainty, which negatively impact long-term investment.

Lower developing-country investment rates

Financial liberalization had been expected to help engineer a revival of investment rates

The start of global financial liberalization in the early 1980s coincided with the developing-country debt crises, which saw severe drops in investment rates in Latin America and Africa. Financial liberalization had been expected to help engineer a revival of investment rates. The performance, however, did not match the expectation. As figures V.3 and V.4 show, real investment in countries with open capital markets either stagnated or fell (as in Latin America) or ratcheted up during boom periods only to collapse during busts (as in Asia). In Latin America and the Caribbean, middle-income countries experienced rates of investment in fixed capital that were temporarily higher than world averages during the debt boom precipitated by the private bank recycling of petrodollars in the 1970s, but that fell below this rate during the debt crisis and never exceeded the world average again (despite the high level of capital inflows during the 1990s) (see figure V.3). In contrast, the performance of lower-income developing countries, which experienced much smaller levels of financial inflows, showed slow but steadier improvements relative to world rates (as well as to those of middle-income countries). In the context of open capital accounts, the decision of Latin American countries to pursue macroeconomic stability as indicated by their lower inflation and reduced fiscal deficits led to more volatile real economic growth rates (see box V.1).

Middle income East Asian economies experienced a spike in investment in the mid-1990s

Asia's lower middle income developing countries, many of which maintained some form of capital controls throughout the period (such as China and India), achieved investment rates in the 1970s and 1980s that were higher than those of the world as a whole and managed to sustain these rates or raise them further in the 1990s and early

Figure V.3
Fixed investment rates, world and Latin America and the Caribbean, 1971-2007

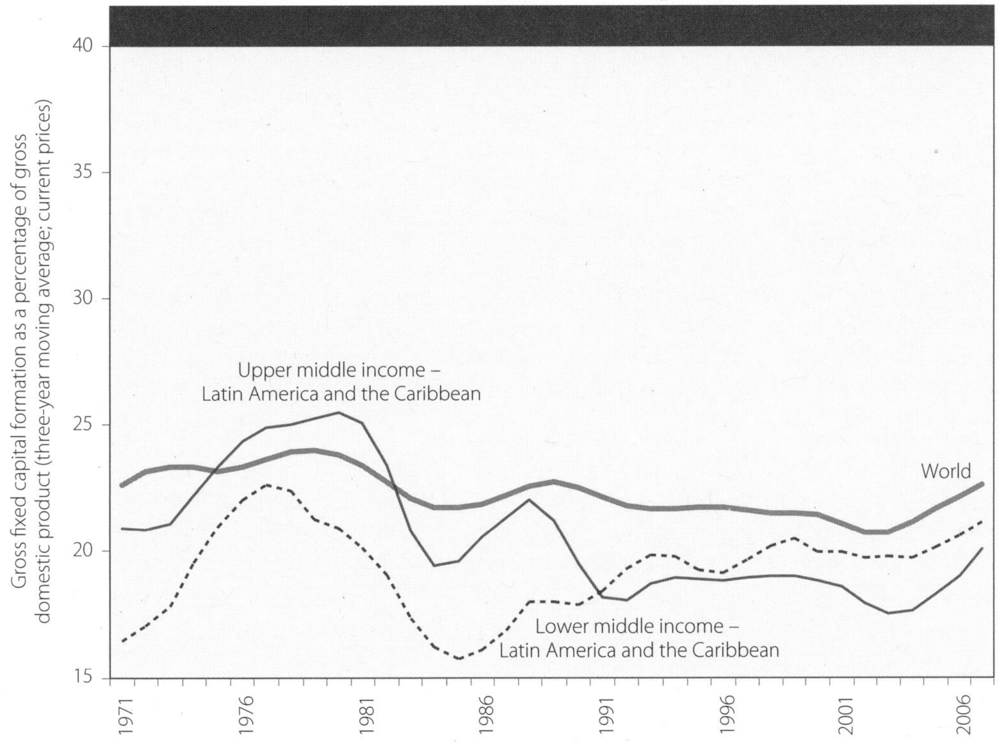

Source: UN/DESA.

Figure V.4
Fixed investment rates, world and Asia and the Pacific, 1971-2007

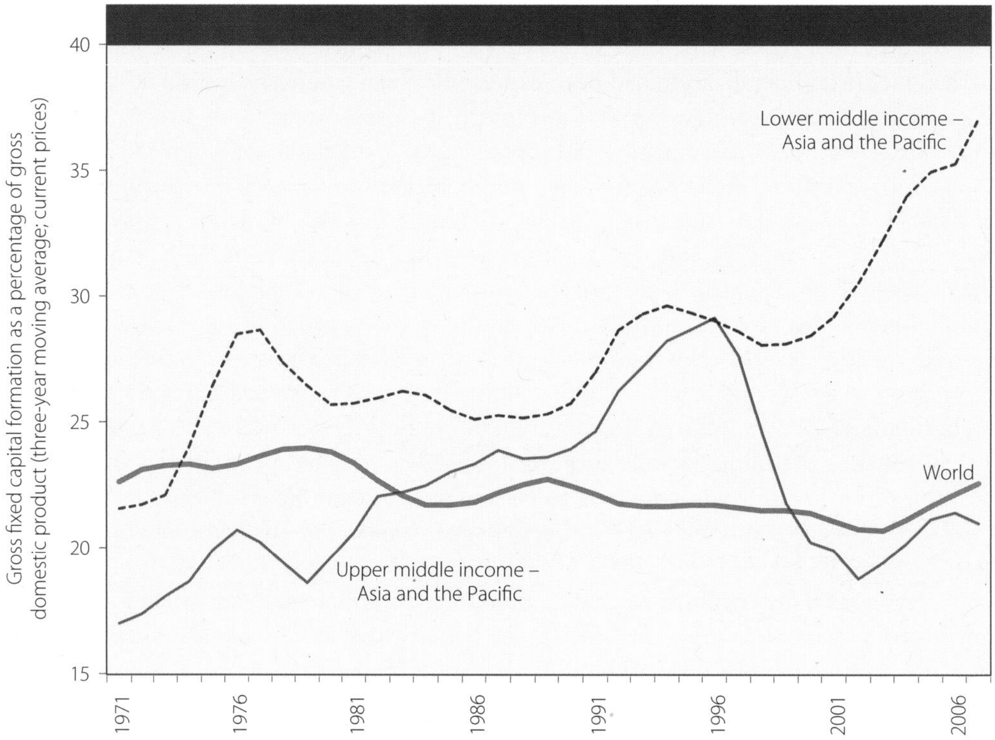

Source: UN/DESA.

Box V.1

Regional financial cooperation in Asia and Latin America

Debates on reforms of the international financial architecture often pay too little attention to the possible role of regional arrangements in macroeconomic policy coordination and the development of regional institutions able to perform the functions traditionally assigned to the international financial organizations. There are nevertheless a number of supporting arguments in favour of regional cooperation in macroeconomic and financial areas, since the current globalization process is also one of "open regionalism"; and increased regional interdependence requires a certain degree of coordination and mutual surveillance of macroeconomic policies. The regional nature of the severe currency crises of the 1990s created a strong stimulus for countries to engage in regional cooperation in order to elaborate commonly agreed targets and mutual surveillance mechanisms and provide financial assistance to each other in order to avoid the contagion effects of a financial crisis. There are also barriers to such cooperation, however, such as the inadequate capacity of countries to provide the necessary financial services, the lack of a proper institutional framework and the possibility of inequitable distribution of the benefits of such cooperation.

Within a context where financial crises tend to be regional, regional financial cooperation can play a relevant role that is complementary to that of new global mechanisms for managing the world economy. The large currency and financial crises in emerging market economies since the 1990s have had important regional dimensions. Countries should have a vested interest in helping to put out a fire in neighbouring countries—before it spreads to them. Pooling foreign-exchange reserves regionally will likely also reduce costs to individual countries, just as universal health insurance reduces costs to individuals. After the East Asian crisis, Japan had proposed the creation of an Asian monetary fund, but this proposal—while well received in the region—was not pursued after objections were presented from outside the region. The collective liquidity support provided under the Chiang Mai Initiative, involving bilateral currency swap arrangements among the Association of Southeast Asian Nations (ASEAN) member countries plus China, Japan and the Republic of Korea,

Box V.1 (cont'd)

was converted to a multilateral regional arrangement in January 2010 (United Nations, Economic and Social Commission for Asia and the Pacific, 2010); the effectiveness of the Chiang Mai Initiative in dealing with financial crises is still to be tested. This regional framework is complementary to the International Monetary Fund (IMF) global facilities and does not negate the need for a crisis prevention framework for IMF itself.

In Latin America and the Caribbean, apart from the Inter-American Development Bank, the main subregional financial institutions include the Latin American Reserve Fund (FLAR) established in 1978 and several development banks, including the (Central American Bank for Economic Integration (BCIE), in operation since 1961; the Andean Development Corporation (CAF), in operation since 1970; the Caribbean Development Bank (CDB), in operation since 1969; and the Latin American Integration Association (ALADI), established in 1980. In spite of increased financial integration among the region's countries, mutual support for balance-of-payments financing remains extremely weak and the only viable institution in the area of liquidity financing is the Latin American Reserve Fund. The scope of the Fund's operation is limited, however, although it did provide counter-cyclical financing during several crisis episodes in the region, (see figure; and United Nations, Economic Commission for Latin America and the Caribbean, 2010). The fact that Mexico is not a member of the Fund did not contribute to a resolution of the 1994 tequila crisis.

Annual credits granted by the Latin American Reserve Fund (FLAR) for balance-of-payments support and liquidity provisioning, 1980-2009

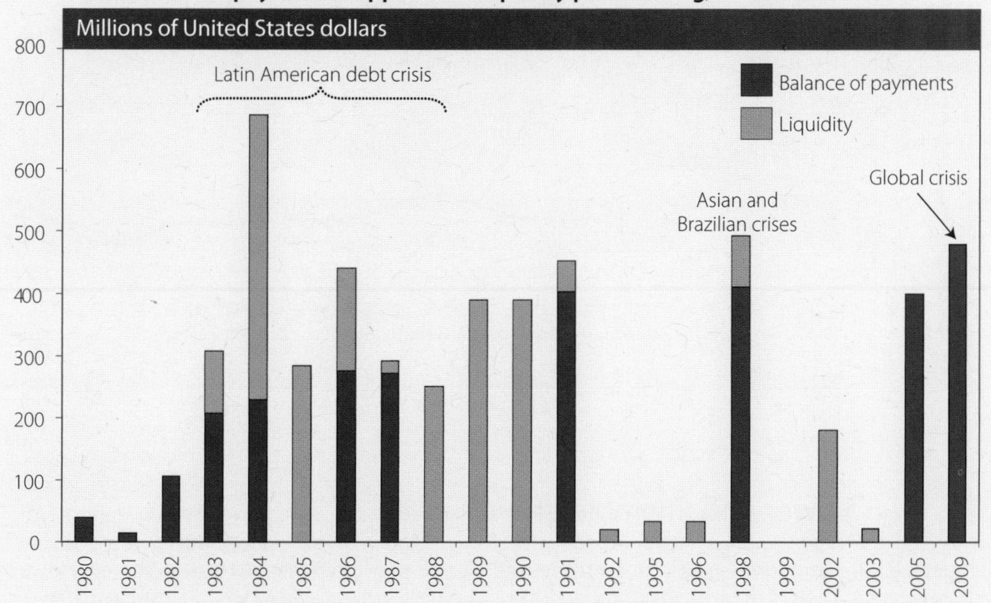

Source: United Nations, Economic Commission for Latin America and the Caribbean (2010), figure 8.

The implications of regional financial cooperation for the international financial system will vary from region to region. Efforts to deepen and expand regional monetary cooperation may be viewed as policy responses that are being driven by the dilemmas spawned by increased trade linkages within the region, as had been the case earlier in Europe, and by the systemic uncertainties created by the present global financial payments system. As part of broader reforms of the international financial architecture, these regional efforts have the potential to bolster the international system's capacity to consult and coordinate on collective issues and assist in their implementation. A more active use of regional financial arrangements is desirable as a complement to the role of IMF. More intensive macroeconomic policy dialogue and stronger forms of regional surveillance and policy consultations could internalize, at least in part, the externalities that national macroeconomic policies impose on regional partners. Thus, while IMF should play a central role in policy coordination at the global level, there is much room for regional and subregional processes of a similar nature. In a similar vein, while regional and international contagion effects in financial markets and management of the main balance-of-payments crises should be the main concern of IMF, regional funds could constitute effective rescue mechanisms for smaller and more local financial crises.

2000s (figure V.3). Middle-income countries in Asia and the Pacific (mainly in South-East Asia) experienced a spike in investment during the period of financial liberalization of the mid-1990s (during the Asian real estate bubble), but then suffered a steep drop in investment to below world rates (the drop began in 1997 during the financial crisis).

Africa's investment rates (figure V.5) had been higher than world average in the 1970s during the commodities boom, then fell below the world average in the era of liberalization and began to recover only during the 2000s commodity boom, which was brought to an end in 2008 by the global crisis.[2]

Figure V.5
Fixed investment rates, Africa, 1971-2007

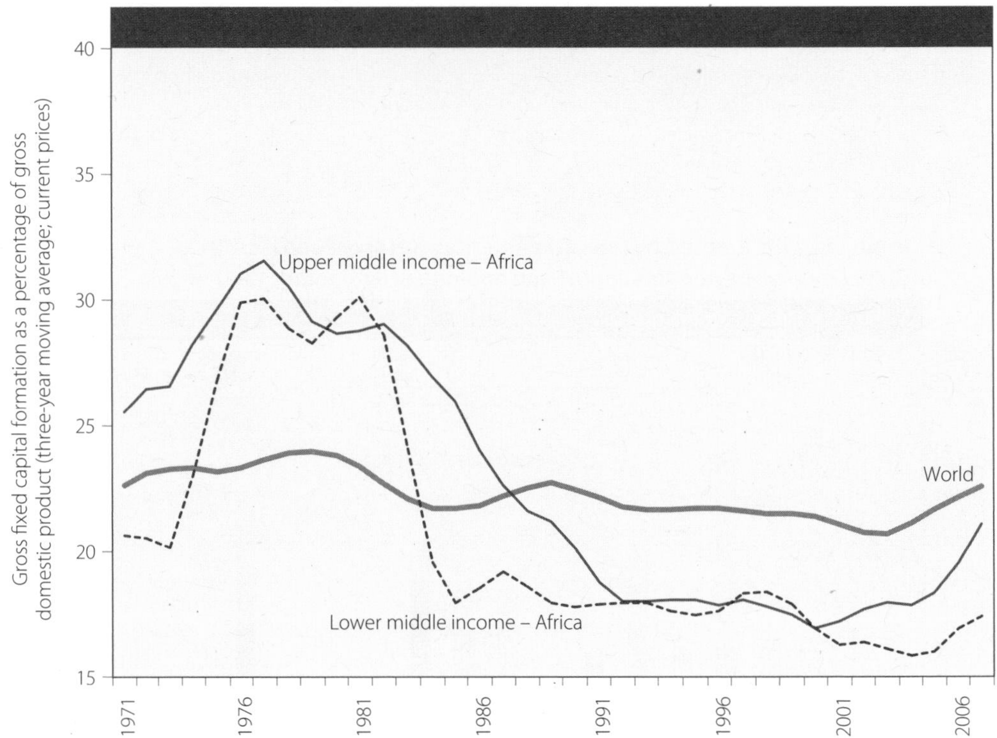

Source: UN/DESA.

Lower and unstable growth rates

The key channel of impact on long-term growth of private capital flow volatility is investment volatility

Fluctuations in capital markets are reflected in the pro-cyclical pattern of the cost of borrowing, the availability of financing, and maturities (Griffith-Jones and Ocampo, 2007). The result is short-term volatility and the short periods of interruption of financing observed during the crises in Mexico, Asia and the Russian Federation. More importantly, they also involve medium-term cycles and losses of real gross domestic product (GDP) growth, as the experience of the past four decades indicates. The key channel of impact on long-term growth of private capital flow volatility is investment volatility. Figure V.6

2 The investment rate is the product of many factors, not the least of which is output stability in the case of demand-constrained economies (Hailu and Weeks, 2009). Among Latin American middle-income countries, the demand constraint imposed by the debt-service treadmills in the 1980s had been critical. Commodity price fluctuations played an important role in economies of Africa (and thus global economic growth for those economies is critical under demand-constrained dynamics), as did the economic dislocations attendant on the profound shift in development strategy beginning in the 1980s.

Figure V.6
Growth of GDP and investment volatility among developing countries, 1971-2000

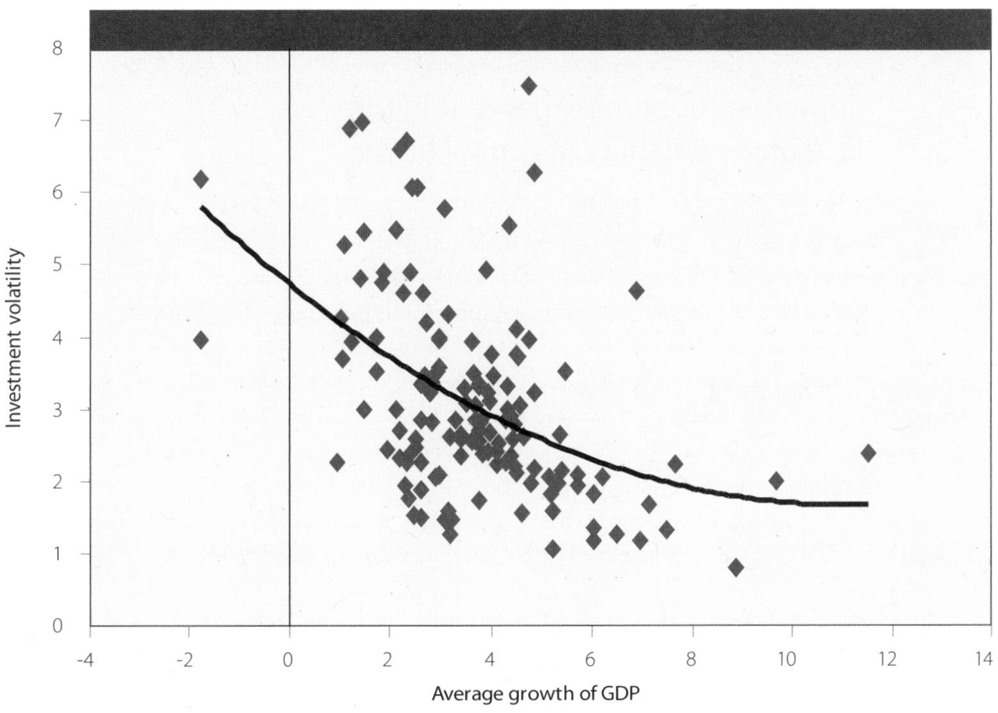

Source: United Nations (2008), chap. II, figure II.1.

Note: At constant prices of 2000 for the period 1971-2006.

Investment volatility is measured by the coefficient of variation (CV) of the annual growth rate of gross capital formation at 2000 prices in 1971-2006. The coefficient of variation is defined as the standard deviation divided by the mean for the period.

indicates a robust non-linear relationship between higher investment volatility and lower GDP growth. As discussed in greater detail in *World Economic and Social Survey 2008* (United Nations, 2008), a predictable macroeconomic environment is an essential component of a strong investment climate. A volatile business climate can increase uncertainty, making investors reluctant to expand capacity; this in turn can slow productivity growth, thereby increasing the potential for further uncertainty.

Volatility of international private financial flows

Capital regulations in the developed countries exacerbate pro-cyclical private flows

There are a host of factors that account for the short-term behaviour of international investors, including rational responses to uncertainty and risk in developing markets, implying that countries should increase transparency, take steps to reduce uncertainty and develop their local capital markets. Alternative explanations for the short-term nature of capital flows have to do with the pro-cyclicality of international finance, which is exacerbated by financial deregulation in developed countries (Stiglitz and others, 2006).[3] In addition, the compensation packages of bankers and investors provide them with incentives to engage in short-term behaviour and risk-taking. Investors, for example, who are usually hedge fund and mutual fund managers, are paid annually based on performance, thus limiting their

3 See Griffith-Jones and Ocampo (2007). These regulations encouraged ultimately unsustainable short-term lending to East Asian countries which had to be intermediated in the domestic financial sector in the lead-up to the region's 1997 financial crisis (Montes, 1998). The explosion of short-term lending followed the region's capital-account liberalization in the early 1990s, a trend promoted by Bretton Woods staff. See, for example, Claessens and Glaessner (1998), Claessens and Jensen, eds. (2000), Caprio and Honohan (2001) and Honohan (2004).

time-horizon to one year.[4] The implication is that reforms made to international capital requirements and compensation packages should also help to reduce the pro-cyclicality and volatility of international capital flows.

Capital-account management in the face of the volatility of capital flows

During the Asian crisis, many countries were pressured by IMF to tighten fiscal deficits that were already at prudent levels

Managing the macroeconomic volatility induced by private financial flows has become a key challenge for countries that have opened their capital markets. It is difficult for policymakers to loosen monetary policy during a crisis, especially when the economy is characterized by currency mismatches. When the currency devalues, foreign currency liabilities rise relative to domestic currency assets, which has the potential to cause widespread private sector and/or sovereign defaults. Thus, central banks are often forced to raise interest rates to stem capital outflows. This has a feedback effect with respect to fiscal deficits, especially in countries with large amounts of short-term debt, as the cost of borrowing increases. Often, credit dries up as foreigners refuse to lend, forcing policymakers to reduce spending during the downturn. During the Asian crisis, for example, many countries were pressured by the International Monetary Fund (IMF) to tighten fiscal deficits that were already at prudent levels and to raise interest rates.

Developing countries had moved ahead of the international financial institutions by self-insuring

The IMF first acknowledged the link between open capital markets and increased volatility several years later in a paper published by the Fund's research department (see Prasad and others, 2003). Capital market liberalization commitments continued nonetheless to be encouraged in practice and, as discussed in chapter IV, began to be included in bilateral trade agreements between the United States and other countries, even countries like Chile, which had previously used capital market restrictions effectively. Furthermore, Prasad and his colleagues later softened their earlier views. In 2006, the same authors (Kose and others, 2006) suggested that financial liberalization had "collateral benefits", such as increased financial market and institutional development, that were difficult to prove through econometric analyses of the data. This was maintained despite the fact that the majority of research showed that the volatility associated with capital market liberalization often had a destabilizing effect on both financial market and institutional development. In February 2010, IMF staff published an unofficial note in which they acknowledged that capital market interventions, such as taxes and other controls, are legitimate policy tools which can be used to reduce volatility associated with international capital flows (see Ostry and others, 2010). By that time, however, developing countries had already devised other means of coping with volatility; many, motivated in part by the desire to build self-insurance against future shocks, took advantage of the relative calm of the period 2003-2007 to accumulate reserves.

Countries with accumulated reserves had greater capacity for stimulus when the crisis struck

The strategy of building up international reserves—a costly one, particularly in terms of the opportunity cost of forgone domestic investment—paid off for economies whose reserves were ample when the 2008-2009 financial crisis struck. Such reserves were used to help moderate currency volatility, provide dollars to the local market, and create fiscal policy space. Reserves enabled seven East Asian economies, for example, to operationalize stimulus packages amounting to over 5 per cent of GDP.

4 Hedge fund managers receive annual performance fees. Mutual fund companies generally earn management fees based on asset size, but the growth of assets is usually tied to recent performance, and individual managers are generally compensated by the company based on the performance of their funds (see Sharma and Spiegel, forthcoming).

Reserve accumulation and ensuing global imbalances: a fallacy of composition?

International reserve accumulation by monetary authorities represented the most prominent policy shift

As indicated above, international reserve accumulation by monetary authorities constituted the most prominent policy shift effected in the wake of the Asian financial crises of the late 1990s. Reserve accumulation had risen to 11.7 per cent of world GDP by 2007, compared with 5.6 per cent of world GDP at the time of the Asian crisis (United Nations, 2009d). For developing and emerging countries, this policy served several purposes. For one thing, it provided self-insurance against sudden capital flow stoppages and in so doing, reduced the likelihood, should such stoppages occur, of a recourse to IMF pro-cyclical adjustment. (To avoid such a course was an objective pursued even by countries without strong export surpluses.) The policy also protected export-oriented stances by preventing exchange appreciation.

The obverse of this shift towards raising reserves was an increase in the demand for dollars and the provision of financing for widening current-account deficits incurred by the United States. There emerged a pattern of widening global imbalances including the unsustainable flow of investment resources from (paradoxically) poor countries as a group to the developed world (figure V.7).

The strategy of reserve accumulation to self-insure against volatile private capital movements is not sustainable because it suffers from a fallacy of composition. It would be sustainable only if there were at least one country large enough and willing to run consistent and ever larger current-account deficits. That the United States was providing the dominant reserve asset and had unlimited capability to do so meant that the process would continue long enough to become a global crisis.

Figure V.7
Global imbalances: net financial transfers to developing countries and economies in transition, 1997-2009

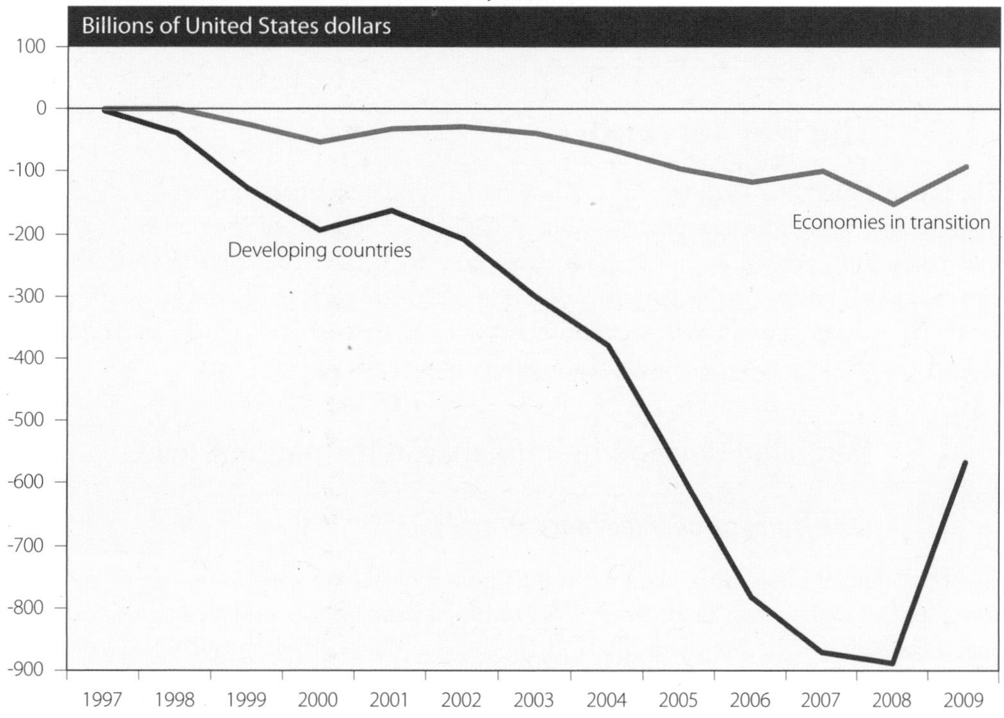

Source: UN/DESA.
a Estimate.

To reverse global imbalances, developing countries would need to decrease, not increase, self-insurance. Yet, the success of self-insurance as protection during the crisis suggests that it will probably become even more popular going forward. It is unlikely that countries will become less dependent on self-insurance without a real decline in the vulnerabilities associated with volatile international capital flows.

The crisis demonstrates that the accumulation of deficits by reserve currency countries is not self-correcting

The current system requires that the country (or countries) providing the global currency run deficits to ensure sufficient liquidity to support the growth of global output and trade. The 2008-2009 global economic crisis demonstrates that the accumulation of deficits by the reserve-currency country, sustained by other countries because of their national policy objectives, is not self-correcting and leads to a crisis of global proportions whose costs are incurred by many innocent parties. The extent to which the authorities in major industrialized economies feel compelled to accumulate assets, for reasons related either to exchange rates or to self-insurance, will determine in turn the magnitude of the inevitable deflationary impact of such accumulation on developing economies' macroeconomic performance.

There are several instances where externalities arising from United States monetary policy have gone on to impact the rest of the world

One of the drawbacks associated with making the dollar the reserve currency is that the global economy becomes tied to United States monetary policy, while the United States Federal Reserve manages monetary policy based only on the state of the United States economy. There are several instances where externalities arising from United States monetary policy have gone on to impact the rest of the world. Perhaps the most significant case occurred in the early 1980s, when the Federal Reserve raised interest rates to 20 per cent to combat stagflation in the United States, thereby making it extremely expensive for developing countries to refinance their debt, and ushering in the 1980s developing-country debt crisis. During the present crisis, the Federal Reserve has kept interest rates low. One of the externalities associated with this policy is a huge increase in global liquidity from the Federal Reserve (and the European Central Bank), which is finding its way back into developing-country markets, thus creating a new surge in capital flows and potentially fuelling new bubbles. As a result, there have been new calls across the developing world for capital market regulations.

The way forward

The international financial system is failing to deliver sufficient and stable development financing

The international financial system is failing to deliver development financing in sufficient volume and with sufficient predictability to facilitate the kind of long-term investment and risk-taking needed to enable poor economies to achieve structural transformation. Reversing this unsustainable pattern will require the introduction of reforms to the global financial architecture, as well as a redirection of macroeconomic stances in developing countries and the retooling of monetary and fiscal policies.

Retooling development finance at the national level

Development-oriented macroeconomics

Development-oriented macroeconomics protects long-term investment plans in the face of downturns

The challenge of integrating macroeconomic policy objectives with those related to social development and poverty eradication was examined in chapter II. A development-oriented macroeconomic stance is predicated on the notion that current spending, particularly private and public sector investments, is the "bridge" to future employment and output growth. Promoting current investment so long as it provides a reasonable probability of future return in terms of more output and durable jobs would be a consistent priority. Development-oriented macroeconomics protects long-term investment plans even in the face of increased public deficits induced by a downturn as long as it meets the criterion of ensuring permanently increased domestic capability in desired sectors in the future. This contrasts with the approach that prioritizes the achievement of fixed public deficit targets, independent of the cycle and the nature of the investment projects that have to be postponed or eliminated to meet them. It also contrasts sharply with the view that all current private-sector investments (investment implies that current-period private spending exceeds current-period income) that can be financed (most unsafely from external financing because of the potential for currency mismatches) must be protected, independent of the business cycle and the nature of the project involved.

A particularly cogent example of such a stance was China's macroeconomic response to the Asian crisis which began in 1997. According to Lin (2009, p. 31):

> The Chinese government adopted a fiscal stimulus package in 1998-2002 to remove bottlenecks in infrastructure. In 1997 China had only 4,700 kilometers of highway, by 2002 this had increased more than five times to 25,000 kilometers. The transportation capacity improved greatly as did port facilities and the electricity grid. With that kind of fiscal stimulus, China maintained its average annual growth rate at 7.8 percent. More importantly, after the crisis the growth rate accelerated. Between 1979 and 2002, the average annual growth rate in China was 9.6 percent. And between 2003 and 2008, the growth rate actually increased from 9.6 percent to 10.8 percent. This growth was made possible by investment targeted to freeing-up bottlenecks, that is, those sectors constraining growth in the economy. As a result, though government debt as a percentage of GDP initially rose from about 30 percent of GDP to 36 percent in 2002 it then declined as growth increased. By 2006-2007, government debt had fallen to 20 percent of GDP.

Counter-cyclical macroeconomic policy facilitates long-term private sector risk-taking and investment

Counter-cyclical macroeconomic policy in developing countries is desirable (see chap. II, as well as Ocampo (2003) and Ocampo and Vos (2008)) because it facilitates long-term private-sector risk-taking and investment. Most importantly, macroeconomic policy in developing countries should be endogenously counter-cyclical in order to protect necessary long-term public investments and other public spending on such future capacities as would be built into core social development programmes.

Developing countries must construct the space for development-oriented macroeconomic policy

The implication of this stance is that, first of all, developing countries must construct the space and capability for development-oriented macroeconomic policy. This will be discussed below under the rubric of retooling monetary policy and retooling fiscal policy and stabilization funds. Second, in the context of limited investment resources in low-income countries, development-oriented macroeconomic policy requires constant management of external financing deficits, both public and private. In recent years, however, developing countries as a group were, instead, managing surpluses against developed countries; this state of affairs would be incoherent with respect to such a stance.

Retooling monetary policy

Monetary policy must take on a broader set of targets

In developing countries particularly, monetary policy must be directed towards a broader set of targets. A basic reason why is that economic performance in developing economies is more dependent on the external sector. Another reason is that, as history suggests, benign institutional development in the domestic monetary and financial system does not occur without State leadership and regulation. Enhancing the domestic capacity to intermediate between savers and investors, particularly through the development of the domestic bond markets, increases the potency of monetary policy (United Nations, 2006b). States have had key roles to play in the establishment of liquid bond markets. Policies oriented towards expanding access by the population to financial services, as part of the social development effort discussed in chapter II, should be part of the monetary policy toolkit.

Inflation targeting has tended to sacrifice employment, wages and output

Inflation targeting, both in actual practice and as a still-to-be-achieved standard, has become the basis for a dominant monetary framework in both developed and developing countries. Its attraction lies in its "one (pre-announced) target/one policy instrument" approach, coupled with mechanisms holding monetary officials publicly accountable for meeting the target—after a period, in many developing countries, of structural reform establishing central bank political "independence". Because inflation targeting has been applied utilizing very low inflation targets[5] and has focused only on restraining prices of real goods and services, it has tended to sacrifice growth of employment, wages and output in favour of price stability. Interest rate-setting under inflation targeting reduces the scope for exchange-rate targeting, which is critical to sustaining exports and protecting domestic production and employment. Inflation targeting, coupled with central bank independence, also limits the ability of the government to borrow from the central bank in order to sustain development and social expenditures, which may affect growth in the long run.

It is often argued that inflation is harmful for the poor, but in fact it is the prices of food and other essential goods and services, and not aggregate inflation, that have the most direct impact on poverty. However, monetary policy is not the best tool for stabilizing prices of food and essential goods. In most cases, stabilization of prices of food and essential goods requires subsidies and hence falls within the domain of fiscal policy. Thus, it requires greater coordination between monetary and fiscal policy, especially when subsidies require government borrowing from the central bank.

Monetary policy should embrace a more diversified set of targets and instruments

Retooling monetary policy will require reinstating a more diversified set of targets and instruments for monetary policy. There should also be a reconsideration of targeted credit programmes, particularly those with large poverty reduction and low inflation impact. In a recent set of country studies from Latin America, the authors, writing from historical experiences of high inflation, expressed their belief that inflation as a sole target was inadequate and emphasized the importance of the real exchange rate as a key focus of monetary policy.[6] Studies from Asia and Africa have suggested employment targeting, which would make monetary policy congruent with normal fiscal policy objectives.

Paying attention to asset price inflation is important

The global financial crisis highlights the importance of paying attention to the role of asset price inflation in monetary policy. The fact that asset price increases received little attention (and almost none under inflation targeting) facilitated the expansion of credit and leverage in the boom phase, which often increased systemic risk. Expansion of the use of tools of monetary policy to increase margin requirements so as to reduce leverage or to impose ceilings for lending in specific sectors (a case of selective credit dis-allocation) has often been needed in resisting asset price bubbles. The role of prudential regulation in limiting systemic risk arising from asset bubbles is discussed below.

Open capital accounts subject developing countries to asset price-driven cycles

Open capital accounts subject developing countries to asset price-driven cycles, reducing the power of monetary policy. With open capital accounts, developing countries have seen even perverse outcomes of the implementation of interest-rate policies. For example,

5 Recently, in a staff paper (Blanchard, Dell'Ariccia and Mauro, 2010) reflecting a change of heart, IMF opined that an inflation rate of 2 per cent was too low and proposed a target of 4 per cent.

6 Multi-country evidence can be found in Epstein and Yeldan, eds. (2009).

attempting to prick a domestic asset bubble by raising the interest rate can provoke more capital inflows from the global savings pool and further inflate the domestic bubble. Putting in place effective capital controls helps to re-establish monetary policy tools.

Retooling fiscal policies and stabilization funds

Domestic resource mobilization is the key challenge

Retooling fiscal policy must be directed at recovering its capacity to mobilize financing for long-term public investment and social development, as discussed in chapter II. Domestic resource mobilization is the key challenge. For many countries, continued reliance on trade taxes is consistent with a still underdeveloped tax system, on the one hand, and social and industrial development objectives, on the other, which reverses the priorities of recent decades. Precipitous tariff reductions, particularly in least developed countries, have not only reduced tax revenues that have not been made up by value-added taxes, but have also increased the vulnerability of small domestic enterprises with respect to competition from foreign imports.[7] Developing countries must steadily broaden their tax bases to include, in particular, income and property taxation. An increased reliance on revenues from income and property, in contrast with priorities in recent decades, ensures that tax revenues more than match economic growth so as to ensure the timely build-up of public capabilities in anticipation of increased demands on these capabilities as the economy grows more complex. Effective income and property taxation would be facilitated significantly by strengthened international tax cooperation (see below) focused on more effective revenue streams from global value chains and reduced tax competition. As automatic stabilizers, a more progressive tax system and a larger publicly supported social sector offer counter-cyclical advantages.

Avoiding pro-cyclical biases in fiscal policy is important (United Nations, 2009d). Targeting the "structural deficit" (the budget balance if cyclical fluctuations are not included) implies that public deficits will be allowed to decline in booms and increase in downturns. The desired level of the structural deficit could be set so as to be consistent with medium-term objectives in output and employment.

Establishing stabilization funds could be effective

Establishing stabilization funds could be effective in economies where commodity prices have strong effects on the macroeconomy (United Nations, 2009d). These funds have been utilized successfully in Algeria, Chile, Colombia, Ecuador, Kuwait and Mexico, albeit less successfully in the Bolivarian Republic of Venezuela. The design and operation of these funds are by no means straightforward matters, depending as they do on the strength of fiscal institutions; appropriately designed international compensatory finance mechanisms are therefore indispensable (see below).

Debt management

Developing-country authorities must monitor and regulate private sector external debts

Because of the implications of deficit spending, coherence between a development-oriented macroeconomic policy and debt management will be critical. Developing-country authorities must not only effectively manage their own domestic and external debt obligations, but also monitor and regulate those of the private sector, particularly its external liabilities, given that even completely private debt contracts become public responsibilities in the event of a financial or payments crisis. Regulating private external liabilities will require effective policies associated with capital-account controls. In the case of public liabilities, the mix of external and domestic obligations requires special attention. Policies that expand domestic public debt merely to sustain external service obligations tend to crowd

7 See Baunsgaard and Keen (2005); and Memis, Montes, and Weeratunge (2006).

out domestic investment and induce higher domestic borrowing costs, and hence must be avoided. In such a situation, a more coherent policy would entail restructuring external debt obligations, which only underlines the need for a coherent international debt mechanism, as discussed below.

Financial sector development and prudential regulations

The public sector has to play a leading role in domestic financial market development

The public sector has to play a leading role in domestic financial market development in developing countries. At low levels of development, this is not a matter of choice: Public sector liabilities are often the only generally traded financial assets in the banking sector, which is why effective public sector debt management is a necessary condition for domestic financial development. As development proceeds, a deep and well-functioning domestic financial sector can help scale up financing of government investment priorities.

Domestic prudential authorities have also been under pressure to adopt international prudential standards

Building and retaining both macro- and microprudential regulatory capabilities are critical to financial sector development. As discussed in chapter IV, commitments under the General Agreement on Trade in Services (World Trade Organization, 1994) and free trade and bilateral investment treaties have caused a premature dismantling of capital controls and regulatory oversight over the mix of private financial services.[8] It is important that ongoing global efforts directed at financial regulatory reform clearly demonstrate that domestic authorities' regulatory responsibilities take precedence over commitments under the General Agreement on Trade in Services. Domestic prudential authorities have also been under extreme pressure to adopt international prudential standards, such as those emanating from the Bank for International Settlements, in order to retain access to external financial resources and services. Owing to the limited participation of developing countries in their design, the most recent international banking prudential standards possess many features that are either irrelevant to, or too costly to implement in, developing countries. Moreover, as the crisis has also proved these standards to be highly counter-cyclical, they are now subject to redesign as part of global regulatory reform efforts. This should offer the opportunity to elicit greater developing-country participation in standards design, including the possible incorporation of rule-based differential treatment for countries with less developed financial sectors. Strengthened domestic capacity in prudential regulation will require a domestic capacity to adapt and implement international standards based on local conditions, with a view to ensuring that those regulations are counter-cyclical in nature. Financial regulations should also promote greater access to finance, including through the provision of credit to underserved groups, while protecting consumers.

Regulations can be designed to be counter-cyclical

Regulatory structures should also be designed to reduce asset and liability risks, such as currency mismatches, and these rules need to encompass cases of indirect exposure of firms and other domestic agents that have borrowed from the banking system, as such exposure can have systemic impacts, like those experienced by countries in Eastern Europe during the recent global crisis. There are numerous ways to achieve these objectives (see Stiglitz and others, 2006) including through outright restrictions on foreign-exchange exposures and loans, higher capital requirements for short-term lending in foreign currencies, and adverse tax treatment for foreign currency-denominated borrowing (especially when it is short-term). The goal would be to establish a simplified set of rules which reflect local regulatory capacity. Similarly, Governments can target exposures to risky sectors that

8 Gallagher (2010) provides details on how commitments under the General Agreement on Trade in Services and investment treaties restrict the regulation of financial services.

are prone to speculative bubbles, such as real estate, by imposing restrictions or higher capital requirements on these sectors. These types of regulations can be designed to be counter-cyclical, so that the cost is tied to the proportion of a bank's assets in the sector concerned, based on the forward provisioning discussed above.

Leverage across the financial system and risks generated by large interconnected institutions are a source of systemic risk

Since the 2008 crisis, increased attention has been paid to regulations that focus on systemic risk, such as leverage across the financial system and risks generated by large interconnected institutions. These macroprudential regulations aim at reducing the pro-cyclicality of finance and its effects on the real economy, and are designed to limit credit growth during boom periods and ease credit contractions during economic slowdowns. Hence, in order for macroprudential regulation to be effective, regulators need to be able to monitor systemic risk throughout the entire financial system, including the shadow banking system. The existing regulatory structure needs to be redesigned so as to enable it to address this gap in the system, as well as other failures discussed above.

Financially-driven trading on futures contracts appeared to have had significant and abrupt impacts on commodity prices

Through the complexity, lack of transparency and the increased leverage involved, the growth in derivative products has increased risk in the financial system. This is a key issue for developed-country markets, where multilateral progress in undertaking reforms has been slowed by technical disagreements and competitive pressures among financial centres. For developing countries, what is at stake is the impact of derivatives on the overall stability and flexibility of international financial markets, including their ability to operate development trust funds (see below), and their specific impact on commodity prices. In recent years, financially driven trading on futures contracts appeared to have had significant and abrupt price impacts which in turn introduced difficulties related to balance of payments, fiscal deficits and the availability of fuel and food in many developing countries.

Capital controls

As argued above, capital flows to developing countries are often short-term in nature and appear not to have contributed to higher rates of long-term investment. Rather, they have tended to contribute to economic volatility in many developing-country contexts. The pro-cyclical nature of these flows makes macroeconomic management more challenging.

There are several different types of capital controls

Since the Asian crisis of the late 1990s, a primary policy response of developing countries with respect to mitigating the effects of volatile capital flows has been to amass large international reserves. However, the cost of this form of self-insurance has been high and potential unwinding, in this regard, is an additional source of global instability, as discussed above. Capital controls could be regarded as an alternative and possibly less costly policy tool for addressing capital flow volatility.

There are several different types of capital controls, including price-based ones, such as taxes on inflows, that act as "speed bumps", similar to the forward-looking provisioning discussed earlier. By making capital inflows more expensive, these controls reduce the volume of inflows during a boom, thereby limiting the expansion of the bubble. Chile and Colombia used price-based controls effectively in the late 1990s, and Brazil implemented them in the fall of 2009, in the face of resurging short-term capital inflows. Alternatively, some countries, like Malaysia during the Asian crisis, instituted quantity-based controls on inflows, outflows or both. What type of controls work best depends on the specificities of the country's markets, as well as the strength of its administrative capacity to apply capital controls. Countries often have been reluctant to use capital controls, fearing a possible backlash from the markets. Regional coordination, with a group of countries implementing controls at the same time, could help shield any one country from having to bear solely the stigma associated with such an undertaking, but it would not reduce the perception in the markets of increased risk. IMF could have a significant role to play here. Given the wider recognition that capital-account liberalization is proper only for economies that have reached a certain level of development (Kose, Prasad and Taylor, 2009) and the fact that the Fund is still bound by its Articles of Agreement to enforce capital controls, it is time for this and other institutions to enhance their capacity to monitor the workings of private international asset markets—including through increasing staff skills—so as to be in a position to assist countries in implementing effective capital-account controls.

Closed-end trust funds for development financing

Trust funds constitute one means of putting developing countries in the driver's seat in respect of the use of external assistance

As first mentioned in chapter III, establishing closed-end trust funds is a potentially effective means of putting developing countries in the driver's seat in terms of the application of external funding and the management of aid and capital flows for macroeconomic stability. The setting up of trust funds for individual countries and for subsets of countries already has precedents and can be expanded.

Ensuring that these funds were controlled by recipients would be a key requirement. The funds could issue "A" voting shares and "B" non-voting shares, with rules on how many of each type parties of different kinds could purchase. They could also issue their own bonds to provide private investors with one non-speculative means of possibly sharing in the development of a country. As in the case of advance market commitments, these funds could become the preferred destination of official development assistance (ODA.) In establishing these funds, there should be clear rules regarding what kinds of flows they would receive and for what kinds of purposes their resources could be utilized and under what conditions.

Recycling resources in international reserves to domestic investment is one possibility

Trust funds could be a depository of commodity stabilization funds and part of a country's reserves could be invested in trust funds (D'Arista and Erturk, 2010). The trust funds could issue GDP-linked bonds, in which multilateral financing institutions might consider taking portfolio positions. In the Asia and Pacific region, there have been proposals on establishing financing mechanisms designed to redirect the substantial international reserves accumulated by some developing countries in developed-country financial instruments towards financing regional infrastructure requirements (United Nations, Economic and Social Commission for Asia and the Pacific, 2006).

A closed-end structure for these funds is consistent with its development assistance purpose

The advantages of a country-controlled trust fund mechanism designed to absorb aid flows are particularly attractive. Bilateral donors and existing global funds would contribute to trust funds, which would disburse funds to and collect resources from recipient countries in accordance with programmatic and budgetary needs. Donors would be able to disburse their aid without necessarily undermining the macroeconomic stability of the recipient countries since the trust fund could serve as a smoothing mechanism for the use of donor funds. A closed-end structure for the fund is most consistent with its development assistance purpose: a closed-end fund is not obligated to service redemptions even though its shares could be traded in financial markets. Countries could invest part of their international reserves in the fund which would in effect serve as a means of recycling their savings for their own development needs. Trust funds could be administered by professional investment advisers and controlled by the country government in which donors would be adequately but not overwhelmingly represented.

The trust funds could also be allowed to purchase government securities of developing countries so as to tie aid to future domestic resource mobilization efforts. Experience exists in this area: in a number of cases, multi-year aid commitments have been converted into bond purchases to fund and front-load resources for tropical medicines. Recipient countries, in turn, could also be allowed to periodically deposit part of their savings into these funds as insurance against shocks, and draw upon them in response to shocks. In the same vein, the trust funds could serve as a vehicle for channelling resources made available through international compensatory financing mechanisms and allocations of special drawing rights (SDRs). This would help align use of short-term financing needs with long-term development objectives. In fact, one proposal contained in the Monterrey Consensus of the International Conference on Financing for Development (United Nations, 2002) was to use SDRs for development purposes and the ODA trust funds could provide the institutional setting within which to do so.

There are precedents for turning multi-year aid commitments into bond purchases

D'Arista and Erturk (2010) present other possible features of these funds as related to their structure, their governance and their investment strategies.[9] These funds could issue their own liabilities in a variety of national currencies and use the proceeds to pay for stocks and bonds of private enterprises and public agencies denominated in local currencies across a wide spectrum of developing countries. The funds' liabilities would be marketed both to private institutional investors in advanced economies and to official investors from emerging economies and would also qualify as international reserves guaranteed by a multinational agency and its member countries. Investing the reserves of developing countries in these funds would redirect external savings back into the economies of the countries that owned the reserves rather than into the financial markets of strong-currency countries. Moreover, their closed-end structure would ensure that long-term funds were provided and that sales of the funds' liabilities by investors did not force redemptions that could disrupt development projects.

Retooling the international financial architecture

Global monetary and financial arrangements are inconsistent with the requirements of development-oriented macroeconomic policy. These rules and mechanisms will need to be transformed if policy coherence is to be achieved. This being said, it must be emphasized that the reforms discussed below constitute an ensemble of interlocking pieces which have to be set in place simultaneously.

Required reforms constitute an ensemble of interlocking pieces which have to be set in place simultaneously

Multilateral macroeconomic coordination and surveillance

There is a need to revise multilateral surveillance and direct it towards taking on board international spillovers of national economic policies. Surveillance by IMF had previously focused on problems in emerging markets and developing countries, while devoting insufficient attention to major financial centres and the vulnerabilities within global financial markets. The global financial crisis has made clear the fact that there is an urgent need to strengthen vigilance over risks emanating from the major developed countries, especially the reserve currency-issuing countries. This will require better cooperation on the part of monetary and financial authorities from mature financial markets and advanced economies, which must bear the burden of greater responsibility for systemic stability.

Surveillance activities need to devote more attention to major financial centres

9 The following description is based on the paper of D'Arista and Erturk (2010, p. 21) which was commissioned for this publication.

Surveillance must differentiate among countries in terms of their influence on systemic stability, and must be more rigorous for countries issuing major reserve currencies.

Institutionalizing macroeconomic coordination avoids conflicts over surveillance activities

Strengthening and institutionalizing international macroeconomic coordination are essential to reducing the policy conflicts over surveillance activities. Macroeconomic coordination must be development-oriented. First, it must ensure that the composition of aggregate demand assigns greater weight to investment in support of future productivity growth and the transformation needed to establish low-emissions and renewable energy sectors and infrastructure required to meet the challenge of climate change (see box V.2). Second, demand across countries will have to be rebalanced in such a way as to ensure that financing is actually channelled to developing countries, rather than to developed countries. Sustaining strong demand in the developing countries, particularly investment demand, would be consistent with a development-oriented macroeconomics. In the current situation, rebalancing demand by relying on consumption demand in the United States would also be undesirable—and unlikely—since United States households already increased savings to

Box V.2

Challenges in financing the global climate change response

The estimated additional investments needed to address the adaptation to and mitigation of climate change are large in absolute terms. It is often pointed out that these constitute only a small fraction of world output, in the order of 1 and 2 per cent of world gross product (WGP) per annum by 2030. At present levels of WGP, this would amount to between $0.6 trillion and $1.2 trillion per annum in new investments. As analysed in detail in *World Economic and Social Survey 2009: Saving the Planet, Promoting Development* (United Nations, 2009a), rather than delayed until 2030, many of these investments will need to be front-loaded, both to effectuate the urgent shift to a low-emissions economy and to minimize the damage from unavoidable changes in the climate.

Climate change is already affecting livelihoods in many countries, especially developing countries and small island developing States, including through more frequent and intense weather shocks. Measures for climate change adaptation therefore need to be implemented now so as to avert major impacts in the form of greater food insecurity, water scarcity and lives lost through natural disasters, among others. Technologies to generate clean energy for climate change mitigation do exist, but are still utilizable only at a multiple of the cost of those technologies using coal and fossil fuels which are the main source of greenhouse gas (GHG) emissions. To make renewable energy more affordable and accessible in amounts sufficient to meet higher demand from developing countries as they try to accelerate economic progress and to ensure that GHG emission-reduction targets are met in a timely manner, clean energy production will need to be carried out on a much larger scale, which would require massive investments starting today.

Front-loading of such investments will put pressure on the financial system in respect of mobilizing the required resources. *World Economic and Social Survey 2009* (United Nations, 2009a, table VI.2) estimates that 34-57 per cent of the additional global investments for climate change mitigation and most of those for adaptation would need to take place in developing countries. Despite the recent proliferation of climate-related funds, the amount currently promised and expected to be available for meeting the climate challenge in the near term, from bilateral and multilateral sources, is woefully inadequate. Current dedicated climate resources have been estimated at about $21 billion and are very heavily skewed towards mitigation. Estimates of the annually required total amount of climate financing for developing countries vary, but on all counts they are a large multiple of that figure and total up to as much as about five times the 2008 levels of official development assistance (ODA). The difficulty involved in reaching even those levels of ODA suggests that global financing for climate change will require a much more determined effort on the part of advanced countries to provide bold leadership on the climate issue and bolster international cooperation. And it will also require an effort on the part of developing countries to mobilize a larger share of their resources for cleaner investments along a new, sustainable growth path.

Box V.2 (cont'd)

The purpose of a sustained injection of external financing in amounts large enough to give the "big push" needed to embark on a low-emissions development path is to simultaneously accelerate and sustain growth in developing countries at levels higher than in the past. As discussed in the 2009 *Survey*, this initial big push from official sources of finance, in combination with various policy mixes, including price incentives, regulation and targeted industrial policies, would begin to raise domestic sources of finance for investment in both the public and the private sectors. The evolving mix of public and private investment will no doubt vary among countries, but for many developing countries, and possibly for some developed countries, public investment would have to take the lead, along with stronger regulations, before large-scale private investment began to materialize.

The need for sizeable external financing to address climate change in developing countries appears to be at odds with present patterns of global resource transfers. Net financial transfers to developing countries have been negative over the past two decades at least (see figure V.7). The resource flow from poor to rich countries exceeded half a trillion dollars annually in the last three years. A big push oriented towards investing in clean energy in developing countries would thus require reversing this trend. It also follows that the mobilization of climate financing will need to be aligned with coordinated policy efforts to deal with the problem of global imbalances.

The United Nations Framework Convention on Climate Change[a] commits developed countries to: (a) providing "new and additional financial resources to meet the agreed full costs incurred by developing countries" in complying with their national communication requirements under article 12 of the Convention (article 4, para. 3); and (b) providing "such financial resources, including for the transfer of technology" needed by developing countries "to meet the agreed full incremental costs" of implementing mitigation and adaptation actions and other commitments identified in article 4, para. 1.

At the fifteenth session of the Conference of the Parties to the United Nations Framework Convention on Climate Change, held in Copenhagen from 7 to 19 December 2009 (the United Nations Climate Change Conference 2009), the Conference of the Parties took note of the non-legally binding agreement entitled the "Copenhagen Accord".[b]

The Accord, which had been agreed by the Heads of State, Heads of Government, Ministers and other heads of delegations present at the Conference, contains voluntary goals and actions on climate change that address key components of the Bali Action Plan, adopted by the Conference of the Parties at its thirteenth session, held in Bali, Indonesia, from 3 to 15 December 2007.[c] The Accord tackles one of the major stumbling blocks introduced in prior negotiations by recognizing the need to mobilize new and additional predictable financial resources. As steps in the direction suggested above, the additional financial resources for addressing climate in developing countries would need to reach $30 billion for the period 2010-2012 and to be scaled up to $100 billion per year by 2020 (para. 8). The Accord also acknowledges the need for the establishment of a Copenhagen Green Climate Fund as an operating entity of the financial mechanisms of the United Nations Framework Convention on Climate Change to support projects, programmes, policies and other activities in developing countries related to mitigation, adaptation, capacity-building, technology development and transfer (para 10).

Aside from having to contend with the insufficient scale of funding, climate change financing must also wrestle with the proliferation of funds and a spaghetti bowl of funding mechanisms and conditions (Opschoor, 2010; and United Nations, Economic and Social Council, 2010). The related problems are akin to those associated with the broader aid architecture discussed in chapter III. The World Bank alone has three specific funds: a Clean Technology Fund, a forest fund and an Adaptation Fund. In the climate negotiations, developing countries have proposed that all climate change-related funding be placed under the umbrella of the United Nations Framework Convention on Climate Change. Whether this proposal will be adopted or not, the establishment of the Copenhagen Green Climate Fund should be seen as offering the opportunity to get a head start on the much-needed reform of the climate change financing architecture at large, including the streamlining and consolidation of funding mechanisms, in order to create greater cohesion, transparency and accountability in the allocation of the required resources.

a United Nations, *Treaty Series*, vol, 1771, No 30822.

b See FCCC/CP/2009/11/Add.1, decision 2/CP.15.

c See FCCC/CP/2007/6/Add.1, decision 1/CP.13.

about 3 per cent of GDP during 2009 (from almost zero in the years leading to the crisis). Since rates of capacity utilization are at historic lows, private investments are also expected to remain weak in the major developed economies. With the prospective phasing out of the fiscal stimulus, net exports of the major deficit countries would need to increase. Starting with China and other parts of developing Asia, major surplus countries will need to absorb the rising exports of deficit countries. In surplus countries, this could be through fiscal stimulus. According to *World Economic Situation and Prospects 2010* (United Nations, 2010, p. 31):

> The stimulus packages that are in place are already supportive of this kind of rebalancing but are as yet not strong enough, and the change will only come gradually. GDP of the countries of emerging Asia is roughly half that of the United States, so they would need to lower their combined current-account surpluses by about 6 per cent of their combined GDP to lower the United States deficit by, say, 3 per cent of its GDP.

Monitoring of business cycles at the global level should be institutionalized

The objective of the Group of Twenty (G-20), which is to achieve a strong, sustainable and balanced world economic growth, can be operationalized only within this kind of framework. Sustainable rebalancing of the world economy will take many years and such a framework cannot be left to ad hoc consultations at the G-20 level. The monitoring of business cycles at the global level and the triggering of multilateral discussions and responses should be institutionalized within the multilateral system. The technical capacities of global agencies with macroeconomic and financial mandates, in respect of designing counter-cyclical policy, must be enhanced. Enforcement mechanisms will need to be designed to make policy coordination effective and accountable.

International coordination of financial regulation

Financial markets are now global and a failure in the financial system in one country can impose negative externalities on others

Delivering sufficient long-term finance for development can be achieved only within the context of a sound international financial system. Financial markets are now global and a failure in the financial system in one country can impose negative externalities on others, as was seen in the emerging market crises of the 1990s and the 2000s and in the more recent global crisis. Inasmuch as countries are all unique, some regulations will likely always be developed to fit the circumstances of a specific country. However, without global coordination, there is the danger that investors will engage in regulatory arbitrage between different regulatory frameworks, often through complicated derivative products, thereby disseminating increased risk throughout the global financial system.

Financial market regulation should aim at ensuring the safety and soundness of the financial sector, while maintaining a broad focus on systemic stability. Authorities in larger mature financial markets bear the onus of responsibility for ensuring that their market activities do not unduly destabilize the international economy. Many features of the existing risk assessment methods and prudential rules, such as Basel I and Basel II, such as loan-loss provisioning, have been seen to exacerbate cyclicality (United Nations, 2008). In the Asian financial crisis of the late 1990s, Asian countries particularly were adversely affected by prudential rules in the major financial markets, and as a result experienced a credit crunch on top of the sudden stop in short-term capital inflows. There is a need for a global mechanism capable of setting standards applicable to all. The conversion of the Financial Stability Forum to the Financial Stability Board represents a step in this direction. However, the Financial Stability Board suffers from inadequate representation and inadequate enforcement power. An evolution towards a World Trade Organization-like regime, with enforceable rules, has also been suggested. The Commission of Experts of the President of the United Nations General Assembly on Reforms of the International Monetary and Financial System proposed taking steps to lay the groundwork for a global financial authority charged with coordinating financial regulation, including oversight of global rules in certain areas, such as money-laundering and tax secrecy.

Counter-cyclical financing to mitigate external shocks

Providing for support in response to external commodity price shocks has been critical

Protecting economic growth from commodity price changes in such a manner as not to introduce debt vulnerabilities has long been identified as a financing-for-development need. There are two general kinds of external shocks: commodity price shocks and global demand shocks. The IMF Compensatory Financing Facility, which had been a mechanism of long standing designed to deal with the first kind of shock, was particularly valuable for low-income countries. The Facility was gutted in 2001 and folded into the poverty reduction strategy, which effectively made access to finance in order to deal with commodity shocks conditional on domestic economic policy and governance reforms, even though the balance-of-payments problem in the case of commodity price shocks is not due to domestic policies or mis-governance.

The principles according to which such financing should be provided are clear enough. Resources should be made available: (a) in a timely manner, (b) in sufficient quantity to permit the affected country to finance essential imports and (c) with no conditionality with respect to covering an external deficit that had nothing to do with domestic policy. Recent reforms of IMF credit facilities, in effect restoring many of the features of the previous "compensatory financing" facilities, will need to be institutionalized as far more than a crisis response, and in a form that would include increased access for all low-income countries.

The provision of properly designed compensatory financing mechanisms as described above is particularly relevant to commodity shocks. For global demand shocks, there exists a need for the capacity to provide—and by extension create—global liquidity through the possibly increased use of SDRs—a capacity that, as the current crisis demonstrates, is available only on an ad hoc basis (see below for a further discussion).

Commodity-dependent countries should be building up stabilization funds during an upturn

There are associated policies, which by nature are also counter-cyclical, whose introduction would improve macroeconomic performance. In respect of traditional external commodity price shocks, countries should be building up stabilization funds during periods when prices are high in order to ride out the periods of price slumps. In the long run, developing countries must acquire sufficient policy space and demonstrate sufficient audacity if they intend to diversify domestic production so as to progressively reduce dependence on commodity earnings (see chaps. II and IV). Incorporating state-contingent features in external assistance programmes and debt contracts can be critical to debt-distressed commodity-dependent countries (Nissanke and Ferrarini, 2007).

International tax cooperation

Cooperation is required to strengthen the capacity of countries to collect their fair share of taxes

The potential for increasing development finance simply through a strengthening of the capacity of developing countries to collect their proper share of taxes—particularly from international private enterprises (part of global value chains) (see chap. IV) that operate within their borders and in turn pay taxes in countries that provide ODA—was examined in chapter III. The conservative estimate[10] of $250 billion per year as representing additional tax revenues from these sources that could be made available to developing countries would be equivalent to a tripling of the resources now being provided through ODA (FitzGerald, 2010).

With the widespread dismantling of capital controls, the international relocation of assets not only for tax purposes but also for regulatory arbitrage, if not evasion, has been facilitated by the infrastructure built up as the international financial industry grew. Heightened capital mobility, in the absence of tax harmonization and financial regulatory coordination among countries, has in turn spurred regulatory and tax competition among jurisdictions, which has resulted, whether intentionally or not, in a clear-cut diminishment of the capacities of tax and financial authorities to secure the information required for financial supervision and tax collection.

Strict reporting and regulation in one country can be circumvented without the cooperation of other countries

In the context of transnational economic activities, developing countries have to find a "balance between maximizing their share of revenues and maintaining a climate that attracts inward investment" (FitzGerald, 2010, p. 5). A basic principle should be that, whatever tax and regulatory stances sovereign countries choose, they must not be undermined by the tax and regulatory stances of other countries. Strict reporting and regulation in one country can be circumvented in the absence of the cooperation of others because of the ease with which assets can be transferred. Because State revenue generation must keep in step with the growth process if State capabilities are to develop, reliance on income and capital taxation is unavoidable. However, with the international mobility of assets and the capabilities of transnational corporations with respect to reapportioning income to their own tax advantage using transfer pricing, "effective income taxation . . . becomes an international rather than a national development issue" (ibid., p. 6).

Strengthened international information exchange and cooperative enforcement will be required. Greater capacity on the part of and cooperation among Governments with respect to monitoring transnational financial activities—a need heightened by the global crisis will be required to protect both their tax bases and the viability of their financial regulations. Undertaking this task within a broader framework than that possible under the auspices of the Organization for Economic Cooperation and Development (OECD) will thus be critical. This need is already being realized through the coordination of financial regulation spearheaded by the G-20. It will be necessary to widen the scope of multilateral tax cooperation along the same lines, which might require greater reliance on the framework provided by the United Nations.

International debt contractual arrangements and resolution

Sovereign restructurings have been incomplete

Another set of important reforms centre on the issue of sovereign debt restructuring. As is the case for banks that are "too big to fail", there is no legal framework within which a country can restructure its debt. The result is that sovereign restructurings have been incomplete, chaotic or both and have entailed huge costs, as discussed above. The uncertainty surrounding the restructuring process is another reason why countries have been building self-insurance in the form of reserves (Herman, Ocampo and Spiegel, 2010; and Ocampo and others, 2010). To address this issue, some form of sovereign bankruptcy

10 The estimate is based on the assumption that one half of the stock of assets from developing countries held abroad [in turn, estimated using flow data calculated by the Global Financial Integrity study (Kar and Cartwright-Smith, 2008) for the mid-2000s] is owned by developing-country residents. A 7 per cent rate of return and a 20 per cent tax rate are then applied to assets held abroad by developing-country residents in order to arrive at lost tax revenues.

framework, with a fair arbiter, needs to be developed. There have been many proposals put forward regarding the form that such a court or arbitration mechanism should take,[11] but to date the international community has not moved forward on any of them. Owing to the new crisis in the euro area sparked by the obligations of Greece, the issue of sovereign debt restructuring has been raised once again. This gap in the financial architecture must be filled if the global system is to become more stable.

Debt relief approaches have paid insufficient attention to growth requirements

Current debt-relief and restructuring approaches, and their associated conditionalities, have not paid sufficient attention to basic growth requirements and the corresponding expansion of policy space genuinely needed to make possible the overcoming of debt distress (United Nations, 2005; United Nations, General Assembly, 2007). The present arrangement at the Paris Club of Industrial Country Creditors violates commonly accepted norms of good governance which would call into question any process in which an ad hoc committee of creditors passes judgement on debtor country obligations (United Nations, General Assembly, 2007) that are enforced under the auspices of IMF. This process also conflicts with the spirit of political agreement reflected in the Monterrey Consensus, which affirms that "[D]ebtors and creditors must share the responsibility for preventing and resolving unsustainable debt situations" (United Nations, 2002, para. 47).

There is a need for a fair and internationally accepted debt workout mechanism

Moreover, the arduous Paris Club process does not result in a true resolution of debt claims. Other donors and lenders, who are not associated with the Paris Club, are becoming significant players in this arena and must find other means to enforce their claims. Debt-relief commitments under the Heavily Indebted Poor Countries (HIPC) Initiative are hobbled by the non-participation of these other creditors. In the absence of an international legal regime responsible for adjudicating debt claims, some private parties, who have come to be called "debt vultures," have managed to institute legal proceedings in financial sector jurisdictions with a view to profiting from sovereign debt distress. There is thus a need for a fair and internationally accepted debt workout mechanism for official debt obligations that applies to all creditors.

On the lending side, improved international financial regulation is needed to stem excessive risk-taking and capital flow volatility. A 2007 report of the United Nations Secretary-General warned that "limited progress has been achieved in surmounting the incentive structure that has seen overextension of private credit to developing countries during episodes of greatly increased global liquidity" and that the "present liquidity conditions are not expected to persist much longer" (United Nations, General Assembly, 2007, para. 107). Indeed, the global liquidity conditions have shifted drastically. As indicated by the Group of Thirty (2009), there is a critical need to plug gaps and weaknesses in the coverage of prudential regulation and supervision; to improve the quality and effectiveness of prudential regulation and supervision, including through appropriate capital controls and macroprudential regulatory reforms; to impose counter-cyclical biases in rules for reserve requirements and loan-loss provisioning; and to strengthen institutional policies and standards, including in accounting and public disclosure, and the transparency of financial markets and products.

Global reserve and payments system

The build-up of global imbalances may be traced back to a trap in the global reserve and payments system

As discussed above, the build-up of global imbalances to global crisis levels may be traced back to a trap inherent in the reserve and payments system, whereby reserve-creating countries are able to run payments deficits as long as other countries find it in their

11 See Herman, Ocampo and Spiegel (2010) for alternative proposals.

interest to keep building up their international reserves in the currencies of the reserve-creating countries. If this trap is not eliminated, all financial regulatory reform will come to nought, because the mechanism facilitates an almost unlimited supply of credit from reserve-accumulating countries, resulting in increased global liquidity, which in turn has to be intermediated by the financial industry. What is required is a reserve and payments system that does not rely on national deficits to provide reserve assets.

Before the crisis, there had already been a move towards a multi-currency reserve system, which became more pronounced with the introduction of the euro. At this point in time, it is impossible to predict how the situation will evolve, absent an explicit political process. Currently, authorities managing both the euro and the dollar find themselves heavily restrained from attempting to prop up their currency's reserve status. While a multi-currency system could be the default outcome, further evolution in that direction would be undesirable, since it might revive the instabilities seen in the 1930s and exacerbate the instabilities already in play among the major currencies.[12] For developing countries, such instabilities would hamper exchange rate setting as a policy tool, unless they continued to accumulate international reserves. First, a multi-currency system would make it harder to target a real exchange-rate level consistent with stable growth in the face of the gyrations in exchange values among the major currencies. Second, under a multi-currency system, short-term capital flow movements stimulated by interest-rate differentials or business sentiment or both in the major markets tend to be sizeable and thus the dominant determinant of exchange-rate fluctuations. A system of more stable exchange values, whether anchored on one currency (as was the case for the system that existed before 1971) or on a special drawing right-type asset, would moderate these flows and reduce developing-country exchange rate setting dilemmas (United Nations Conference on Trade and Development, 2009b).

A feasible evolutionary path towards a more stable system is one along which there is an increased use of SDRs, within a system of nationally supplied reserve assets, dominated by the dollar. The current crisis has already seen a more than 10-fold ad hoc increase in the total quantity of SDRs in existence. The SDR, already the unit of account of IMF, is a basket of four currencies—the dollar, the euro, the Japanese yen and the pound sterling. The weight of each currency in the basket, last revised in November 2005, is based on the value of the exports of goods and services and the amount of reserves denominated in the respective currencies held by other members of IMF. In the future and given the changing weights in the global economy, other currencies, including those of emerging market economies, would need to be included in the SDR basket.

The members of IMF could start a process directed towards increasing the use of SDRs as a currency for central bank operations among themselves (though under the present rules, the United States has a single-country blocking vote on the issue of increased SDR allocations). SDRs could be increased through periodic allocations in line with the expansion of international commerce. The Commission of Experts of the President of the United Nations General Assembly on Reforms of the International Monetary and

12 Attempting to stabilize exchange rates among the major currencies in a multi-currency system is particularly difficult. According to D'Arista and Erturk (2010, p. 14):

> When a central bank bought another country's currency to push up that currency's value, it invested its holdings in credit market assets such as bank deposits or government securities issued by that country and thus added to the recipient country's credit supply. Assuming the acquired currency had fallen in value as a result of expansive monetary or fiscal policies, intervention would have the pro-cyclical effect of augmenting that expansion.

Financial System proposed regular or counter-cyclical issuance of SDRs (United Nations, General Assembly, 2009b; D'Arista and Erturk, 2010). IMF could begin by using only SDRs in its standby lending and extinguishing them as loans are paid back. SDRs could also be invested in bonds issued by regional development banks.[13] The Commission also advocates using SDRs to support regional financing requirements (United Nations, General Assembly, 2009b).

Proposals to shift to the allocation of SDRs based on need or performance, instead of on the economic significance that determines voting shares in IMF, are of great interest. Ocampo (2009) proposes giving larger allocations to countries with the highest demand for reserves and allowing IMF to use unutilized SDRs to buy bonds from developing countries. Ocampo proposes generous overdraft or "drawing" facilities which could be used on an unconditional basis by all member countries and recommends that IMF be authorized to suspend the right of countries with large surpluses or excessive reserves to receive SDR allocations.

To turn the SDR into an investment asset or a unit of value (roles that the United States dollar plays at this time), more institutional changes and more time would be required, along with possibly giving IMF the role of a market maker for the buying and selling of SDRs at spreads comparable to those on the United States dollar (Eichengreen, 2009). Additional international agreements (regarding what kind of debts SDRs might discharge, for example) could also increase its viability as an investment asset.

To summarize, reducing dependence on the dollar through increased use of a created currency made up of a basket of currencies such as the SDR could be a significant step towards greater stability in the world economy. Greater SDR use would constitute an additional tool for creating the international liquidity needed for the conduct of a global counter-cyclical policy, for which there is already a precedent, as reflected in the April 2009 decision of the G-20. Greater reliance on the SDR could also open up the possibility of utilizing such a created currency for development or other global purposes. SDRs can be used to swap for bonds of developing countries or backstop the issuance of global bonds whose proceeds could be used for specific purposes. This latter approach basically describes the mechanism for climate change financing proposed in a recent IMF staff paper (Bredenkamp and Pattillo, 2010). Developed countries would pledge their SDR allocations to a "green fund" which would then float bonds backed by the SDRs to fund climate change spending.

Regional arrangements

A flurry of initiatives have arrived on the scene based on regional monetary and financial cooperation, including in the areas of macroeconomic and exchange-rate coordination, crisis responsiveness and prevention, and mobilization of development financing. While many of them are best characterized as being long on ambition and short on performance, regional arrangements do offer clear advantages to the international system and international discussions should therefore increasingly recognize their potential (Ocampo, 2001).

In the area of monetary and financial cooperation, regional arrangements could exploit pooling advantages, both in terms of risk and in investment. Notwithstanding the fact that regions are subject to contagion, risk pooling of international reserves can be a first line of defence, especially in the context of regional surveillance and mutual commitments

13 It might be necessary to activate the substitution account mechanism to facilitate the conversion of SDRs into actual currencies.

among pool members regarding remedial action.[14] Pooling to create larger bond markets and investment funds has been discussed as a response to infrastructure requirements, including for increased integration in the Asia and Pacific region (see box V.3).

Box V.3

Funding of regional development gaps in Asia and the Pacific

The global economic crisis has underlined the need for regional cooperation in funding development gaps—a process in which Governments coordinate their fiscal spending around a commonly shared paradigm of inclusive and sustainable development. Countries in Asia and the Pacific have accumulated vast amounts of foreign-exchange reserves, motivated in part by the desire to create a buffer in case of large external shocks. Yet, holding such reserves comes with costs. This is so in part because the region's reserves are currently being invested in low interest earning deposits in the developed world, while a significant share of the reserves accumulated between 2001 and 2008 (about half) were in fact "borrowed" (that is, through running capital-account surpluses) at rates typically higher than the return on reserves. There may also be important opportunity costs, as there are at the same time important long-term investment needs to be financed. These opportunity costs likely outweigh the benefits of holding reserves for precautionary needs when the stock of reserves goes beyond the minimally required level and when long-term financing is scarce. Reserve holdings in Asia have increased to from two to three times the stock of three months of imports and the stock of short-term external debt, hence it is likely that their size extends well beyond the size of what would be considered a comfortable buffer.

Capital markets for long-term financing in the region remain relatively underdeveloped and there is vast scope for using official reserves to foster such markets. There have been some moves in recent years towards greater integration of regional equity markets and promoting the development of local-currency bond markets at the regional level, but progress has remained limited. Intraregional investment in local currency bonds has remained subdued owing to the existence of too many legal and institutional impediments, as well as a lack of investment information (Arner, Lejot and Rhee, 2005). The move forward of the Asian Bond Market Initiative, intended to foster the growth of local currency bond markets, has only been slow, as countries have remained preoccupied with addressing issues of harmonization of rules and regulations and there has been a lack of transparency in its investment targets and fund performance.

One priority target for alternative uses of excess official foreign-exchange reserves, both for domestic development and for increasing regional integration, would be the massive unmet infrastructure funding needs across Asia and the Pacific (United Nations, Economic and Social Commission for Asia and the Pacific, 2006). It is estimated that the region, with an annual shortfall of more than $200 billion, needs an annual investment of more than $600 billion in transport, energy, water and telecommunications. One option for countries in the region would be to allocate a part of their reserves to a trust fund set up to guarantee bond issues for infrastructure financing. In May 2010, for example, countries members of the Association of Southeast Asian Nations, joined by China, the Republic of Korea and Japan ("ASEAN+3"), set up a $700 million bond fund backed by $130 million dollars from the Asian Development Bank and a total of $570 million from member countries. The trust fund will provide guarantees for long-term local currency-denominated bonds. Progress in the creation of these kinds of trust funds has been limited so far, however, because of a lack of agreement on the allocation of voting rights in such funds.

A financial architecture within the Asia and Pacific region could grow out of successful regional experiences in establishing and operating such funds. These funds would provide a more effective intermediation between the region's growing savings and foreign-exchange reserves and its established investment requirements than is currently being achieved through the recycling of reserves to finance developed-country deficits at substantial opportunity cost.

14 The Economic and Social Commission for Asia and the Pacific (United Nations, Economic and Social Commission for Asia and the Pacific, 2010) examines the challenges that have beset the Chiang Mai Initiative which is being converted from a set of bilateral agreements into a regional foreign reserve pool totalling $120 billion.

There are important complementarities between world and regional mechanisms. Regional institutions could "play a useful role in setting norms, in the adaptation of international norms to regional conditions (given different regulatory traditions), and in reducing learning costs and sharing experience with institutional development" and could "also establish mechanisms to ensure surveillance of their regulatory systems and, eventually, regional currencies" (Ocampo, 2001, p. 21). Regional institutions have the potential to provide programmes that are better tailored to the regional situation and the situation of small countries, inasmuch as global institutions tend to be more responsive to systemic players. Finally, regional mechanisms can use the fact that they offer their participants a greater voice to help aggregate commitment to and coordination with global mechanisms.

Conclusions

The agenda encompassing the reform challenges set out in this chapter is an enormous one. Furthermore, it entails urgent political requirements. As discussed above, the set of reforms must be seen as a whole whose parts must be mutually reinforcing. Fiscal policy and monetary policy should not operate at cross-purposes domestically and both must sustain investment. Both types of policy must in turn be coherent with international arrangements (and vice versa), most particularly the controls exerted over international private asset flows, which are part of prudential regulation. What political resources the international community can count and draw on in order to address these challenges is a question examined in chapter VI.

Chapter VI
A feasible globalization

Summary

- Globalization is not likely to be economically sustainable if it proceeds as it has. In fact, it could come to a sudden and catastrophic stop unless properly governed. Thus, a more effective system of global economic governance needs to be built, through an intrinsically political process, involving the adjustment of the boundaries between national sovereignty and global mechanisms.
- Existing mechanisms for global economic governance were designed to a large extent to respond to the global realities being faced more than 60 years ago. Since then, the world has changed beyond recognition, but the multilateral institutions for economic governance have changed little or have adapted slowly. To respond to today's challenges, major reforms will be needed. For one thing, democratic deficits as regards voice and voting power need to be redressed in recognition of the growing weight of developing countries in the global economy. But the actual functions of the major institutions also need to be reformed. The principle of common-but-differentiated responsibilities should be a major guide throughout the reform process which is crucial for a fairer and sustainable globalization.
- The food, financial and climate change crises have highlighted fundamental weaknesses which require not only a retooling of the multilateral trading regime and a deep-reaching reform of the international financial architecture, but also the closing of present gaps so as to eliminate inconsistencies in the existing mechanisms of global economic governance. This may necessitate the creation of new mechanisms for dealing with some of the deficiencies, such as specialized multilateral frameworks through which to govern international migration and labour mobility, international financial regulation and sovereign debt workouts. Most importantly, what is needed is a strong mechanism for global economic coordination which establishes coherence across all areas of global economic governance.

Business as usual is not an option

Drastic changes in the mechanisms of global economic governance are under way

Enormous changes in the workings of and the mechanisms of governance over the international economy are under way as a result of the current global crisis, the deepest the international community has faced since the Great Depression more than 75 years ago. However, the actual shape of the outcome is uncertain. While there are powerful interests pressing to restore the system's configuration before the crisis, even these will be thwarted by the significant economic trends that are already in evidence and the unprecedented restructuring that is already in train. The current recession could persist for some time, even if it does not turn into a depression, because of the thoroughgoing recapitalization and de-leveraging in the major financial sectors that has to take place. Even if the world were simply to be rebooted worldwide so as to function exactly as it had, one might expect the scale of private flows to be more subdued in years to come. Yet, more limited flows could still cause additional severe damage in an unreformed system. The enhanced risk for sovereign debt crises in Europe that emerged in early 2010 was matched by equally risky surges in short-term capital flows to emerging markets which triggered renewed financial turmoil worldwide. The fact that policymakers have been slow to respond highlights once more the glaring gaps in global economic governance.

Even with the stronger experience in supranational coordination, the European sovereign debt crisis appears to have spiralled out of control

If nothing else, the events of the last few years have revealed inadequacies in international coordination mechanisms. While a number of responses to the current crisis appear to have had some effect, these were mostly ad hoc and insufficient to address the more systemic weaknesses in the world economy.

The European sovereign debt crisis which erupted in May 2010 is a case in point. This crisis revealed, first, that unaddressed inconsistencies between international private lending in periods of global liquidity (chap. V), on the one hand, and uncontrolled national deficit spending, on the other, served as the basis for a crisis whose systemic repercussions could have been more limited if there had been more adequate international financial regulation and macroeconomic policy coordination. Second, in the throes of the crisis, there was no international mechanism in place for debt resolution that would not endanger the whole global financial system and/or would provide a credible national adjustment path for debtor countries over the medium term. Such debt resolution processes, while quite demanding, have long-standing precedents in national contexts through a burden-sharing process between the debtor and the community of creditors. Third, even with the already existing practice of European supranational cooperation, the crisis appears to have spiralled out of control because of coordination delays among nations operating under disparate political conditions. These issues merely underline the urgent need for a global governance system that can address the treacherous conditions endangering the world economy and ensure a more stable context for development so as to enable it to foster and build a sustainable future for all.

Addressing the multiple global crises will need to go hand in hand with governance reforms

As emphasized in chapter I, the world community must wrestle with the economic and financial crisis on top of an already ongoing crisis of food and energy insecurity. The harmful effects of climate change are already being felt in many parts of the world and must also be addressed. These crises had been simmering for decades and their resolution will require many years of concerted efforts. Since the economic crisis erupted, there has been frequent reference to the truism that a global crisis requires a global solution. The problem is that the current global governance arrangements do not seem to be up to the task at hand, so that addressing these crises must be undertaken simultaneously with overcoming widespread weaknesses of multilateral mechanisms.

The present chapter will discuss the challenge of rebuilding global governance, while seeking to identify key requirements based on the survey of issues provided in the previous chapters. The key challenge is to establish a global governance system that will harness, instead of cowering before the forces of globalization. If the experience of the global economy's last great crisis in the 1930s is any guide, the globalization process itself will come to a sudden and catastrophic stop unless properly governed. Its sustainability and feasibility can be guaranteed only by an effective global governance system.

A piecemeal approach will not do.

The international community is currently engaged in a piecemeal reform of global governance. This chapter argues that reforms need to be comprehensive. The focus will be on key areas for reform and the directions that reform should take when addressing these areas in an integral way. Inevitably, certain areas may not be covered in this discussion. While the piecemeal approach has the advantage of gathering and relying on the support of dominant incumbent global players, it has the disadvantage of possibly being unable to keep up with the pace of the continuous morphing of the crisis into more complex forms (as in the European example). Being piecemeal, it also has the potential disadvantage of introducing new elements of incoherence. From a purely logical point of view and one that recognizes the need to build confidence, a deliberate and deliberative global process entailing programmed preparatory conferences focused on various areas of concern, which would lead to the strengthening or the creation of international mechanisms—a Bretton Woods II, as it were—is clearly superior.

The appeal to the Bretton Woods experience reflects the political economy-related uncertainties that beset global economic governance reform efforts (see box VI.1). Rebuilding global governance will require adjustments involving the derogation of powers and privileges of nation States within international bodies. This means that the process is highly political and must be conducted in circumstances where technical questions are not yet completely settled. Thus, while the pressures to reform cannot be evaded, the overall outcome cannot be anticipated in the present discussion.

Box VI.1

The Bretton Woods conference and economic development

The Bretton Woods conference, officially called the United Nations Monetary and Financial Conference, was a gathering of 730 delegates from all 44 Allied nations[a] in Bretton Woods, New Hampshire. The conference was held from 1 to 22 July 1944, less than a month after the Normandy landings and with more destruction and countless deaths yet to come before the Second World War ended. The negotiations at Bretton Woods towards the establishment of the International Bank for Reconstruction and Development (IBRD) and the International Monetary Fund (IMF) followed two years of preparatory work entailing background studies and discussions between the United States Treasury and the Chancellor of the Exchequer of the United Kingdom.

The Bretton Woods experience highlights the fact that, in creating new international mechanisms, full representation of all parties and stakeholders (India and the Philippines, although not yet independent States, still attended) is essential. The British proposal that the negotiations over global arrangements be conducted only by the United States of America and the United Kingdom of Great Britain and Northern Ireland (the 1940s version of the "G2", with the United States as the rising power) was not accepted by the United States.

Policymakers at the Conference were driven by the desire to assert the role of public authority within the realm of international finance in the wake of a major international financial meltdown. This overall goal culminated in three sets of proposals: (a) those designed to regulate international financial markets more tightly, (b) those aimed at addressing global economic imbalances and (c) those promoting international development. The third set of proposals, sometimes overlooked, constituted a fundamental part of the envisioned new international order.

These proposals reflected the belief that the promotion of the economic security of individuals throughout the world would provide a crucial foundation for post-war political stability, domestically and internationally. These sentiments were strongly supported not only by the United States and British delegations, but also by many other delegations represented at Bretton Woods, particularly those from developing countries. In fact, well over half the countries attending were from non-industrialized regions. Strong support for the development function of the Bank came from Latin America, China and still colonized India.

In this regard, article I(i) of the IBRD Articles of Agreement[b] affirmed that one of the purposes of the Bank was to encourage "the development of productive facilities and resources in less developed countries". Far from being an accident, the Bank's mandate to promote development was strongly supported at the time. Article I of the IMF Articles of Agreement[c] sets out the same objectives, albeit with slight differences in wording.

Fifty years later, GATT member countries created the World Trade Organization through the Agreement Establishing the World Trade Organization.[d] The parties to the Agreement recognized "that their relations in the field of trade and economic endeavour should be conducted with a view to raising standards of living, ensuring full employment and a large and steadily growing volume

a Besides 19 Latin American countries, other non-industrialized countries from outside Europe that were represented in the conference included China, Egypt, Ethiopia, India, Iran (Islamic Republic of), Iraq, Liberia, the Philippines and South Africa.

b Available from http://go.worldbank.org/WAUZA5KF90.

c Available from http://www.imf.org/external/pubs/ft/aa/aa01.htm.

d Available from http://www.wto.org/english/docs_e/legal_e/legal_e.htm

Box VI.1 (cont'd)

of real income and effective demand, and expanding the production of and trade in goods and services, while allowing for the optimal use of the world's resources in accordance with the objective of sustainable development, seeking both to protect and preserve the environment and to enhance the means for doing so in a manner consistent with their respective needs and concerns at different levels of economic development" and "that there is need for positive efforts designed to ensure that developing countries, and especially the least developed among them, secure a share in the growth in international trade commensurate with the needs of their economic development".

Three other issues were in the agenda governing the Bretton Woods negotiators' efforts to integrate development goals into the post-war international financial architecture, although they were not incorporated in the purposes set out in the final agreements: (a) the problem of capital flight from poor countries, (b) the question of restructuring the debts of poorer countries and (c) the promotion of government policies (particularly in Latin America) designed to build more diversified, industrialized and inward-focused national economies. The last-mentioned objective was to be attained by endorsing the use of capital controls, activist monetary policy aimed at domestic goals, adjustable exchange-rate pegs and government-controlled central banks.

In the face of increasing global inequality, pervasive financial crises and climate change, the pursuit, through such efforts, of a fairer and sustainable globalization, should be resumed.

Source: UN/DESA, based on Helleiner (2009).

Global governance: quo vadis?

The world has changed enormously since the current system of global governance was put together with the founding of the United Nations and the creation of the International Monetary Fund (IMF), the World Bank and the General Agreement on Tariffs and Trade (GATT). While the governance system has not stood still, adjustments have not kept pace with requirements of increasing interdependence among national economies through trade, investment, finance, international migration, and the technological advances in transport and communications.

On many occasions, the international community has issued pronouncements on the purposes of the global economic governance system. One of the earliest statements of purpose, subsequently restated with slight changes in the agreements establishing other international institutions, such as the World Trade Organization, appeared in the IMF Articles of Agreement. Article I(ii) thereof affirms that one purpose of the Fund was to "facilitate the expansion and balanced growth of international trade, and to contribute thereby to the promotion and maintenance of high levels of employment and real income and to the development of the productive resources of all members". Such phrases, in this specific case applicable to IMF but subsequently associated with other institutions, can be read as embodying the international community's view that the expansion of international interaction must in the first place support high and stable employment. Most importantly, by calling for the development of the productive resources of all member countries, the international community has put development at the centre of multilateral cooperation and global governance.

Overcoming the asymmetries that characterize the world economic system is critical

In a recent parsing of this overall objective, Ocampo (2010) comes up with finer criteria for evaluating global governance arrangements. They should (a) manage interdependence, (b) further the development of societies and (c) overcome the asymmetries that characterize the world economic system. This proposal recognizes that the construction of international public processes and institutions may entail facing the inevitability of certain context-specific trade-offs. Through the putting in place of public institutions and mechanisms, the global community has conveyed its commitment to prioritizing the fulfilment of these criteria (thereby going beyond adherence to the standard economic formulation that public goods exist only in a situation of non-rival and non-excludable consumption).

The formulation of "common but differentiated responsibilities" is treaty language that encapsulates an international approach to reconciling the three above-mentioned goals. While some international arrangements will emphasize one goal more than the others, reconciling all three will be critical. There is a need to allocate agendas and responsibilities, first, between global mechanisms and nation States and, second, among the international processes, in a coherent and mutually reinforcing way. The focus of previous chapters has centred mainly on the first two goals. This chapter will highlight the issue of global asymmetries.

Globalization and national policy space

Nation States must assume the primary responsibility for their own development (United Nations, 2002, para. 6), a conception that corresponds to the second key pillar of global governance provided by Ocampo (2010). Close on the heels of the current economic crisis and the multiple threats from climate change, food insecurity and increased political instability, a full-blown restoration of the Government's indispensable economic role is very much under way.

The decline in the responsibilities and corresponding capabilities of national authorities paralleled the rise of economic interdependence and globalization. This trend was "man-made": States surrendered some of their powers, along with the corresponding responsibilities, to the market, on the principle that market outcomes were superior to State interventions. Rodrik (2002) takes up a phrase—the "golden straitjacket"—introduced by a popular columnist to capture the naivety of this view. There were asymmetries between developed and developing countries in the context of the State's retreat from market oversight. Advanced countries tend to have a superior informational infrastructure and superior legal powers for monitoring market developments. In developing countries, an early deregulation often precludes achievement of the institutional development needed to govern the market. Reporting requirements on capital-account transactions, which would be necessary not only for macroeconomic policymaking but also for prudential financial regulation, are a key example of such development. As discussed in chapter V, the golden straitjacket in financial deregulation subjected developing countries to greater volatility in capital flows.

Increased economic interdependence has reduced the scope for national policies

Part of the above-mentioned decline has been induced by unavoidable constrictions arising from increased economic interdependence and the spread of largely unregulated private transnational economic operations through global value chains (see chap. IV). Countries that manage to impose restrictions on capital inflows, for example, risk saddling neighbouring countries or economies in the same investment class with increased flows. The financial crisis saw bank depositors withdrawing their balances in distressed countries and investing these in other centres perceived to be more stable. International financial institutions withdrew balances and credit lines in overseas branches when they needed to shore up their balance sheets in their mother institutions based in developed countries.

Rebuilding the international governance system will require rebuilding the capabilities of the State, both domestically and internationally. States must be allowed to keep the powers that will prove necessary if they are to take the primary responsibility for their own development. Primary responsibility applies not only to the implementation but also to the design of development strategy (see chap. II). As discussed in chapter III, this principle requires that external assistance programmes align behind national development strategies. Sovereign States must respect and not undermine the domestic resource mobilization efforts of other States (see chaps. III and V).

Preserving adequate policy space for national Governments will need to be a key objective of the rebalancing of global governance responsibilities

The 15 November 2008 Declaration of the G-20 Leaders Summit on Financial Markets and the World Economy (Washington, D.C., 14 and 15 November 2008)[1] underlined the role of nation States in global regulation by affirming that "[r]egulation is first and foremost the responsibility of national regulators who constitute the first line of defense against market instability" (para. 8). While this formulation clearly recognizes and assigns responsibilities and powers to national authorities, it does not ultimately resolve the difficult issue of rebalancing powers between global mechanisms while preserving adequate policy space for national Governments. The issue of the economic impact of individual States' policies on those of others cannot be completely resolved by a "first line" approach.

Managing financial interdependence will require setting up minimum global standards and commitments to adjust domestic policies which will reduce national policy space. It will require that each layer of international governance be provided with sufficient space and monitoring and enforcement capability to fulfil its role. As elaborated on in chapter V, a key objective of opening up policy space for developing countries is reducing the volatility of private flows to which they have been subjected from international markets.

One could list some important priorities identified in previous chapters: social development (chap. II), controlling aid donor activities (chap. III), industrial development and economic diversification (chap. IV) and re-establishing capital-account controls and prudential regulation (chap. V).

Protecting the space for domestic policy experimentation is important

The key national policy issue for developing countries concerns the space for experimenting with the utilization of a broader range of development tools, while building on existing domestic institutions and capabilities and proceeding along the lines suggested in chapter II. The international community finds itself at the end of the era in which global development was promoted through thoroughgoing social engineering approaches for the purpose of creating the preconditions for the emergence of vibrant private markets. The experience in many successor economies of the former Soviet Union suggests that building private markets and releasing private initiative for development are context-specific and that the rapid importation of Western legal and administrative institutions can be costly in human terms. For example, rapid privatization of State enterprises not only led to asset stripping but also dismantled the informal social support mechanisms that had been built up around these enterprises in the socialist period, which led to rapid increases in indigence, especially in the first phases of the economic transition (Ellerman, 2010).

The negative experiences arising from the transition matters just as much as the positive ones. The major lesson to be learned from the post-communist transition is precisely that State institutions are of crucial importance. Whereas the example of the Soviet Union had proved that a non-market economic system with an all-prevailing State cannot be efficient, the transformational recession of the 1990s proved that the market without a strong State results in the substitution of unaccountable state power for unregulated private wealth accumulation, leading to economic and social decline (Holmes, 1997).

---

1 Available from http://www/g20.org/Documents/g20_summit_declaration.pdf.

Reforming global economic governance

In 2002, in the Monterrey Consensus of the International Conference on Financing for Development, the international community made a commitment to "good governance at all levels" (United Nations, 2002, para. 4), recognizing that striving for good governance at the national level is incoherent if not matched by good governance in international bodies and mechanisms. Commonly accepted norms for good governance might need to be applied systematically to international bodies and processes.

Transparency, accountability, effectiveness, fairness and ownership are key features of good governance

As embraced by the Bretton Woods institutions in their lending operations, good governance is commonly thought to have the following characteristics: transparency, accountability, efficiency (or effectiveness, in common parlance), fairness and ownership (Woods, 2000). The situations in which these general values are relevant are very much overlapping and they need to be applied to the specific operational issues confronting international organizations. Conflicts-of-interest issues may result in the undermining of the values of transparency and accountability. These conflicts of interest exist, for example, in international debt resolution mechanisms where the Bretton Woods institutions, themselves creditors with a material interest in maintaining debt service, have a key role in the Paris Club process, which passes judgements on the sovereign debt obligations (see chap. V). Unfocused agendas and expansion of activities beyond their assigned role in international governance or core competencies violate principles of accountability and efficiency. The expansion of the areas under World Trade Organization disciplines into financial services and investment rules, as discussed in previous chapters, is one product of an unfocused agenda (see chap. IV). Effectiveness and fairness require that all stakeholders, particularly minorities and small economic players, be assured of having a voice. The question of sufficient voice and participation of developing countries in the design of prudential standards, highlighted in chapter V, is one aspect of this. Fairness and ownership are evidenced through an emphasis on participation and democratic processes. Efforts to accelerate progress in reallocating voting weights in the Bretton Woods institutions to reflect the increased significance of developing countries are consistent with promoting good governance.

Specialization and coordination

The international system relies on specialized institutions

By design, the international system relies on specialized institutions and processes to address specific global issues. As discussed in previous chapters, the proliferation of the agendas of existing institutions is a key source of system incoherence. In order to eliminate costly duplication and conflicting policy agendas, the process of defining more precisely the roles of existing institutions and refocusing their existing activities on core competencies—a process that has already begun—needs to be accelerated. The previous chapters have indicated the general directions in which reform efforts can proceed, but have not provided a blueprint. Similarly, in this chapter, general directions—not a blueprint—for strengthening governance, are offered.

The World Trade Organization

The World Trade Organization should remain the champion of the multilateral trading system. Its singular role of proscribing engagement in discriminatory trade practices by powerful trading nations should be strengthened. This will require more rigorous disciplines over free trade agreements and economic partnership agreements which not only tend to generate unwanted trade diversion but also rechannel commerce into venues where developing countries tend to be at a disadvantage.

The main thrust of the reform process should be towards helping developing countries secure access to the markets and technologies available in developed countries on a non-reciprocal and preferential basis. Some concrete suggestions relating to the realization of such an aim, were presented in chapter IV, particularly in regard to strengthening and democratizing the World Trade Organization's dispute resolution process. As discussed in chapter IV, the World Trade Organization's agenda has expanded to include trade-related areas, such as financial regulation and migration, whose challenges would be better addressed in more specialized venues.

Most likely, the global regime that emerges from climate change negotiations combined with individual-country climate change policies will have a significant impact on the global trade regime. For example, there are many proposals for border adjustment measures to make up for the negative impact on international competitiveness of domestic environmental regulations. Disciplines under the trade-related aspects of intellectual property rights could prove too restrictive or expensive to facilitate a big push in clean energy investment in developing countries. Reconciling climate change imperatives with existing World Trade Organization disciplines will pose challenges but, as argued in chapter IV, the process of seeking greater coherence between the two regimes should begin with a conferring of primacy on the objectives of averting the threat of climate change.

Similarly, attempts at strengthening financial regulation and creating more national policy space through capital control are creating tensions with rules of the World Trade Organization regarding liberal trade of financial services under the General Agreement on Trade in Services, where—as suggested in chapters IV and V—primacy in rules setting would seem to lie more appropriately with objectives of global financial stability pursued as part of financial regulatory reforms.

The International Monetary Fund

IMF must play a critical role in operating and managing a reformed global reserve and payments system and must be the venue for multilateral cooperation in exchange rate setting through its surveillance function, under the principles elaborated in chapter V.[2]

IMF responsibilities and capacities will need to be significantly augmented if macroeconomic policy coordination is to be institutionalized and surveillance strengthened (see chap. V). This will involve extending the purview of IMF to include capital movements. In the years immediately following the Second World War, when the World Bank and IMF were being set up, the focus was on the current account. An emphasis on flexibility evolved into a fostering of unsafe volatility as IMF adopted a hands-off—and even a cheerleading—stance with regard to expansion of private financial flows. As indicated in chapter V, IMF could play a constructive role in assisting countries instal, operate and coordinate controls in the capital account.

IMF programmes should simplify conditionality and refrain from imposing trade and domestic governance conditions that are relevant to payments and exchange-rate issues only in the very long term. A more even-handed international debt resolution approach, as suggested in chapter V, would determine that IMF should not be the

2 The Commission of Experts of the President of the United Nations General Assembly on Reforms of the International Monetary and Financial System proposed to replace IMF with a totally new organization, having the capability from its inception to create global liquidity (see United Nations, 2009d).

sole source of macroeconomic programming since it would be a member of the group of creditor-claimants. Debtors, as members of a "cooperative" pool, could accord IMF claims some level of seniority, and on the grounds that IMF is a public entity. The same conflict-of-interest argument would require that IMF, as one of the players in international lending, should not be the coordinator of financial regulation.

IMF must seek to be perceived as an organization basically intent on helping countries deal with payments difficulties while preserving the growth of their economies, consistent with its articles of incorporation. A more even-handed approach to surveillance, applied particularly to countries whose macroeconomic policies have an impact on developing countries, as discussed in chapter V, is critical in governance terms for protecting the integrity of IMF as an organization that intervenes solely in the interest of ensuring systemic stability. A redistribution of the IMF capital contributions, with greater weight for developing countries, may prove helpful in bringing about the desired reorientation.

Multilateral development banks

Multilateral development banks have a critical role to play in contributing to an adequate flow of financing for development by leveraging global private savings to support critical development projects. In the last decade, the flow of non-concessional financing from the World Bank particularly has been found to be inadequate (if not negative, net of repayments on existing loans), especially with regard to middle-income countries. Increased reliance on private lending by the Bank's potential borrowers has been necessitated by the competitive costs of private loans which do not come with policy conditionality. Rethinking the role of policy conditionality and, by extension, of the kinds of purposes for which multilateral bank resources should be applied is therefore critical to ensuring that these banks are able to fulfil their critical role. There is in fact a possibility that refocusing the activities of multilateral development banks so as to align their lending to national development strategies, including a withdrawal from policy lending, could actually increase the volume and quality of the finance that these banks are able to intermediate for developmental purposes. Genuinely finance-oriented multilateral development banks would steer clear of policy conditionality and this would also be consistent with the donor-accepted principle of country ownership (see chap. III).

In the case of the World Bank, as a result of reform efforts and shifting pressures from donors, reflecting evolution in approaches to development (see chap. II), its resources are being applied in a wide variety of areas. Currently, the World Bank, inter alia, is a repository of knowledge regarding development, sets standards in the area of debt distress and debt resolution, operates a variety of donor-driven trust funds beyond the reach of its shareholders, and finances not only development projects but also governance reforms in developing countries.

Refocusing the activities of multilateral development banks towards the financing of large-scale infrastructure projects is one approach

One possible target of refocusing would be the financing of large infrastructure projects, as was the case when the World Bank was first founded. Similarly, the Bank could have a role to play as an implementing arm of large-scale energy and infrastructure projects in the area of climate change mitigation and adaptation. First, even with liberalized financial markets, and financial innovations like build-operate-and-transfer and build-operate-and-operate, the private sector has not managed to generate the kinds of volumes required to finance infrastructure requirements without requiring elaborate government guarantees and standard-setting. Moreover, the fact that large infrastructure projects, such as dams and road construction, are often accompanied by social adjustments and political controversy raises the risks to private financiers. As a public institution, the World Bank can, in its operations, be asked to assist the private sector in the design and co-financing of large development projects within the framework of addressing the adjustment and social issues that naturally arise from these. It can build on capacities already established through incorporating environmental impact assessments in its operations and can apply these techniques in handling other social priorities.

For coherence, such large-scale infrastructure projects must be aligned with national development strategies

For purposes of coherence, large infrastructure projects financed by the World Bank would need to be part of national development plans in recipient countries (see chap. II). A focus on large infrastructural projects implies that the World Bank could move out of the area of policy conditionality. Policy conditionality had been introduced almost as an accident of history in the 1980s to ramp up financing for developing countries beyond project lending levels. This was perceived to be a means of rescuing deposit money banks in danger of bankruptcy from the sovereign debt crisis through more rapid loan disbursements aimed at funding institutional reform programmes for market-oriented development strategies. Reforming sovereign debt mechanisms (see chap. V and below) should obviate the need for this type of policy conditionality.

Multilateral development banks can also increase the volume of their development finance through bond purchases and bond guarantees, particularly at the regional level, for funds devoted to infrastructure and energy development. Because of the increased probability of the emergence of secondary bond markets facilitated by such intervention, this approach could actually help lead to the development of financial markets locally and regionally and would be in sharp contrast to the previous approach of policy lending intended to facilitate the emergence of private bond markets through deregulatory and liberalization reforms.

Increased use of special drawing rights (SDRs) could expand the resources available to multilateral development banks

Increased use of special drawing rights (SDRs) would open the possibility of expanding the financing activities of the multilateral development banks beyond intermediating private savings into development projects. Such an approach would be especially appropriate if development-oriented macroeconomic policy indeed became more widespread and the requirements for large scale financing become more prevalent. This would be particularly applicable to climate change financing, which might be supported by allocation of SDRs, assuming that the projects concerned were in harmony with the global climate change regime.

In undertaking a loan evaluation, the World Bank would necessarily incorporate the probability of repayment based on the best available information. However, in the event of a need for debt resolution, because of the conflict of interest, as a creditor institution itself the World Bank should have the status of being one among other creditors, notwithstanding the element of seniority built into the original loan agreement with a public lending institution. Governance principles suggest that if the Bank recused itself from juries that passed judgement on debtor obligations, it would improve internal incentives for effective loan evaluation.

Regional development banks could have an advantage in supporting institutional development

Regional development banks could consider incorporating these same governance imperatives. They could co-finance large-scale infrastructure projects with the World Bank and also focus on development of regional and national financial markets by taking bond positions in those markets (see chap. V). These banks are better placed to participate through their expertise in institutional development in their regions. According to Ocampo (2010, p. 14), "[i]nstitutional development, the creation of mechanisms of social cohesion, and the accumulation of human capital and technological capacities ('knowledge capital') are essentially endogenous processes" and are better developed locally.

Missing or weak international institutions

Surveys in previous chapters have identified critical areas that are characterized by a lack of international mechanisms and institutions.

International financial regulation

The existing international financial architecture relies on private organizations over which public oversight is limited

International financial regulation constitutes the most current challenge. Much of the existing international financial architecture relies on private organizations and, as the current crisis suggests, public oversight over and regulation of those organizations are indispensable. Accounting standards are determined in the private International Accounting Standard Boards, whose activities are mainly financed by large global accounting firms. The international coordination of equity market regulation is dependent on the deliberations of the International Organization of Securities Commissions (IOSCO). There is also a need to improve private oversight over credit ratings agencies. Chapter V emphasized that financial sectors in mature industrialized economies must bear the additional burden of maintaining financial standards so that their activities do not impose instability on other economies. It also suggested the need for an independent international process overseeing international financial regulatory mechanisms, which would take precedence in rule-setting over the World Trade Organization, because expanding global financial services needed to be accompanied by robust regulatory arrangements.

Sovereign debt workout mechanisms

A sovereign debt restructuring is critical to developing a stable international financial system

As discussed in chapter V, a new framework for sovereign debt restructuring is critical to developing a stable international financial system that promotes economic development. The existing ad hoc and piecemeal approaches to both official and market-based sovereign debt restructuring have been inefficient and costly, especially for developing countries. Workouts often take place with undue lags which prolong distress and economic hardship; and outside of the Multilateral Debt Relief Initiative (MDRI), the solutions almost never provide enough debt relief to give debtor countries a "fresh start" in returning to growth. There are two key governance challenges. First, the process should mediate effectively and fairly between debtors and creditors, because this is the best guarantee that enough resources will be made available for a fresh start, which is in the interest of both parties. This means that the adjudication must be lodged with an independent body. Second, the process should be enforceable on all creditors in all jurisdictions, which means that all States must commit to enforcing debt resolution decisions. National courts would have to recognize the legitimacy of the international arbiter and respect its rulings, which would require amendments in domestic contract laws.

Technology transfer

A development-friendly international technological regime is needed

Technology is a critical input to development and a key driver of global inequality and thus is a key arena within which to overcome international assymetries (Ocampo, 2010). Aside from the World Intellectual Property Organization (WIPO) mechanism, which has dealt mainly with disseminating intellectual property standards internationally, the World Trade Organization intellectual property regime is the only enforceable approach applicable to the international transmission of technology. As discussed in chapter IV, developing countries must rely on so-called flexibilities to obtain access to needed technology. The need for a development-friendly international technological regime is an issue being debated in connection with the proposed work programme of WIPO.

Environmental protection and climate policy

The Conference of the Parties to the United Nations Framework Convention on Climate Change[3] is the treaty body dedicated to promoting collective action to reduce global warming and to cope with corresponding temperature increases. The Kyoto Protocol to the United Nations Framework Convention on Climate Change[4] binds 37 participating developed countries and the European community to limits on the emission of greenhouse gases. Of the four agreed pillars of the Framework Convention—mitigation, adaptation, finance and technology—the last two in particular have implications for coherence in global economic governance, as has been pointed out in earlier chapters.

The United Nations Framework Convention on Climate Change has inadequate reach and limited enforcement capability

The United Nations Framework Convention on Climate Change has inadequate reach (not all countries are party to binding commitments) and limited enforcement capability. Ongoing climate change negotiations must address this weakness. A key governance challenge related to the Framework Convention concerns mechanisms of transfer from developed to developing countries, raising resources to the required levels, and implementation and monitoring in this regard (see chap. V, box V.2; and Clark, 2010). The Framework Convention could be assigned the responsibility for setting overall guidelines, based on treaty commitments, for the contribution and the use of funds. If empowered, it could monitor these flows and evaluate country compliance to commitments.

Migration and labour services

Regulation of migration and labour services is too complex an issue to be left to General Agreement on Trade in Services

The challenges of establishing a more humane and mutually beneficial migration process were discussed in chapters II and IV. Labour migration requires difficult social adjustments in receiving and sending countries and does not involve only the issue of filling needed jobs. A dedicated multilateral process to deal with these complex issues is needed. As in the case of climate change, the configuration of a future regime is the subject of international negotiations. The recognition by the World Trade Organization that the principle of liberalization also encompasses the movement of natural persons (under Mode 4) represents a significant step forward, even though in respect of applying this principle, developed countries have so far showed interest mainly in persons with a very high level of education and specialized skills. Meanwhile, based on its many years of work on migration, the International Labour Organization (ILO) has developed a Multilateral Framework on Labour Migration (MFLM), proceeding from a rights-based approach. While focused more on the rights of migrants, the Multilateral Framework also calls for international cooperation to facilitate both temporary and permanent migration. One may note, for instance, that immigrants comprise 88, 71 and 70 per cent of the population in Qatar, the United Arab Emirates and Kuwait, respectively.

Protecting the human rights of migrants should be an immediate priority

Until a more favourable situation emerges for permanent immigration, temporary labour flows could be managed in order to enhance global welfare and protect the human rights of migrants. Given their prior work on migration, ILO and the International Organization for Migration (IOM) might cooperate in creating a global clearing house for

3 United Nations, *Treaty Series*, vol. 1771, No. 30822.

4 Ibid., vol. 2303, No. 30822.

world labour demand and supply. Such a global labour regime could bring order to the currently chaotic situation of spontaneously arising labour flows, some of which are illegal, which impose significant costs on the migrants themselves (they sometimes pay with their lives) and often provoke the ire and resentment of the people in destination countries.

Global economic coordination

No mechanism exists to ensure consistency across the global trade, financial, migration and environmental protection regimes

A corollary of the need for more strongly focused international institutions is the need for a strengthened multilateral coordination mechanism, to ensure that the activities of individual agencies and commissions are not in conflict and do not encroach on each other's purviews. The previous chapters have presented numerous instances of the kinds of agenda-related conflicts that might be adjudicated or even eliminated by such a coordinating council. The mechanisms through which such a council could so act would depend on the kinds of enforcement capabilities with which nation States would be willing to invest it. This shall be discussed below.

Additionally, such a coordinating body could address the cases of missing international institutions, as mentioned above. A coordinating body could advance progress by commissioning research reports and convening discussions among key parties. Such a functioning coordinating body, with its own tradition of procedures and working methods, would be a natural venue within which to address the challenge of braking global crises, such as the food, energy and the financial crises.

Bodies already exist that could discharge this needed function. The Economic and Social Council is the United Nations organ charged with coordinating the economic and social and related work of the 14 specialized agencies, the functional commissions and the 5 regional commissions. Along with the strengthening of governance and international procedures, the Council could be mandated with a coordinating function that encompassed more than just United Nations entities. There have been a variety of proposals regarding the creation of a body along the lines of the United Nations Security Council, the most recent proposal focusing on a global economic coordination council, supported by an international panel of experts (United Nations, 2009d). Among the key arguments underpinning the proposal for the establishment of a more powerful body is that the challenge presented by the current crisis appears to call for a thoroughgoing reform of existing institutions. According to another argument, the kind of interconnectedness of issues that has been discussed in this report requires the presence of such a body.

Voice, legitimacy and effectiveness

Governance reform must consider the growing weight of developing countries in the global economy

The Monterrey Consensus called for the modernized governance structure of global finance institutions to be more consonant with the fundamentally changed structure of the global economy, which stems mainly from the much greater weight of developing countries therein. The developing countries are also home to a much greater proportion of the human population. Functionally speaking, the argument for an increased voice and participation of developing countries in global governance was based on the need for the users of the resources and services to be assured of the effectiveness, relevance and accountability of those mechanisms.

When the original Bretton Woods institutions were established, their potential users had been allocated a weight of voice and governance that was undoubtedly much greater than what could be justified on the grounds of economic significance in a world in which, by any measure, the United States had the overwhelming economic weight. The argument that providing users with an ample voice would be a guarantee of the responsive and accountable agenda-setting and operation of a public institution applies now as it did then; but in terms of both economic weight and accountability to users, developing countries are underrepresented in decision-making in these institutions. Recently proposed reforms (such as the G-20 targets of a voting weight increase in favour of developing countries of at least 5 per cent in the IMF and at least 3 per cent in the World Bank) are being pursued but progress is very slow. In any case, these reforms would not offer the ample weight that potential users were allocated in the beginning. Forthright voting reforms in the World Bank and the Fund are critical because their constituency-based systems, enhanced by a system of basic votes, provide a stake in the organizations for the smallest economies, and could be an important model for other international institutions.

Voting distributions should be appropriate to the purpose of the organization

As a general rule, voting distributions should be appropriate to the purpose of the organization. In the financing of development projects, a scheme of equal weights in voting power of donors and recipients does have precedents, for instance, within the Inter-American Development Bank, and could constitute an appropriate voting allocation within the World Bank as well. Enlarging the resources and capacities of international institutions over the long term will ensure organizational effectiveness, but will also require the exerting of greater influence by the community of developing countries.

Inequality, exit and enforcement

The main underlying reason for the deficiencies of the current institutions of globalization is structural inequality of economic and political power between the developed countries, on the one hand, and the developing countries, on the other (Nayyar, 2010). It is this inequality that pervades various multilateral institutions and bilateral relations between developed countries, on the one hand, and developing countries, on the other. In a sense, this inequality of powers is a legacy of the colonial era.

Inequality

This underlying structural inequality implies that mere changes in formal rules may not be sufficient to counteract the processes of divergence and differentiation and make globalization sustainable. The processes unfolding at the World Trade Organization illustrate this reality. Unlike the World Bank and IMF, where decisions are taken on the basis of subscription- or contribution-weighted voting, the World Trade Organization operates on the basis of the "one-country, one-vote" principle. However, this apparent democratic decision-making process is not doing much to make the World Trade Organization work in favour of developing countries or to make globalization sustainable.

Inequality in economic and political strength stymies and could effectively nullify equality in voting power

The basic inequality in economic and political strength stymies and effectively nullifies the equality in voting power in one forum (the World Trade Organization), and this is much like what happens through the mechanism of interlocking markets which ties sharecropper to landlord in the model of Bhaduri (1973). When a developing country is tied to developed countries in so many other ways through unequal relationships, it is difficult for it to assert its equality in one particular arena. Besides failing to influence the outcome of World Trade Organization negotiations, many developing countries fail to otherwise make use of several avenues for remediation that offer formal equality of access. For example, many developing countries find the World Trade Organization's dispute settlement mechanism to be beyond their reach because of the cost and technical sophistication requirements associated with its utilization (see chap. IV; and Toye, 2010). Indeed, it is difficult for a small developing country to take retaliatory measures against the large, powerful developed countries on which it may depend in so many ways (for example, as a source of remittance income), not to mention the simple fact that retaliation is effective only if the size of the trade volume is large, which is usually not the case for developing countries.

Exit

To progressively reduce global asymmetries, which is the third criterion for global governance arrangements offered by Ocampo (2010), is an indispensable one. The international precedents for application of the principle of differentiated responsibilities stretch back to the GATT; and modernizing the application of affirmative action and protection for the weak is critical to ensuring the increasing engagement of these countries in international commerce. International arrangements arguably would be robust if they provided time-bound opt-out rules (Toye, 2010) for those with a clear incapacity to meet them. The single-undertaking approach of the World Trade Organization makes it difficult to implement such rules (Drache, 2010), and this, combined with its expansive agenda, makes it difficult to reach agreement. Clear, predictable standards with respect to differentiated responsibilities are required.

The trade-off is that if there are too many exceptions, powerful countries will exit international disciplines. Exit, which is the ultimate enforcement mechanism available to economically powerful countries, would have a negative impact on developing countries.

If there are too many exceptions, powerful countries will exit international disciplines

The role of caucuses

The emergence of the G-20 as a self-annointed, self-selected grouping arranged to oversee economic recovery and reform has raised many questions about the role of these kinds of formations in global governance. The G-20, which is an expansion of the Group of Eight (G-8), is often described as an improvement. Caucuses' limited memberships are often seen as necessary for the taking of timely decisions that can be enforced by economic players having the actual power to do so. This criterion of effectiveness in reaching enforceable decisions should indeed be one basis on which all groupings must be judged. In terms of this criterion, the G-20 has succeeded on some fronts but not on others. One notable success is the increase in resources for IMF, which basically involved ensuring that other important economies would support a change in the stance long maintained by the United States regarding the matter.

On other issues, the effectiveness of the G-20 is still in doubt. It has formulated general objectives for macroeconomic coordination without setting out the details of a process of institutionalization (see chap. V). There is no guarantee that the technical designs on international financial regulation requested by the G-20 from the Financial Stability Board and IMF will be accepted by all G-20 members. Countries that are represented both in the G-20 and in official international bodies such as IMF do not have to take the same position in both bodies, making the effectiveness of these kinds of groupings unpredictable. Still, inadequate as they are, only official international bodies have enforcement capability and ultimately caucuses must implement their own decisions through

Effectiveness is an important criterion in evaluating groupings those bodies. Improving the effectiveness of official international bodies with enforcement capability should be a priority shared by all countries and by all caucuses.

Decisions of groups can be implemented only through official bodies

The effectiveness of a caucus or grouping in implementing its decisions through official bodies depends on its own internal cohesion, which depends in turn on the ability of all its members to participate fully in its deliberations and accept the group's decisions as their own. The tendency of these groupings to rely, for technical and staff support, on institutions in which some members may feel they have insufficient influence (the G-20, for example, relies on Organization for Economic Cooperation and Development (OECD) and IMF staff) undermines cohesion.

New platforms have proposed themselves as acting in the global interest

The organization of country groupings is based on a perceived inherent common interest of its members. The fact that new country groupings have presented themselves as acting in the global interest immediately raises the governance issue of representativeness. Using the most expansive determination of the size of the European Community, G-20 members like to point out that they account for 91.5 per cent of world gross domestic product (GDP) and 66.5 per cent of the world's population. These highly documented demonstrations of representativeness still violate principles of fairness and recognition of the rights of the weak and minority interests, which are unlikely to be internalized by members. There do exist representative organizations, such as the United Nations, but their effectiveness has been questioned. That there is a parallel existence of groupings claiming global reach, on the one hand, and of globally representative organizations, on the other, does act as a spur to both types of entities to raise their effectiveness and representativeness. Establishing channels of communication and coordination between these two kinds of global body must be a priority.

Enforcement mechanisms

At this juncture, the international community has only one effective enforcement mechanism in place, namely, the dispute settlement mechanism, which is able to generate binding rulings that authorize countries to impose trade sanctions on others. It happens to be based in the World Trade Organization, and this is one reason why many countries find that it would be in their interest to expand the World Trade Organization agenda. This approach relies on the Westphalian principle that sovereign States are the world's highest-level independent actors.

Can a global economic coordinating council adjudicate cases in the same way that the World Trade Organization's dispute settlement mechanism does?

Chapter IV has discussed how, even within the World Trade Organization, the dispute settlement mechanism is heavily skewed against countries with small markets and small public sectors. As an enforcement mechanism, it appears to be quite effective. Should such a mechanism be applicable in other areas, though perhaps not through the World Trade Organization? Assuming that a strengthened Economic and Social Council or a global economic coordinating council could adjudicate cases in the same way that dispute panels in the World Trade Organization do today, should trade sanctions be the enforcement instrument of choice?

Other proposed enforcement mechanisms either have, historically, been proposed or, like the "scarce currency" powers of IMF, exist but are not applied. The scarce currency sanction (under article VII of the IMF Articles of Agreement) represented a compromise with the original Keynesian proposal that IMF function as a genuine currency union where countries would have to pay a penalty on surplus payments balances. Such penalties would have provided debtor nations with unrestricted access to the clearing fund without having to seek approval or make domestic adjustments. Following the rejection of the idea by the United States, a compromise was reached in the form of the scarce currency clause which authorizes, upon the determination of IMF, capital restrictions and trade discrimination against countries with chronically excessive trade surpluses. *World Economic Situation and Prospects 2010* (United Nations, 2010, p. 94) has presented another type of enforcement mechanism involving the imposition of sanctions on countries for non-compliance with internationally agreed prudential regulations.

In the monetary-financial area, there are effective mechanisms for enforcing changes in domestic policy, but these have been applicable only to debtor countries, through Bretton Woods programmes.[5] Greater enforcement power over countries whose domestic policies have systemic impact could potentially elevate the role of the Bretton Woods institutions internationally: rather than enforcers of the collection of international claims on developing countries, they could become genuine instruments of global governance.

What is to be done?

The risks associated with the deeper interdependence of national economies exposed by the crisis can foster a drastic retreat from globalization. There are, however, feasible approaches to initiating more sustainable globalization processes. The previous chapters have examined various approaches to retooling the existing aid, trade and financial architectures with a view to filling such gaps and eliminating such traps in the international system as undermine development efforts. Overcoming institutional weaknesses in the key international organizations, such as IMF and the World Bank, and eliminating inequities in respect of the access to participation, particularly at the World Trade Organization, are also important. There are glaring inadequacies in the global coordination of economic decision-making, including conflicting agendas and conflicting rules in the areas of trade, aid and debt.

The proposed directions for global reforms are challenging ones

The previous chapters have identified a number of challenging directions for reform, including:

- Providing sufficient policy space for developing countries so as to allow them to deploy a broader range of development policies
- Reforming the technology regime, particularly in the light of the climate change challenge, so as to ensure greater access for developing countries
- Reforming the global regime overseeing international labour flows
- Establishing and resourcing coordinated counter-cyclical mechanisms among economies
- Coordinating international financial regulation and controlling regulatory and tax competition among countries
- Averting climate change

The principle of common-but-differentiated rights and obligations will need to be applied in practice

Retooling the rules of the game for a fair and sustainable global development is necessary, but not sufficient. Retooling is also about the players. Providing developing countries having weaker initial conditions with more of the time, resources and policy space needed for them to become full participants is to be regarded not as an act of charity or goodwill on the part of the powerful but as an imperative for realizing the shared goal of expanding international commerce. The principle of common-but-differentiated rights and obligations which are to be defined as a function of level of development will need to be applied in practice and embedded within a system of clear-cut rules.

5 The conflict between good governance principles and the Paris Club process was discussed in chapter V.

Reshaping rules is easier said than done. Players will need to agree on the common global sustainable development goals to be pursued and will need to be convinced that cooperation will provide net benefits for all—benefits serving present and future generations. However, within any scheme of international cooperation, net benefits may be perceived as not being equal for all; and any expected unevenness in outcomes may impede the reaching of effective global solutions. Because of differences in living standards, and therefore in capacity to pay, some countries will be expected to shoulder larger shares of the total costs of providing global public goods, which may reduce their incentive to cooperate in providing them. Hence, with respect to establishing multilateral agreements, the proposed pattern of burden-sharing is as important as the extent of the benefits to be conferred by the public goods.

The pattern of uneven development brought about by globalization so far has been sustainable neither economically nor environmentally

The international community must face a key fact, namely, that the pattern of uneven development brought about by globalization so far has been sustainable neither economically nor environmentally, nor has it been feasible politically. As this time around, developing countries are much more significant and much better integrated into the world economy, the global crisis has profounder implications and more serious consequences for development. While the present crisis only highlights the ever-present risks associated with the deeper integration of national economies into the world economy, the issue concerns not so much a retreat from globalization, as a feasible reshaping of the globalization process. The proposed means of retooling the existing aid, trade and financial architectures aim at overcoming present shortcomings. It is equally important to overcome institutional shortcomings in current decision-making in the key organizations of global economic governance, such as IMF and the World Bank, and to eliminate inequities in respect of the access to participation in other organizations, such as the World Trade Organization.

A coordination mechanism to ensure coherence in global economic governance is needed more urgently than ever

There is a need to strengthen the global coordination of economic decision-making so as to minimize the number of cases where rules dealing with trade, aid, debt, finance, migration, environmental sustainability and other development issues come into conflict. At present, there is no international agency dealing systematically with questions of coherence and consistency in multilateral rules-setting. The global crisis has provided painful evidence of the weaknesses of the present system. The issues of climate change and demographic changes demand even greater coherence among the spheres of global governance and between decision-making processes at the global and national levels. Whatever its shape, the foundation to be established for international coordination based on shared principles and transparent mechanisms is more urgently needed than ever.

Bibliography

Adhikari, Ratnakar, and Yumiko Yamamoto (2007). The textiles and clothing industry: adjusting to a post quota world. In *Industrial Development for the 21st Century: Sustainable Development Perspectives*. United Nations publication, Sales No. E.07.II.A.1.

Addison, Tony, Channing Arndt and Finn Tarp (2010). The triple crisis and the global aid architecture. Background paper prepared for *World Economic and Social Survey 2010: Retooling Global Development.*

Aguayo Ayala, Francisco, and Kevin P. Gallagher (2005). Preserving policy space for sustainable development: the subsidies agreement at the WTO. Winnepeg, Canada: Trade Knowledge Network, International Institute for Sustainable Development. December. Available from http://www.ase.tufts.edu/gdae/Pubs/rp/TKNSubsidiesDec05.pdf.

Amsden, Alice (1991). Diffusion of development: the late industrializing model and greater East Asia. *American Economic Review*, vol. 81, No. 2, pp. 282-286.

________ (2003). *The Rise of "the Rest": Challenges to the West from Late Industrializing Economies*. Oxford: Oxford University Press.

Arner, Douglas, Paul Lejot and S. Ghon Rhee (2005). *Impediments to Cross-border Investments in Asian Bonds*. Singapore: Institute of Southeast Asian Studies.

Atkinson, Anthony B., ed. (2005). *New Sources of Development Finance.* UNU-WIDER Studies in Development Economics. Oxford: Oxford University Press.

Baldwin, Richard (1997). The causes of regionalism. *CEPR Discussion Paper*, No. 1599. London: Centre for Economic Policy Research. March.

Baunsgaard, Thomas, and Michael Keen (2005). Tax revenue and (or?) trade liberalization. IMF Working Paper, No. WP/05/112. Washington, D.C.: International Monetary Fund. June.

Benhabib, Jess, and Mark Speigel (1994). The role of human capital in economic development: evidence from aggregate cross-country data. *Journal of Monetary Economics*, vol. 34, No. 2, pp. 143-173.

Besley, Timothy, and Louise J. Cord, eds. (2007). *Delivering on the Promise of Pro-Poor Growth: Insights and Lessons from Country Experiences*. Washington, D.C: World Bank.

Bhaduri, A. (1973). A study in agricultural backwardness under semi-feudalism. *The Economic Journal*, vol. 83, No. 329, pp. 120-137.

Bhagwati, Jagdish (2010). Banned aid: why international assistance does not alleviate poverty. *Foreign Affairs*, vol. 89, No. 1 (January/February), pp. 120-125.

Bils, Mark, and Peter Klenow (2000). Does schooling cause growth? *American Economic Review*, vol. 90, No. 5, pp. 1160-1183.

Blanchard, Olivier J., Giovanni Dell'Ariccia and Paulo Mauro (2010). Rethinking macroeconomic policy. IMF Staff Position Note, No. SPN/10/03. Washington, D.C.: International Monetary Fund. 12 February.

Booth, Anne (1999). Education and economic development in Southeast Asia: myths and realities. *ASEAN Economic Bulletin*, vol. 16, No. 3 (December), pp. 290-307.

Bourguignon, François (2004). The poverty-growth-inequality triangle. Paper presented at the Indian Council for Research on International Economic Relations. New Delhi, 4 February.

________, and Christian Morrison (2002). The size distribution of income among world citizens. *American Economic Review*, vol. 92, No. 4, pp. 207-209.

Bredenkamp, Hugh, and Catherine Pattillo (2010). Financing the response to climate change. IMF Staff Position Note, No. SPN/10/06. Washington, D.C.: Strategy, Policy and Review Department, International Monetary Fund. 25 March. Available from http://www.imf.org/external/pubs/ft/spn/2010/spn1006.pdf.

Caprio, Gerard, and Patrick Honohan (2001). *Finance for Growth: Policy Choices in a Volatile World*. Washington, D.C.: World Bank; and New York: Oxford University Press.

Chang, Ha-Joon (2009). Should industrial policy in developing countries conform to comparative advantage or defy it? a debate between Justin Lin and Ha-Joon Chang. *Development Policy Review*, vol. 27, No. 5, pp. 483-502.

Chen, Shaohua, and Martin Ravallion (2001). How did the world's poorest fare in the 1990s? *Review of Income and Wealth*, vol. 47, No. 3, pp. 283-300.

________ (2008). The developing world is poorer than we thought, but no less successful in the fight against poverty. World Bank Policy Research Working Paper, No. 4703. Washington, D.C.: World Bank. August.

Chenery, Hollis B. (1986). *Industrialization and Growth*. New York: Oxford University Press.

________, and others (1974). *Redistribution with Growth: Policies to Improve Income Distribution in Developing Countries in the Context of Economic Growth*. Oxford: Oxford University Press.

Chowdhury, Anis, and Iyanatul Islam (1993). *The Newly Industrialising Economies of East Asia*. New York: Routledge.

Claessens, Stijn, and Thomas Glaessner (1998). The internationalization of financial services in Asia. World Bank Policy Research Working Paper, No. 1911. Washington, D.C.: World Bank. April.

Claessens, Stijn, and Marion Jensen, eds. (2000). *Internationalization of Financial Services, Issues and Lessons for Developing Countries*. The Hague: Kluwer Law International.

Clark, Michael T. (2010). Governance challenges in financing green and sustainable energy policies. FES Briefing Paper, No. 2. New York: Friedrich-Ebert-Stiftung, New York Office. April.

Clemens, Michael A., and Todd J. Moss (2005). Ghost of 0.7%: origins and relevance of the international aid target. CGD Working Paper, No. 68 (September). Washington, D.C.: Center for Global Development.

Clunies-Ross, Anthony (2004). *Imminent Prospects for Additional Finance: What Might be Done Now or Soon and Under What Conditions. WIDER Research Paper*, No. 2004/45. Helsinki: United Nations University—World Institute for Development Economics Research. July.

Coady, David, Margaret Grosh and John Hoddinott (2004). *Targeting of Transfers in Developing Countries: Review of Lessons and Experience*. World Bank Regional and Sectoral Studies. Washington, D.C.: World Bank and International Food Policy Research Institute.

Cornia, Giovanni Andrea (2006). Potential and limitations of pro-poor macroeconomics: an overview. In *Pro-Poor Macroeconomics: Potential and Limitations*, Giovanni Andrea Cornia, ed. New York: Palgrave Macmillan.

________ (2010). Economic integration, inequality and growth: theory and comparative assessment. Background paper prepared for *World Economic and Social Survey 2010: Retooling Global Development*.

________, ed. (2006). *Pro-Poor Macroeconomics: Potential and Limitations*. New York: Palgrave Macmillan.

Culpeper, Roy (2005). Millennium Development Goals: are they adequate? In *Helping the Poor? The IMF and Low-Income Countries*, Jan Joost Teunissen and Age Akkerman, eds. The Hague: FONDAD.

Cummings, William K. (1995). The Asian human resource approach in global perspective. *Oxford Review of Education*, vol. 21, No. 1, pp. 67-81.

D'Arista, Jane, and Korkut Erturk (2010). Reforming the international monetary system. Background paper prepared for *World Economic and Social Survey 2010: Retooling Global Development*.

Dag Hammarskjöld Foundation (1975). What now? The 1975 Dag Hammarskjöld report on development and international cooperation. Uppsala, Sweden.

de Brauw, Alan, and John Hoddinott (2008). Must conditional cash transfers be conditioned to be effective? the impact of conditioning transfers on school enrolment in Mexico. IFPRI Discussion Paper, No. 757. Washington, D.C.: International Food Policy Research Institute. March.

De Gregorio, José, and others (1999). *An Independent and Accountable IMF*. Geneva Reports on the World Economy 1. Geneva: International Centre for Monetary and Banking Studies; and London: Centre for Economic Policy Research.

de Haan, Arjan (2009). Aid: the drama, the fiction, and does it work? ISS Working Paper, No. 488. The Hague: Institute of Social Studies. December. Available from http://biblio.iss.nl/opac/uploads/wp/wp488.pdf.

Dell, Sidney (1985). The origins of UNCTAD. In *UNCTAD and the North-South Dialogue*, Michael Zammit Cutajar, ed. New York: Pergamon Press.

Dembinski, Paul H. (2007). Enhancing the role of SMEs in global value chains. Paper submitted to the Expert Meeting on Enhancing the Participation of Small and Medium-sized Enterprises in Global Value Chains, Geneva, 18 and 19 October 2007. Available from http://www.unctad.org/sections/wcmu/docs/com3em31p016_en.pdf.

Dijkstra, Geske (2010). The new aid paradigm: a case of policy incoherence. Background paper prepared for *World Economic and Social Survey 2010: Retooling Global Development*.

Dommen, Caroline, and Kamol Kamoltrakul, eds. (2004). *Practical Guide to the WTO for Human Rights Advocates*. Geneva: 3D and Forum-Asia.

Drache, Daniel (2010). The nasty business of protectionism: new state practices at a time of system disturbance – the expectation for global demand management. Background paper prepared for *World Economic and Social Survey 2010: Retooling Global Development.*

Easterly, William (2006). *The White Man's Burden: Why the West's Efforts to Aid the Rest Have Done So Much Ill and So Little Good.* New York: Penguin Group.

Eichengreen, Barry (2009). Out of the box thoughts about the international financial architecture. IMF Working Paper, No. WP/09/116. Washington, D.C.: International Monetary Fund.

Ellerman, David (2010). Pragmatism versus economics ideology in post-Socialist transition: China versus Russia. *Real World Economics Review*, No. 52 (10 March), pp. 2-27.

Epstein, Gerald A., and Erinc A. Yeldan, eds. (2009). *Beyond Inflation Targetting: Assessing the Impacts and Policy Alternatives.* Cheltenham, United Kingdom: Edward Elgar Publishing.

Escaith, Hubert (2008). Measuring trade in value added in the new industrial economy: statistical implications. MPRA Paper, No. 14454. Munich: Munich Personal RePEc Archive, Munich University Library. June. Available from http://mpra.ub.uni-muenchen.de/14454/1/MPRA_paper_14454.pdf.

________ (2009). Trade collapse, trade relapse and global production networks: supply chains in the great recession. Conference paper presented at the OECD Roundtable on Impacts of the Economic Crisis on Globalization and Global Value Chains, Paris, 28 October 2009. Available from http://mpra.ub.uni-muenchen.de/18274/1/MPRA_paper_18274.pdf.

European Commission (2009). Aid effectiveness agenda: benefits of a European approach. Project No. 2008/170204 - Version 1. Hemel Hempstead, United Kingdom: HTSPE Limited. 14 October.

Ffrench-Davis, Ricardo (2006). *Reforming Latin America's Economies: After Market Fundamentalism.* Basingstoke, United Kingdom: Palgrave Macmillan.

Fiess, Norbert (2002). Chile's new fiscal rule. Mimeo. Washington, D.C.: World Bank. May.

Filho, Alfredo Saad (2010). From Washington Consensus to inclusive growth: the continuing relevance for pro-poor alternatives. Background paper prepared for *World Economic and Social Survey 2010: Retooling Global Development.*

Fiszbein, Ariel, and Norbert Schady (2009). *Conditional Cash Transfers: Reducing Present and Future Poverty.* World Bank Policy Research Report. Washington, D.C.: World Bank.

FitzGerald, Valpy (2010). International tax cooperation and international development finance. Background paper prepared for *World Economic and Social Survey 2010: Retooling Global Development.*

Ford, Nathan, and others (2004). The role of civil society in protecting public health over commercial interests: lessons from Thailand. *The Lancet*, vol. 363, No. 9408 (February), pp. 560-563.

Gallagher, Kevin P. (2005). Globalization and the nation-state: reasserting policy autonomy for development. In *Putting Development First*, Kevin P. Gallagher, ed. London: Zed Books.

_________ (2010). Policy space to prevent and mitigate financial crises in trade and investment agreements. G-24 Discussion Paper Series, No. 58. New York and Geneva: Intergovernmental Group of Twenty-four on International Monetary Affairs and Development and United Nations Conference on Trade and Development. April.

_________, ed. (2005). *Putting Development First*. London: Zed Books.

Gamberoni, Elisa, and Richard Newfarmer (2009). Trade protection: incipient but worrisome trends. Trade Notes, No. 37. Washington, D.C.: International Trade Department, World Bank. 2 March. Available from http://siteresources.worldbank.org/NEWS/Resources/Trade_Note_37.pdf.

Glewwe, Paul (2002). Schools and skills in developing countries: education policies and socioeconomic outcomes. *Journal of Economic Literature*, vol. 40, No. 2, pp. 436-482.

Gottschalk, Ricardo (2005). The macro content of PRSPs: assessing the need for a more flexible macroeconomic policy framework. *Development Policy Review*, vol. 23, No. 4 (July), pp. 419-442.

Griffith-Jones, Stephany, and José Antonio Ocampo (2007). A counter-cyclical framework for a development-friendly international financial architecture. DESA Working Paper, No. 39. New York: Department of Economic and Social Affairs of the United Nations Secretariat. June. ST/ESA/2007/DWP/39.

Grindle, Merilee S. (2010). Social policy in development: coherence and cooperation in the real world. Background paper prepared for *World Economic and Social Survey 2010: Retooling Global Development*.

Group of Thirty (2009). Financial reform: a framework for financial stability. January. Washington, D.C. Available from http://www.group30.org/pubs/reformreport.pdf.

Hailu, Degol, and John Weeks (2009). Can low-income countries adopt counter-cyclical policies? One pager, No. 92. Brasilia: International Policy Centre for Inclusive Growth. August. Available from http://www.ipc-undp.org/pub/IPCOnePager92.pdf.

Haque, Irfan ul (2007). Rethinking industrial policy. UNCTAD Discussion Paper, No. 183. Geneva: United Nations Conference on Trade and Development. April.

Harrison, Ann, and Margaret McMillan (2007). On the links between globalization and poverty. *Journal of Economic Inequality*, vol. 5, No. 1, pp. 123-134.

Hausmann, Ricardo, and Bailey Klinger (2006). Structural transformation and patterns of comparative advantage in product space. CID Working Paper, No. 128. Cambridge, Massachusetts: Harvard University, Center for International Development.

Helleiner, Eric (2009). Contemporary reform of global financial governance: implications of and lessons from the past. In *Reforming the International Financial System for Development: Lessons from the Current and Recent Crises in Developing Countries*, Jomo Kwame Sundaram, ed. Washington, D.C.: G-24 Secretariat, pp. 1-24.

Helleiner, Gerry K. (2005). Panel on donor coordination: framework for holding donors to account. Oxford: Global Economic Governance Programme at University College, University of Oxford. Available from http://www.globaleconomicgovernance.org/wp-content/uploads/Helleiner%20on%20Tanzania.pdf.

Herman, Barry, José Antonio Ocampo and Shari Spiegel (2010). The case for a new international reform effort. In *Overcoming Developing Country Debt Crises*, Barry Herman, José Antonio Ocampo and Shari Spiegel, eds. New York: Oxford University Press.

Holmes, Stephen (1997). What Russia teaches us now: how weak states threaten freedom. *The American Prospect*, vol. 8, No. 33 (July-August), pp. 30-39.

Honohan, Patrick (2004). Financial development, growth and poverty: how close are the links? World Bank Policy Research Paper, No. 3203. Washington, D.C.: World Bank. February.

Howell, David R., ed. (2005). *Fighting Unemployment: The Limits of Free Market Orthodoxy*. New York: Oxford University Press.

Hudson Institute, Center for Global Prosperity (2009). *The Index of Global Philanthropy and Remittances 2009*. Washington, D.C.

International Labour Organization (1976). *Employment, Growth, and Basic Needs: A One World Problem*. Geneva: International Labour Office.

________ (1977). *Employment, Growth, and Basic Needs: A One World Problem: The International "Basic Needs Strategy" Against Chronic Poverty*. New York: Praeger.

________ (2007). Decent work for a fair globalization: broadening and strengthening dialogue. Overview paper prepared for the ILO Forum on Decent Work for a Fair Globalization, Lisbon, 31 October-2 November 2007, Geneva: International Labour Office.

Jolly, Richard, and others (2004). *UN Contributions to Development Thinking and Practice*. Bloomington, Indiana: Indiana University Press.

Kapur, Devesh, John P. Lewis and Richard Webb (1997). *The World Bank: Its First Half Century, Volume 1: History*. Washington, D.C.: The Brookings Institution.

Kar, Dev, and Devon Cartwright-Smith (2008). Illicit financial flows from developing countries: 2002-2006. Washington, D.C.: Global Financial Integrity, Center for International Policy.

Kharas, Homi (2008). Measuring the cost of aid volatility. *Wolfensohn Center for Development Working Paper*, No. 3. Washington, D.C.: The Brookings Institution.

Kose, M. Ayhan, Eswar S. Prasad and Ashley D. Taylor (2009). Thresholds in the process of international financial integration. NBER Working Paper, No. 14916. Cambridge, Massachusetts: National Bureau of Economic Research. April. Available from http://www.nber.org/papers/w14916.

Kose, M. Ayhan, and others (2006). Financial globalization: a reappraisal. IMF Working Paper, No. 06/189. Washington, D.C.: International Monetary Fund. August.

Kuznets, Simon (1955). Economic growth and income inequality. *American Economic Review*, vol. 45, No. 1 (March), pp. 1-28.

Laird, Sam (2007). Aid for trade: cool aid or Kool-aid? G-24 Discussion Paper, No. 48, prepared for the Intergovernmental Group of Twenty-Four on International Monetary Affairs and Development. Geneva: United Nations Conference on Trade and Development. November. Available from http://www.unctad.org/en/docs/gdsmdpbg2420076_en.pdf.

Lall, Sanjaya (2005). Rethinking industrial strategy: the role of the state in the face of globalization. In *Putting Development First*, Kevin P. Gallagher, ed. London: Zed Books.

Lamy, Pascal (2009). Climate first, trade second: GATTzilla is long gone. Simon Reisman Lecture, organized by the Norman Paterson School of International Affairs, Carleton University, and the Department of Foreign Affairs and International Trade of Canada, Ottawa, 2 November 2009. Available from http://www2.carleton.ca/newsroom/speech/pascal-lamy-simon-reisman-lecture/.

Lin, Justin Yifu (2009). Policy responses to the global economic crisis. *Development Outreach*, vol. 11, No. 3 (December), pp. 29-33.

Linnerooth-Bayer, J., and R. Mechler (2007). Insurance against losses from natural disasters in developing countries. Background paper prepared for *World Economic and Social Survey 2008: Overcoming Economic Insecurity.*

Lister, Stephen, and others (2006). Evaluation of general budget support: Uganda country report. A Joint Evaluation of General Budget Support 1994-2004. Birmingham, United Kingdom: International Development Department, School of Public Policy, University of Birmingham. Available from http://www.dfid.gov.uk/Documents/publications/evaluation/gbs-uganda.pdf.

Lustig, Nora, ed. (1995). *Coping with Austerity: Poverty and Inequality in Latin America.* Washington, D.C.: The Brookings Institution.

Maslow, Albert H. (1943). A theory of human motivation. *Psychological Review*, No. 50 (March), pp. 370-396.

Mason, Edward S., and Robert E. Asher (1973). *The World Bank Since Bretton Woods.* Washington, D.C.: The Brookings Institution.

Mayer, Jorg (2008). Policy space: what, for what and where? UNCTAD Discussion Paper, No. 191. Geneva: United Nations Conference on Trade and Development. October.

Meier, Gerald M., and Dudley Seers, eds. (2001). *Pioneers in Development.* New York: Oxford University Press.

Memis, Emel (2009). *The Potential for Cooperative Regional Industrial Development Strategies in Asia and the Implications of Emerging China and India.* Policy paper. Colombo: United Nations Development Programme Regional Centre, Asia Pacific Trade and Investment Initiative.

________, and Manuel F. Montes (2006). Assessing RTAs in the context of the flying geese framework. UNU-CRIS Occasional Paper, No. O-2006/18. Bruges, Belgium: United Nations University and Comparative Regional Integration Studies. Available from http://www.cris.unu.edu/UNU-CRIS-Working-Papers.19.0.html?&tx_ttnews%5Btt_news%5D=120&tx_ttnews%5BbackPid%5D=19&tx_ttnews%5Bpointer%5D=1&cHash=d8b75be3b0.

________ (2008). Who's afraid of industrial policy. Discussion paper. Colombo: United Nations Development Programme Regional Centre, Asia Pacific Trade and Investment Initiative.

Memis, Emel, Manuel F. Montes and Chatrini Weeratunge (2006). Public finance implications of trade policy reforms: Lao PDR case study. Unpublished manuscript. Colombo: United Nations Development Programme Regional Centre. July.

Mesa-Lago, Carmelo (2007). Social security in Latin America: pension and health care reforms in the last quarter century. *Latin American Research Review*, vol. 42, No. 2, pp. 181-201.

Milanovic, Branko (2005). *Worlds Apart: Measuring International and Global Inequality*. Princeton, New Jersey: Princeton University Press.

Miroudot, Sebastien, Rainer Lanz and Alexandros Ragoussis (2009). Trade in intermediate goods and services. OECD Trade Policy Working Paper, No. 93. Paris: Organization for Economic Cooperation and Development.

Mkandawire, Thandika (2010). Aid, development and the State. Background paper prepared for *World Economic and Social Survey 2010: Retooling Global Development*.

Montes, Manuel F. (1998). *The Currency Crisis in Southeast Asia*. Singapore: Institute of Southeast Asian Studies.

Morduch, Jonathan (1994). Poverty and vulnerability. *The American Economic Review*, vol. 84, No. 2, pp. 221-225.

________ (1999). The microfinance promise. *Journal of Economic Literature*, vol. 37, No. 4, pp. 1569-1614.

Morley, Samuel A., and David Coady (2003). *From Social Assistance to Social Development: Targeted Education Subsidies in Developing Countries*. Washington, D.C.: Center for Global Development.

Nayyar, Deepak (2010). Reinventing globalization: fair is feasible. Background paper prepared for *World Economic and Social Survey 2010: Retooling Global Development*.

Nelson, Gerald C., and others (2009). *Climate Change: Impact on Agriculture and Costs of Adaptation*. Food Policy Report. Washington, D.C.: International Food Policy Research Institute.

Ngowi, Daniel (2005). Effects of budgetary process reforms on economic governance: evidence from Tanzania. Dar es Salaam: Economic and Social Research Foundation. June. Available from http://www.tzonline.org/pdf/effectsofbudgetaryprocessreformsoneconomic.pdf.

Nissanke, Machiko, and Benno Ferrarini (2007). *Assessing the Aid Allocation and Debt Sustainability Framework: Working Towards Incentive Compatible Aid Contracts*. UNU-WIDER Research Paper, No. 2007/33. Helsinki: United Nations University - World Institute for Development Economics Research. June. Available from http://www.wider.unu.edu/stc/repec/pdfs/rp2007/rp2007-33.pdf.

North-South Institute (2004). Economic policy choices for poverty reduction. Paper based on Wilton Park Conference 750, West Sussex, United Kingdom, 11-15 June 2004.

Ocampo, José Antonio (2001). *International Asymmetries and the Design of the International Financial System*. Temas de Coyuntura Serie, No. 15. Santiago: Economic Commission for Latin America and the Caribbean. April. United Nations publication, Sales No. E.01.II.G.70.

________ (2003). Capital account and counter-cyclical prudential regulation in developing countries. In *From Capital Surges to Drought: Seeking Stability for Emerging Markets*, Ricardo Ffrench-Davis and Stephany Griffith-Jones, eds. London: Palgrave Macmillan, pp. 217-244.

________ (2008). A broad view of macroeconomic stability. In *The Washington Consensus Reconsidered*, Narcis Serra and Joseph E. Stiglitz, eds. New York: Oxford University Press.

________ (2009). Special drawing rights and the reform of the global reserve system. In "Reforming the international financial system for development", K. S. Jomo, ed. Washington, D.C.: Intergovernmental Group of Twenty-Four on International Monetary Affairs and Development.

________ (2010). Rethinking global economic and social governance. *Journal of Globalization and Development*, vol. 1, No. 1, pp. 1-26.

________, and Rob Vos (2008). *Uneven Economic Development*. New York: United Nations; London: Zed Books; Hyderabad, India: Orient Longman; and Penang, Malaysia: Third World Network.

Ocampo, José Antonio, and Mariangela Parra-Lancourt (2010). The terms of trade for commodities since the mid-19th century. *Revista de Historia Económica* (Second Series), vol. 28, No. 1, pp. 11-43.

Ocampo, José Antonio, Kwame Sundaram Jomo and Rob Vos (2007). *Growth Divergences: Explaining Differences in Economic Performance*. Penang, Malaysia: Orient Longman, Zed Books and Third World Network.

Ocampo, José Antonio, and others (2010). The great recession and the developing world. IPD Working Paper. New York: Initiative for Policy Dialogue, Columbia University. 12 April. Available from http://www0.gsb.columbia.edu/ipd/pub/Crisis_Complutense%5B1%5D_Great_Recession.pdf.

Oliver, Raylynn (1999). Fertility and women's schooling in Ghana. In *The Economics of School Quality Investments in Developing Countries: An Empirical Study of Ghana*, Paul Glewwe, ed. London: Macmillan Press.

Opschoor, Hans (2010). Policy and financial coherence in the post-Copenhagen climate negotiations. Background paper presented at the twelfth session of the Committee for Development Policy, New York, 22-26 March 2010. CDP/2010/PLEN/7.

Organization for Economic Cooperation and Development (2009). *OECD Transfer Pricing Guidelines for Multinational Enterprises and Tax Administrations*. Paris.

________, Development Co-operation Directorate (DCD-DAC) (2010). Development database on aid from DAC Members: DAC online. Available from http://www.oecd.org/document/33/0,2340,en_2649_34447_36661793_1_1_1_1,00.html.

Ostry, Jonathan D., and others (2010). Capital inflows: the role of controls. IMF Staff Position Note, No. SPN/10/04. Washington, D.C.: Research Department, International Monetary Fund. 19 February.

Pack, Howard, and Kamal Saggi (2001). The case for industrial policy: a critical survey. London: Department for International Development. Available from www.dfid.gov.uk/pubs/files/itd/industrial-policy.pdf.

Page, Sheila (2007). The potential impact of the Aid for Trade initiative. G-24 Discussion Paper Series, No. 45, prepared for the Intergovernmental Group of Twenty-Four on International Monetary Affairs and Development. Geneva: United Nations Conference on Trade and Development. April. Available from http://www.unctad.org/en/docs/gdsmdpbg2420073_en.pdf.

Prasad, Eswar, and others (2003). Effects of financial globalization on developing countries: some empirical evidence. Washington, D. C: International Monetary Fund. 17 March. Available from http://www.imf.org/external/np/res/docs/2003/031703.pdf.

Pew Center on Global Climate Change (2009). Response of the Pew Center on Global Climate Change to the Committee on Energy and Commerce and its Subcommittee on Energy and Air Quality of the United States House of Representatives on the Climate Change Legislation Design White Paper: Competitiveness Concerns/Engaging Developing Countries. Arlington, Virginia: Pew Center on Global Climate Change. Available from http://www.pewclimate.org/docUploads/Pew%20Center%20on%20Competitiveness-Developing%20Countries-FINAL.pdf.

Pritchett, Lant (2001). Where has all the education gone? *World Bank Economic Review*, vol. 15, No. 3, pp. 367-391.

Public Citizen (2009). Trade agreements cannot be allowed to undermine needed financial service-sector reregulation: to rescue Main Street, we need to curb the WTO. Washington, D.C.: Global Trade Watch program, Public Citizen. Available from http://www.citizen.org/documents/FinanceReregulationFactSheetFINAL.pdf.

Ravallion, Martin (1997). Can high-inequality developing countries escape absolute poverty. World Bank Policy Research Working Paper, No. 1775. Washington, D.C.: World Bank. June.

________ (2001). Growth, inequality and poverty: looking beyond averages. *World Development*, vol. 29, No. 11 (November), pp. 1803-1815.

________, Guarav Datt and Dominique van de Walle (1991). Quantifying absolute poverty in the developing world. *Review of Income and Wealth*, vol. 37, No. 4 (December), pp. 345-361.

Reinert, Erik S. (2005). Development and social goals: balancing aid and development to prevent "welfare colonialism". *post-autistic Economics Review*, No. 30 (21 March).

Reinhart, Carmen M., and Kenneth S. Rogoff (2008). Banking crises: an equal opportunity menace. NBER Working Paper, No. 14587. Cambridge, Massachusetts: National Bureau of Economic Research. December. Available from http://www.nber.org/~confer/2009/mes09/rogoff.pdf.

Rodrik, Dani (2002). Feasible globalizations. *CEPR Discussion Paper*, No. 3524. London: Centre for Economic Policy Research. August.

________ (2004). Industrial policy for the twenty-first century. *CEPR Discussion Paper*, No. 4767. London: Centre for Economic Policy Research. November.

________ (2007a). Industrial development: some stylized facts and policy directions. In *Industrial Development for the 21st Century: Sustainable Development Perspectives*. United Nations publication, Sales No. E.07.II.A.1.

________ (2007b). *One Economics, Many Recipes: Globalization, Institutions, and Economic Growth*. Princeton, New Jersey: Princeton University Press.

Rollo, Jim (2007). The challenge of negotiating RTA's for developing countries: what could the WTO do to help? Paper presented at the Conference on Multilateralising Regionalism, sponsored and organized by the World Trade Organization - Graduate Institute of International and Development Studies (WTO-HEI), and Centre for Economic Policy Research, Geneva, 10-12 September 2007.

Sen, Amartya K. (1973). Poverty, inequality and unemployment: some conceptual issues in measurement. *Economic and Political Weekly*, vol. 8, No. 31/33, pp. 1457-1459.

Shadlen, Kenneth (2005). Policy space for development in the WTO and beyond: the case of intellectual property rights. Global Development and Environment Institute Working Paper, No. 05-06. Medford, Massachusetts: Tufts University.

Sharma, Krishnan, and Shari Spiegel (forthcoming). Institutional investor compensation structures and excess risk-taking: lessons from mutual funds and hedge funds. IPD Working Paper. New York: Initiative for Policy Dialogue, Columbia University.

Singh, Ajit (2002). Competition and competition policy in emerging markets: international and developmental dimensions. G-24 Discussion Paper, No. 18, prepared for the Intergovernmental Group of Twenty-Four on International Monetary Affairs and Development. Geneva: United Nations Conference on Trade and Development.

Sobhan, Rehman (1993). *Agrarian Reform and Social Transformation: Preconditions for Development*. London: Zed Books.

Standing, Guy (2007). How cash transfers boost work and economic security. DESA Working Paper, No. 58. New York: Department of Economic and Social Affairs of the United Nations Secretariat. October. ST/ESA/2007/DWP/58.

Stewart, Frances, and Michael Wang (2003). Do PRSPs empower poor countries and disempower the World Bank, or is it the other way around? QEH Working Paper, No. 108. Oxford: Queen Elizabeth House, University of Oxford.

Stiglitz, Joseph (2003). *Globalization and Its Discontents* New York: W.W. Norton and Company.

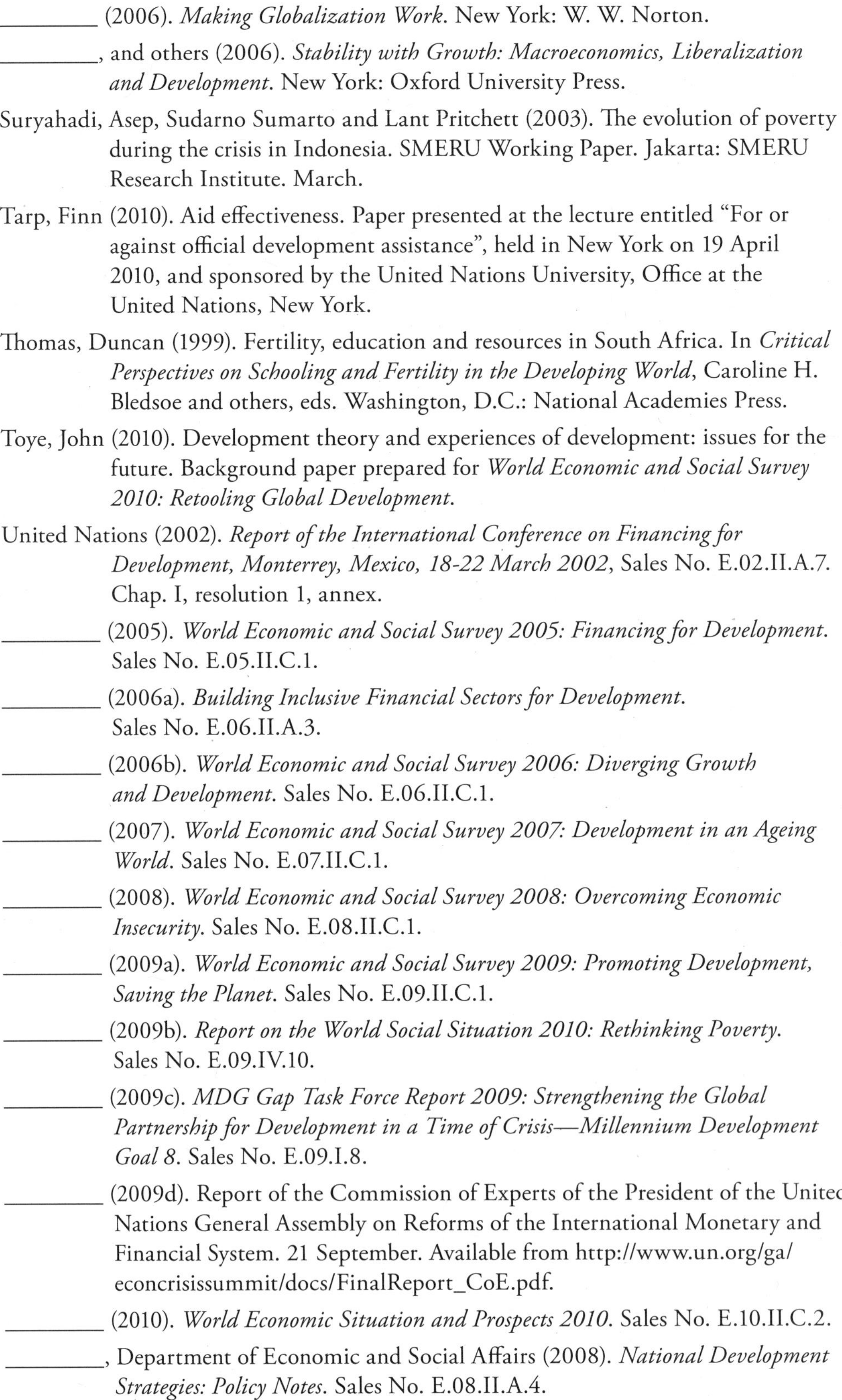

________ (2006). *Making Globalization Work.* New York: W. W. Norton.

________, and others (2006). *Stability with Growth: Macroeconomics, Liberalization and Development.* New York: Oxford University Press.

Suryahadi, Asep, Sudarno Sumarto and Lant Pritchett (2003). The evolution of poverty during the crisis in Indonesia. SMERU Working Paper. Jakarta: SMERU Research Institute. March.

Tarp, Finn (2010). Aid effectiveness. Paper presented at the lecture entitled "For or against official development assistance", held in New York on 19 April 2010, and sponsored by the United Nations University, Office at the United Nations, New York.

Thomas, Duncan (1999). Fertility, education and resources in South Africa. In *Critical Perspectives on Schooling and Fertility in the Developing World*, Caroline H. Bledsoe and others, eds. Washington, D.C.: National Academies Press.

Toye, John (2010). Development theory and experiences of development: issues for the future. Background paper prepared for *World Economic and Social Survey 2010: Retooling Global Development.*

United Nations (2002). *Report of the International Conference on Financing for Development, Monterrey, Mexico, 18-22 March 2002*, Sales No. E.02.II.A.7. Chap. I, resolution 1, annex.

________ (2005). *World Economic and Social Survey 2005: Financing for Development.* Sales No. E.05.II.C.1.

________ (2006a). *Building Inclusive Financial Sectors for Development.* Sales No. E.06.II.A.3.

________ (2006b). *World Economic and Social Survey 2006: Diverging Growth and Development.* Sales No. E.06.II.C.1.

________ (2007). *World Economic and Social Survey 2007: Development in an Ageing World.* Sales No. E.07.II.C.1.

________ (2008). *World Economic and Social Survey 2008: Overcoming Economic Insecurity.* Sales No. E.08.II.C.1.

________ (2009a). *World Economic and Social Survey 2009: Promoting Development, Saving the Planet.* Sales No. E.09.II.C.1.

________ (2009b). *Report on the World Social Situation 2010: Rethinking Poverty.* Sales No. E.09.IV.10.

________ (2009c). *MDG Gap Task Force Report 2009: Strengthening the Global Partnership for Development in a Time of Crisis—Millennium Development Goal 8.* Sales No. E.09.I.8.

________ (2009d). Report of the Commission of Experts of the President of the United Nations General Assembly on Reforms of the International Monetary and Financial System. 21 September. Available from http://www.un.org/ga/econcrisissummit/docs/FinalReport_CoE.pdf.

________ (2010). *World Economic Situation and Prospects 2010.* Sales No. E.10.II.C.2.

________, Department of Economic and Social Affairs (2008). *National Development Strategies: Policy Notes.* Sales No. E.08.II.A.4.

________, Economic and Social Commission for Asia and the Pacific (2006). *Enhancing Regional Cooperation in Infrastructure Development Including that Related to Disaster Management.* Bangkok. Sales No. E.06.II.F.13.

________ (2010). Regional economic cooperation in Asia: current situation and future prospects. Paper presented at the World Economic and Social Survey 2010 workshop, entitled "Towards a new development paradigm? coherence in development policy and international cooperation", held in Geneva on 8 and 9 February. Available from http://www.un.org/esa/policy/wess/wess2010workshop/wess2010_escap.pdf.

United Nations, Economic and Social Council (2008). Trends in South-South and triangular development cooperation. Background study for the first biennial high-level Development Cooperation Forum held in New York on 30 June and 1 July 2008. April.

________ (2010). Report of the Committee for Development Policy on the twelfth session, (22-26 March 2010). *Official Records of the Economic and Social Council, 2010, Supplement No. 13.* E/2010/33.

United Nations, Economic Commission for Latin American and the Caribbean (2010). Policy coherence and stabilization: rebalancing stabilization and developmental policies in Latin America and the Caribbean. Paper presented at the World Economic and Social Survey 2010 workshop, entitled "Towards a new development paradigm? coherence in development policy and international cooperation", held in Geneva on 8 and 9 February. Available from http://www.un.org/esa/policy/wess/wess2010workshop/wess2010_eclac.pdf.

United Nations, General Assembly (2007). Follow-up to and implementation of the outcome of the International Conference on Financing for Development. Report of the Secretary-General. 10 August. A/62/217.

________ (2009a). Progress report of the Secretary-General on innovative sources of development finance. 29 July. A/64/189 and corrigendum.

________ (2009b). Outcome of the Conference on the World Financial and Economic Crisis and Its Impact on Development. Resolution 63/303, annex. 9 July.

United Nations Conference on Trade and Development (2003). *Trade and Development Report, 2003: Capital Accumulation, Growth and Structural Change.* Sales No. E.03.II.D.7.

________ (2006). *Trade and Development Report 2006: Global Partnership and National Policies for Development.* Sales No. E.06.II.D.6.

________ (2009a). *World Investment Report 2009: Transnational Corporations, Agricultural Production and Development.* Sales No. E.09.II.D.15.

________ (2009b). *Trade and Development Report 2009: Responding to the Global Crisis—Climate Change Mitigation and Development.* Sales No. E.09.II.D.16.

United Nations Development Programme (1990). *Human Development Report.* New York: Oxford University Press.

United Nations Millennium Project (2005). *Investing in Development: A Practical Plan to Achieve the Millennium Development Goals.* London: Earthscan.

United Nations Research Institute for Social Development (2006). Transformative social policy: lessons from UNRISD research. *UNRISD Research and Policy Brief*, No. 5. Geneva.

Van Arkadie, Brian (2006). Twenty years of economic development in Uganda. Background paper No. 1. In Ministry of Foreign Affairs of Denmark, *Evaluation of Danish Aid to Uganda 1987-2005*, vol. 3, *Background Papers*. London: Mokoro. Available from http://www.oecd.org/dataoecd/28/62/37894951.pdf.

van der Hoeven, Rolph (2010). Labour market trends, financial globalization and the current crisis in developing countries. Background paper prepared for *World Economic and Social Survey 2010: Retooling Global Development*.

Van Ginneken, Wouter (2009). Social security and the global socio-economic floor: towards a human rights-based approach. *Global Social Policy*, vol. 9, No. 2, pp. 228-245.

Vos, Rob (2009). Green or mean: is biofuel production undermining food security? In *Climate Change and Sustainable Development: New Challenges for Poverty Reduction*, Mohamed Salih, ed. Cheltenham, United Kingdom: Edward Elgar.

________, and Maritza Cabezas (2006). *Illusions and Disillusions with Pro-Poor Growth: Poverty Reduction Strategies in Bolivia, Honduras and Nicaragua*. SIDA Studies, No. 17. Stockholm: Swedish International Development Cooperation Agency.

Vos, Rob, José Antonio Ocampo and Ana Luiza Cortez, eds. (2008). *Ageing and Development*. New York: United Nations; Hyderabad, India: Oriental Longman; and London: Zed Books.

Wade, Robert (1990). *Governing the Market: Economic Theory and the Role of Government in East Asian Industrialization*. Princeton, New Jersey: Princeton University Press.

________ (2005). What strategies are viable for developing countries today? the WTO and the shrinking of development space. In *Putting Development First*, Kevin P. Gallagher, ed. London: Zed Books.

Williamson, John (1990). What Washington means by policy reform. In *Latin American Adjustment: How Much Has Happened?*, John Williamson, ed. Washington, D.C.: Institute for International Economics.

________, ed. (1990). *Latin American Adjustment: How Much Has Happened?* Washington, D.C.: Institute for International Economics.

Wood, Bernard, and others (2008). *Synthesis Report on the First Phase of the Evaluation of the Implementation of the Paris Declaration*. Copenhagen: Ministry of Foreign Affairs of Denmark. July. Available from http://www.oecd.org/dataoecd/19/9/40888983.pdf.

Woods, Ngaire (2000). The challenge of good governance for the IMF and the World Bank themselves. *World Development*, vol. 28, No. 5 (May), pp. 823-841.

World Bank (2001). *World Development Report 2000/2001: Attacking Poverty*. New York: Oxford University Press.

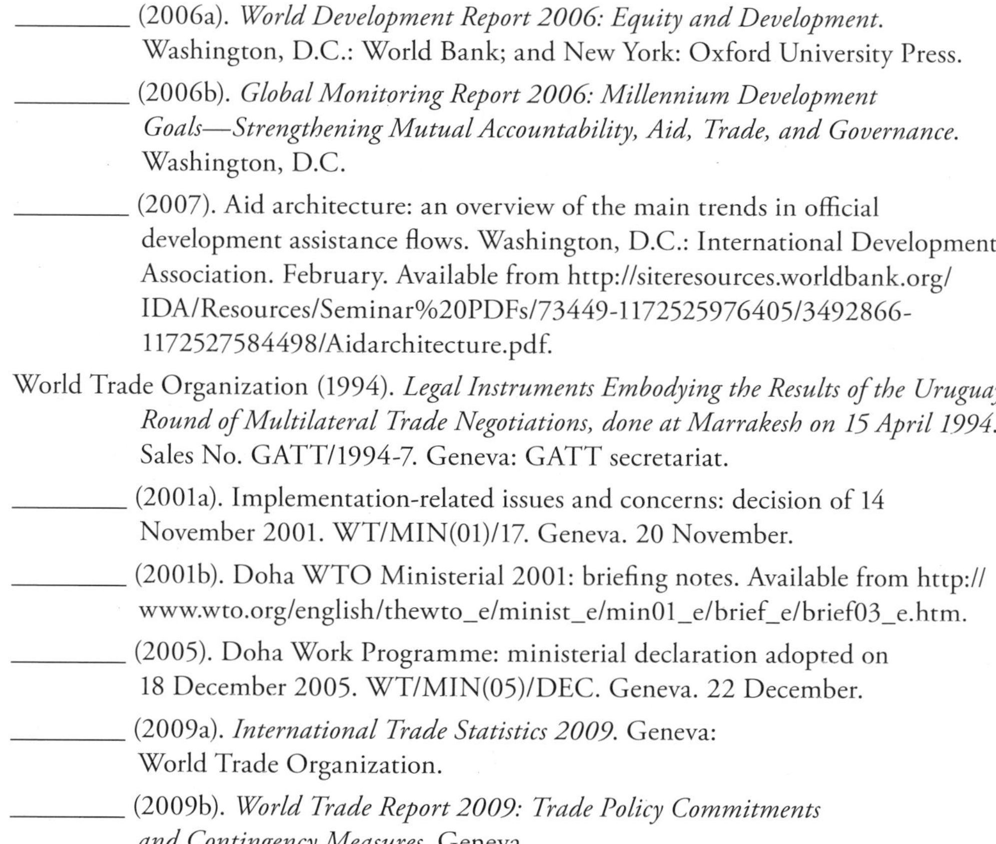

________ (2006a). *World Development Report 2006: Equity and Development.* Washington, D.C.: World Bank; and New York: Oxford University Press.

________ (2006b). *Global Monitoring Report 2006: Millennium Development Goals—Strengthening Mutual Accountability, Aid, Trade, and Governance.* Washington, D.C.

________ (2007). Aid architecture: an overview of the main trends in official development assistance flows. Washington, D.C.: International Development Association. February. Available from http://siteresources.worldbank.org/IDA/Resources/Seminar%20PDFs/73449-1172525976405/3492866-1172527584498/Aidarchitecture.pdf.

World Trade Organization (1994). *Legal Instruments Embodying the Results of the Uruguay Round of Multilateral Trade Negotiations, done at Marrakesh on 15 April 1994.* Sales No. GATT/1994-7. Geneva: GATT secretariat.

________ (2001a). Implementation-related issues and concerns: decision of 14 November 2001. WT/MIN(01)/17. Geneva. 20 November.

________ (2001b). Doha WTO Ministerial 2001: briefing notes. Available from http://www.wto.org/english/thewto_e/minist_e/min01_e/brief_e/brief03_e.htm.

________ (2005). Doha Work Programme: ministerial declaration adopted on 18 December 2005. WT/MIN(05)/DEC. Geneva. 22 December.

________ (2009a). *International Trade Statistics 2009.* Geneva: World Trade Organization.

________ (2009b). *World Trade Report 2009: Trade Policy Commitments and Contingency Measures.* Geneva.

كيفية الحصول على منشورات الأمم المتحدة

يمكن الحصول على منشورات الأمم المتحدة من المكتبات ودور التوزيع في جميع أنحاء العالم . استعلم عنها من المكتبة التي تتعامل معها أو اكتب إلى : الأمم المتحدة ، قسم البيع في نيويورك أو في جنيف .

如何购取联合国出版物

联合国出版物在全世界各地的书店和经售处均有发售。请向书店询问或写信到纽约或日内瓦的联合国销售组。

HOW TO OBTAIN UNITED NATIONS PUBLICATIONS

United Nations publications may be obtained from bookstores and distributors throughout the world. Consult your bookstore or write to: United Nations, Sales Section, New York or Geneva.

COMMENT SE PROCURER LES PUBLICATIONS DES NATIONS UNIES

Les publications des Nations Unies sont en vente dans les librairies et les agences dépositaires du monde entier. Informez-vous auprès de votre libraire ou adressez-vous à : Nations Unies, Section des ventes, New York ou Genève.

КАК ПОЛУЧИТЬ ИЗДАНИЯ ОРГАНИЗАЦИИ ОБЪЕДИНЕННЫХ НАЦИЙ

Издания Организации Объединенных Наций можно купить в книжных магазинах и агентствах во всех районах мира. Наводите справки об изданиях в вашем книжном магазине или пишите по адресу: Организация Объединенных Наций, Секция по продаже изданий, Нью-Йорк или Женева.

COMO CONSEGUIR PUBLICACIONES DE LAS NACIONES UNIDAS

Las publicaciones de las Naciones Unidas están en venta en librerías y casas distribuidoras en todas partes del mundo. Consulte a su librero o diríjase a: Naciones Unidas, Sección de Ventas, Nueva York o Ginebra.

Litho in United Nations, New York
10-28729—May 2010—5,265
ISBN 978-92-1-109161-8

United Nations publication
Sales No. E.10.II.C.1
E/2010/50/Rev.1